PIPE FITTINGS

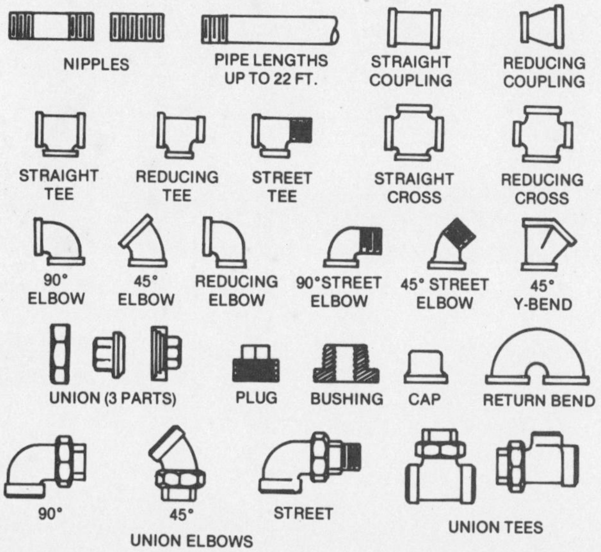

Here are the common steel pipe fittings. Nipples are simply short lengths of pipe threaded on both ends. Reducing fittings join two different sizes of pipe.

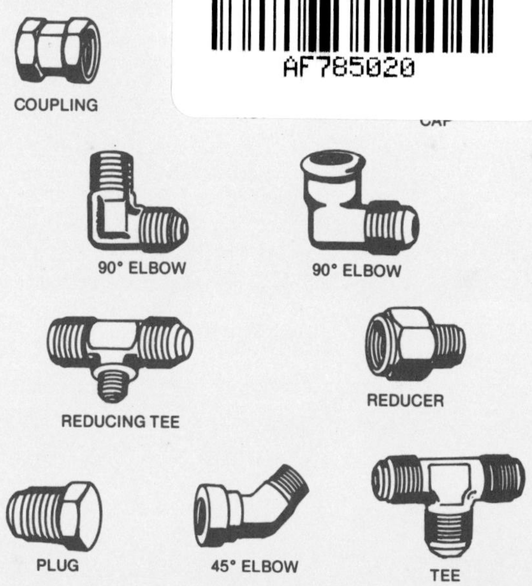

Compression fittings of the flared-tube type are the easiest for the novice to handle when working with copper tubing.

STANDARD STEEL PIPE (All Dimensions in Inches)					
Nominal Size	Outside Diameter	Inside Diameter	Nominal Size	Outside Diameter	Inside Diameter
1/8	0.405	0.269	1	1.315	1.049
1/4	0.540	0.364	1 1/4	1.660	1.380
3/8	0.675	0.493	1 1/2	1.900	1.610
1/2	0.840	0.622	2	2.375	2.067
3/4	1.050	0.824	2 1/2	2.875	2.469

SQUARE MEASURE

144 sq in = 1 sq ft
9 sq ft = 1 sq yd
272.25 sq ft = 1 sq rod
160 sq rods = 1 acre

VOLUME MEASURE

1728 cu in = 1 cu ft
27 cu ft = 1 cu yd

MEASURES OF CAPACITY

1 cup = 8 fl oz
2 cups = 1 pint
2 pints = 1 quart
4 quarts = 1 gallon
2 gallons = 1 peck
4 pecks = 1 bushel

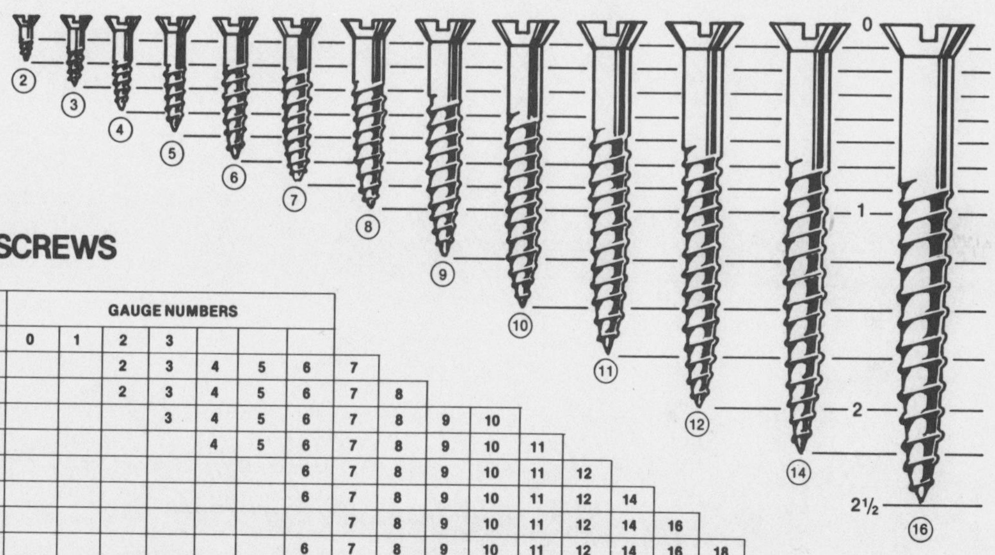

WOOD SCREWS

LENGTH	GAUGE NUMBERS																
1/4 INCH	0	1	2	3													
3/8 INCH			2	3	4	5	6	7									
1/2 INCH			2	3	4	5	6	7	8								
5/8 INCH				3	4	5	6	7	8	9	10						
3/4 INCH					4	5	6	7	8	9	10	11					
7/8 INCH							6	7	8	9	10	11	12				
1 INCH							6	7	8	9	10	11	12	14			
1 1/4 INCH								7	8	9	10	11	12	14	16		
1 1/2 INCH							6	7	8	9	10	11	12	14	16	18	
1 3/4 INCH									8	9	10	11	12	14	16	18	20
2 INCH									8	9	10	11	12	14	16	18	20
2 1/4 INCH										9	10	11	12	14	16	18	20
2 1/2 INCH													12	14	16	18	20
2 3/4 INCH														14	16	18	20
3 INCH															16	18	20
3 1/2 INCH																18	20	24
4 INCH																18	20	24

WHEN YOU BUY SCREWS, SPECIFY (1) LENGTH, (2) GAUGE NUMBER, (3) TYPE OF HEAD—FLAT, ROUND, OR OVAL, (4) MATERIAL—STEEL, BRASS, BRONZE, ETC., (5) FINISH—BRIGHT, STEEL BLUED, CADMIUM, NICKEL, OR CHROMIUM PLATED.

In this volume . . .

BUILD A SWIVEL audio center. Below we show the same unit from two sides. Pivoting on ball bearings, these stacking units hide home entertainment equipment when it's not in use, swing it quickly into view for instant enjoyment. And for a bonus use, see the fourth page on this frontispiece. You'll find complete plans for the easy-to-build unit on page 1444.

TILE YOUR FIREPLACE to give it an elegant, custom look. See page 1468 for details.

CREATE A STRIKING ROOM with strips of lattice. Learn how on page 1462.

THIS EARLY AMERICAN hutch table is a chair, a table, and a sure-fire conversation piece. The two-drawer storage area beneath is a bonus. For complete plans see page 1516.

YOU CAN HAVE a lush greenhouse in your window. Find plans for this handsome unit on page 1492.

SLIDE A FONDUE POT right out of a beautiful piece of furniture, basically made by stacking handsome boxes. See page 1444.

Popular Mechanics

do-it-yourself encyclopedia

in 20 volumes

a complete how-to guide for the homeowner, the hobbyist—
and anyone who enjoys working with mind and hands!

All about:

home maintenance
home-improvement projects
wall paneling
burglary and fire protection
furniture projects
finishing and refinishing furniture
outdoor living
home remodeling
solutions to home problems
challenging woodworking projects
hobbies and handicrafts
model making
weekend projects
workshop shortcuts and techniques
hand-tool skills
power-tool know-how
shop-made tools
car repairs
car maintenance
appliance repair
boating
hunting
fishing
camping
photography projects
radio, TV and electronics know-how
clever hints and tips
projects just for fun

volume 10

ISBN 0-87851-075-3
Library of Congress Catalog Number 77 84920

MANUFACTURED IN THE UNITED STATES OF AMERICA

contents

TWO VIEWS of the same unit show how this novel hi-fi center can change its appearance—and function—at the flick of a finger. Below, it shows off books, magazines, pictures and decorative objects—doesn't look at all like a housing for electronic gear. At right, swung around to its opposite side, it suddenly sports a speaker, tape deck, AM/FM stereo receiver, telephone and other equipment, ready for immediate use. At lower right is a mouth-watering setup for serving party snacks from a Panasonic electric fondue cooker on a slide-out shelf.

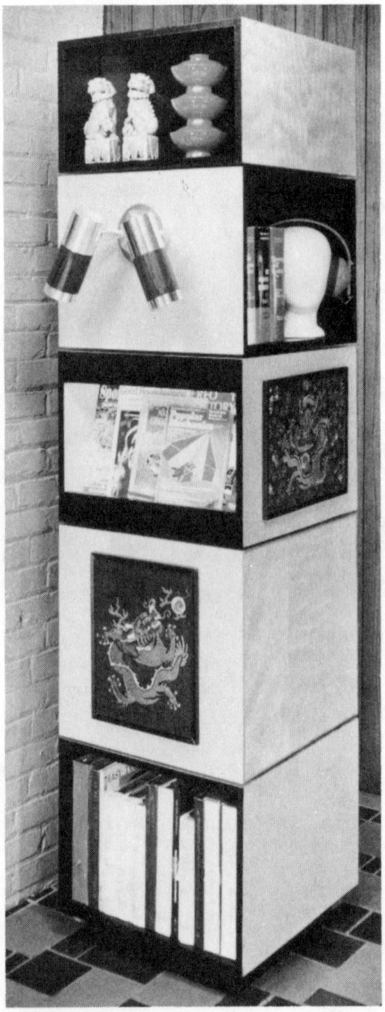

SEE ALSO

Cabinet furniture . . . Cabinets, hi-fi . . . Cassette recorders . . . Cassette tapes . . . Modular furniture . . . Record care . . . Shelves . . . Speakers . . . Storage walls . . . Television antennas

Build a swivel hi-fi center

By SHELDON M. GALLAGER

Turning on ball-bearing pivots, these stacking units can hide home entertainment equipment when it's not in use and swing it quickly into view for instant party fun

A SMART PIECE of furniture by day, an active entertainment center at night—that's the quick-change convenience you get from these stacking enclosures on rotating swivels. Each unit is designed to house one type of equipment on one side and another on the opposite side. Each swings freely on its own pivot, independently of the others. Turned one way, the units provide spaces for books, knick-knacks, pictures and other decorative objects. Swung the other way, the stack changes magically into a hi-fi center with speaker, tape deck, tuner, amplifier, record changer, television set and other electronic gear.

The units are simple boxes—in most cases, open at both ends—so there's no complicated carpentry involved. Three basic modular sizes can be combined in any order and number you wish to handle the particular equipment you have. All have an inside width of 19 inches with a choice of three heights—10½, 14 and 17½ inches. If you like to rack-mount your hi-fi components, you'll note that these dimensions correspond exactly to standard rack-panel sizes—another feature of the modular design. The shallowest unit is handy for small bookshelf-type speakers, receivers, amplifiers and similar low equipment. The middle-sized 14-inch module handles taller items such as a vertically mounted

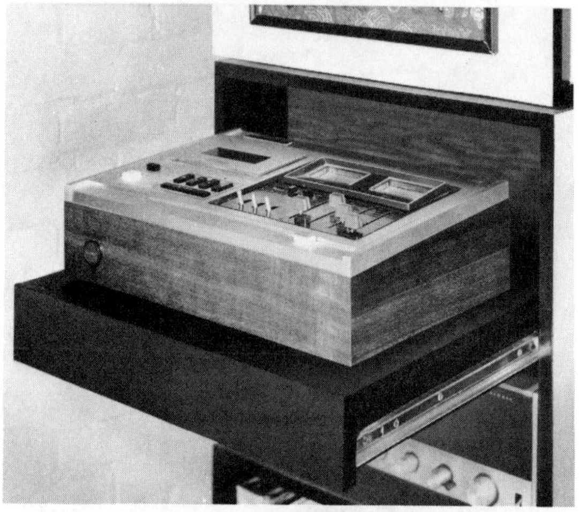

A SLIDE-OUT SHELF is a versatile accessory that can make normally hard-to-reach equipment easily accessible. At the top, it holds a Garrard record changer; at the center, a Panasonic cassette tape deck; at the bottom, a Kodak Carousel slide projector. On the facing page, it doubles as a handy snack server for party guests, sporting one of Panasonic's colorful fondue cookers. The shelf is easy to make using standard 18-inch roller-bearing drawer slides available at hardware stores. A front lip and recessed side rails hide most of the hardware from view. One helpful hint: The rear edges of the shelf must be notched out so you can press down on the release catches to disengage the rails and remove the unit from the cabinet. Otherwise, the shelf will remain locked in once it is inserted.

tape deck, table-model television set or record storage. The still larger 17½-inch unit provides extra overhead clearance for record players with swing-up covers and compact receivers with a turntable on top.

The column shown here is made up of five modules—one 10½-inch size at the top for a speaker, three 14-inchers for general use and one 17½-incher for bulky gear. Their total height comes to 82 inches—just short of 7 feet and about maximum for good appearance in an 8-foot room. All modules are square so they automatically line up with each other no matter which way they're turned. Only the bottom unit doesn't rotate. This rests on a recessed kickboard and forms a fixed, stable base for the swiveling units above it.

All sorts of variations are possible, depending on the particular features you want. You'll note that one unit incorporates a colorful telephone niche, another a sloping magazine rack. The large unit houses a slide-out shelf, handy for quick access to equipment that needs to be reached from the top, such as a turntable, cassette tape deck or slide projector. The shelf can even be used as a mini pull-out bar or snack server for party fun. Internal partitions can be installed wherever needed to divide the units into double-sided enclosures open at either end. The top unit, for instance, houses a speaker on one

SWIVEL ACTION PERMITS the TV set to be turned for the best viewing angle, along with the speaker unit at the top. When not in use, the TV can be hidden from view. The light fixture is one of many dress-up touches.

3 BASIC SIZES OF STACKING CABINETS CAN BE USED IN ANY ORDER

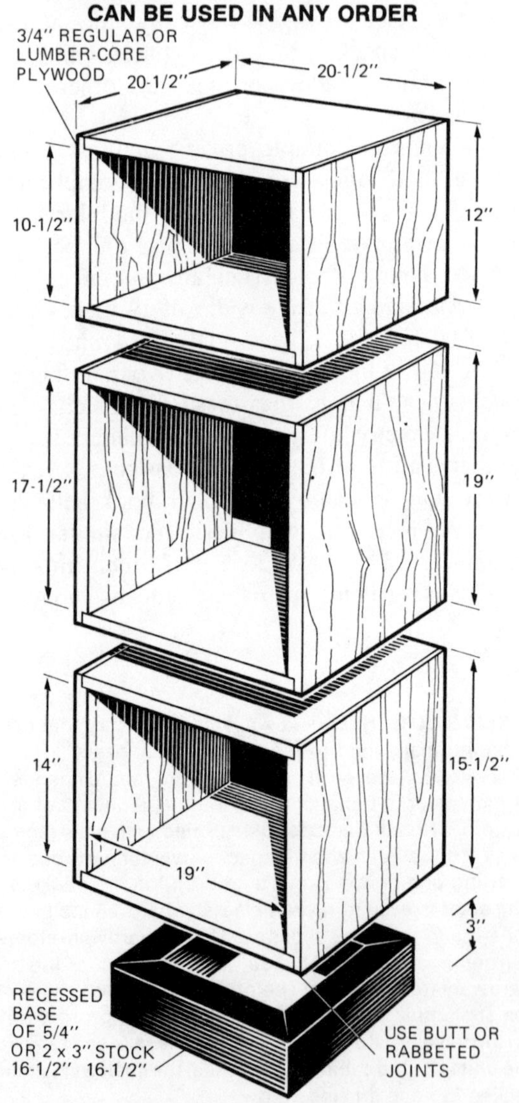

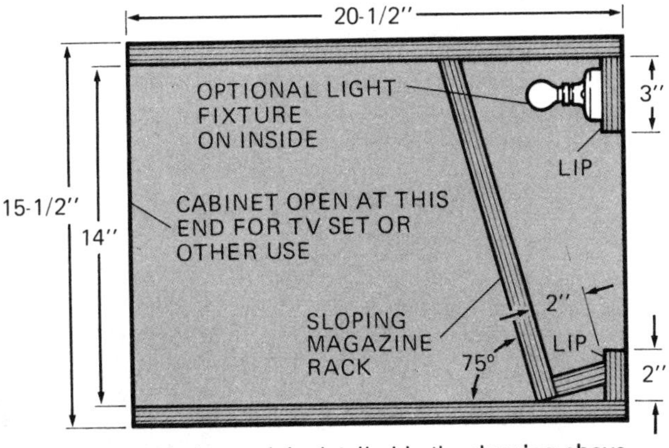

The magazine rack is detailed in the drawing above

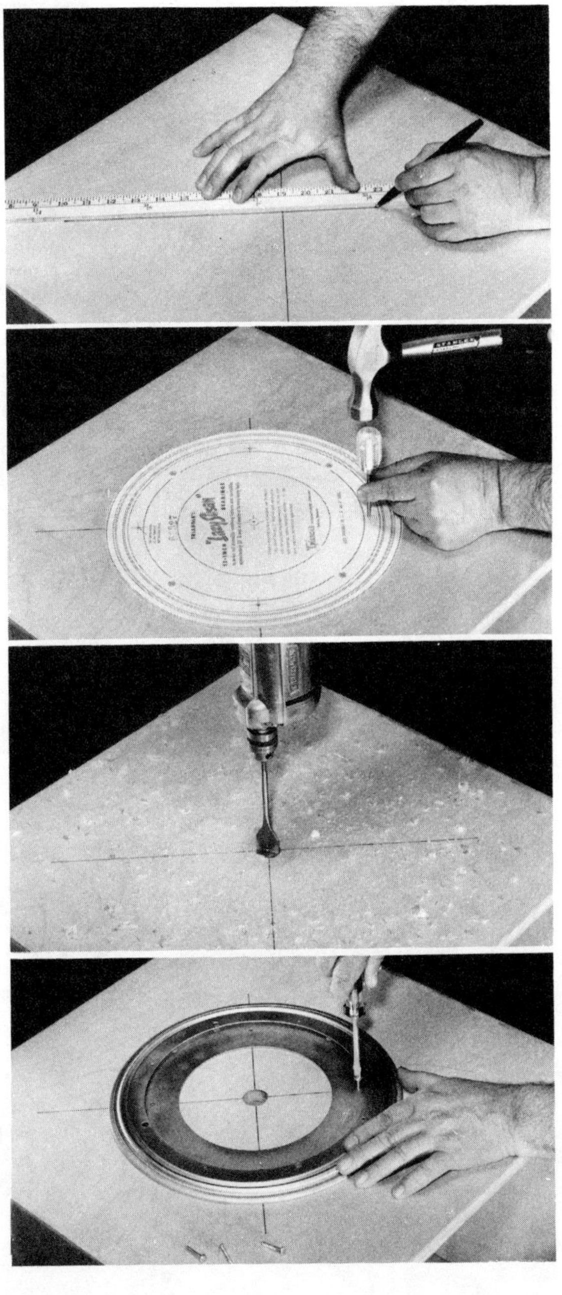

side, a shallow knickknack shelf on the other. The magazine rack hides a TV set in back; an innocent-appearing bookshelf conceals a reel-to-reel tape deck on the opposite side.

The swivels are standard 12-inch-diameter ballbearing types used for making lazy-Susan tables, rotating kitchen shelves and the like. They're available for about $4 each postpaid from Edmund Scientific Co., 300 Edscorp Building, Barrington, N.J. 08007. The swivels can support up to 1000 pounds apiece and turn with surprising ease, even when weighted with heavy hi-fi gear. Attaching them is easy because each comes with a cutout marking template to simplify the location of mounting screws. Power cords, speaker leads, audio cables and antenna wires run down through 1-inch-diameter center holes drilled in the top and bottom of each module. To avoid excessive twisting of the wires, simply remember not to turn the units constantly in the same direction. Rotate them one way to get at one side, then the other way to reach the opposite side.

Constructing the modules is easy because they fit so closely together (the swivels are only ⅜ inch thick) that corner joints are scarcely visible. You can use rabbeted joints if you wish, but simple butts will also do. The units shown here are made of ¾-inch solid-core birch plywood.

THE SWIVELS ARE EASY to mount because they come with marking templates. At the top, the center is found by crisscrossing diagonals from the corners, then the template is used to mark screw holes with a hammer and punch. A center hole is drilled for the wires, then the swivel is screwed on (bottom photo). The photo at the top right shows a Heath speaker and slip-in grille of speaker cloth stapled to a 1 x 2 frame.

An open hi-fi rack

This open, practical hi-fi rack is for people who have good-looking equipment and want to show it off. And for the handyman it's easy to build in his home shop

By JACKSON HAND

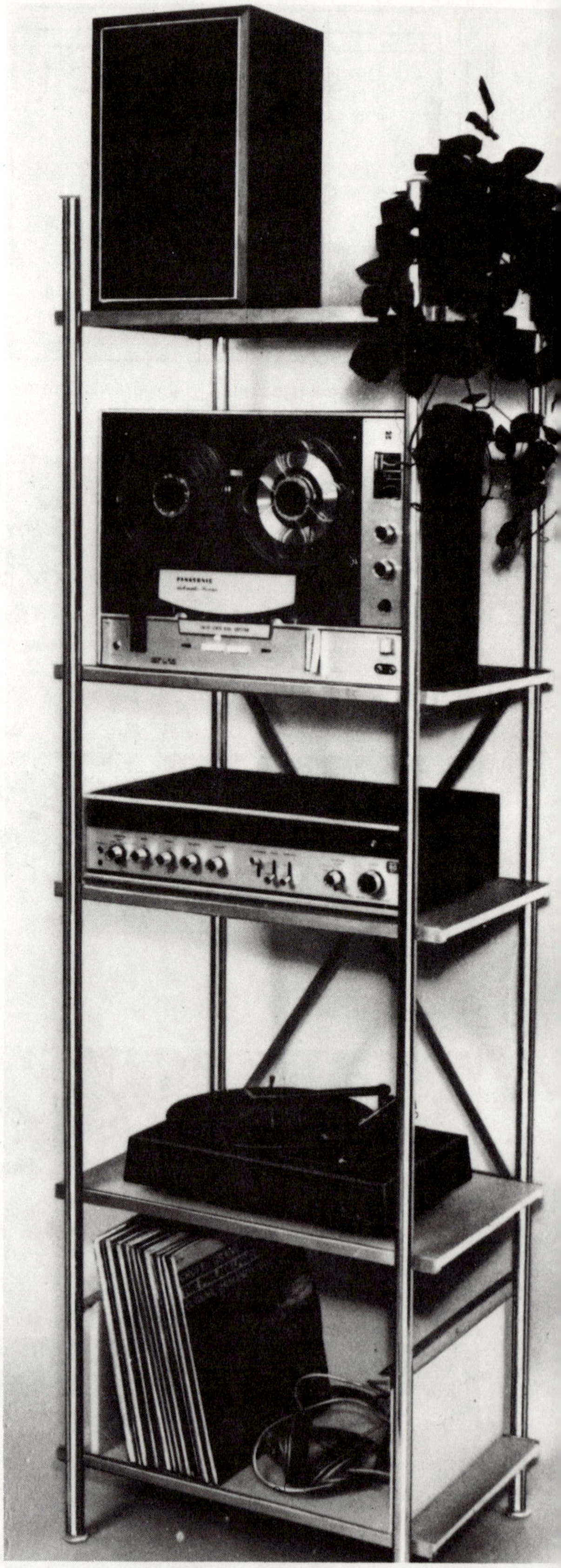

THIS HI-FI RACK is designed to show off your equipment rather than itself. Standing upright, it stacks a lot of gear in a minimum of floor space and puts it out in the open for easy access in making connections and adding or rearranging units. It makes the most of today's smartly styled hi-fi components instead of hiding them behind doors. And it's simple to build.

Basically, the rack consists of tubular aluminum poles for legs with shelves supported between them on aluminum angle cleats. The tubing is the 1-in.-dia. type made by Reynolds and sold at most hardware stores. The aluminum angle is the ¾ x ¾-in. size, also readily available. You buy the tubing in 6-ft. lengths and use them just as they come with no cutting required. The angle is cut into 24-in. sections so you get three even pieces out of each 6-ft. length. The

SEE ALSO
Cabinets, hi-fi . . . Cassette recorders . . . Cassette tapes . . . Etageres . . . Record care . . . Shelves . . . Speakers . . . Storage walls . . . Tubing, metal

THE SHELVES REST in cleats made of aluminum angle (left). One way to fasten the cleats to the uprights is with Pop Rivets (right photos). A pilot hole is drilled in the angle and the angle is clamped to the upright (top). Thus the pilot hole serves to guide the drill for the hole into the round upright. Then the rivet is inserted through both holes and clinched up tight (bottom).

shelves are ½-in. plywood 16 in. deep and 24 in. long. Allowing for a slight overhang at each side, they provide a 20-in. opening between the uprights—wide enough to accommodate all types of hi-fi equipment on the market.

The aluminum has a modern appearance and blends well with the brushed-aluminum panels and trim used on many current hi-fi components. The shelves can be painted black or white for good contrast or stained walnut to match the walnut enclosures popular today.

In attaching the shelf cleats to the uprights, use either Pop Rivets or self-tapping sheet-metal screws that enter only one side of the tubing. Do not run bolts all the way through the tubing as they will tend to crush the walls as they are pulled up tight and will spoil the appearance. Screw the shelves to the cleats from the underside. This has the effect of locking the front and back sections together so they can't pull apart. Extra strength is added by running crisscrossing strips of flat aluminum between the two rear uprights, forming a rigid X-brace. The shelf spacing shown here was designed around a Panasonic tape deck and receiver, but can, of course be adjusted to suit the particular equipment you have. Side pieces on the bottom shelf hold stacks of records or tapes. End caps for the uprights can be made from round wooden drawer pulls, or you can use metal caps. Either will give a finished appearance to this handsome rack.

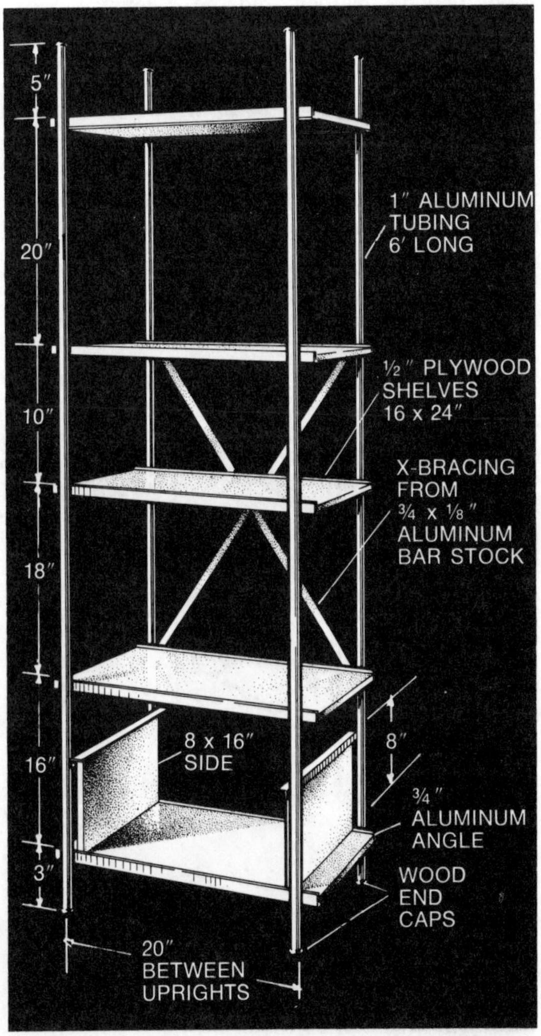

Swing it on the right hinge

There are dozens of hinge types and sizes from which you can choose. Here's how you go about selecting one for your particular purpose

By W. CLYDE LAMMEY

HINGES LET YOU in and out of doors, cabinets and chests, your car, your attaché case—just think of all the things you own that have parts swinging on hinges!

Hinges have come a long way from the thongs, loops of wire, leather, and the squeaky wooden pins and straps used to swing doors and lids not too many generations ago.

Basically a hinge is a simple item consisting of two metal leaves and a pivot pin. The simplest and most common are known as butt hinges. One leaf is ordinarily attached to a fixed member—a door jamb or the back of a box or chest. The other, to the movable member—a lid or door, for example. You could say a hinge lets the movable part move without losing its place.

Hinges of the common types are available with fixed and loose pins and in a wide range of pin styles and leaf shapes. Some are made as reproductions of old types such as the rattail, butterfly and those originally hand-forged at the fire. The latter are finished in attractive simulations of hand-hammered iron. Others are of advanced contemporary design adapting them to use with modern fixtures and furnishings.

Selecting the hinge for the job it is to do is important if it is to give satisfactory service. There are seven points to consider:

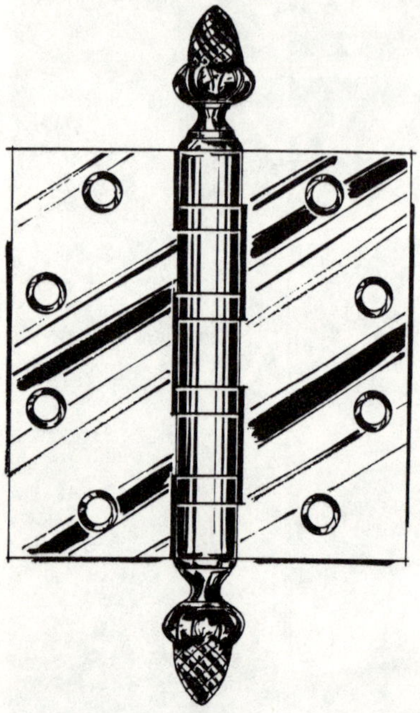

THE SIMPLEST hinges have plain fixed pins, their ends often invisible. But common butt hinges also come with removable pins with flat or ballshaped heads or heads in a great variety of decorative styles such as those below. In such cases, one leaf has a matching head attached so top and bottom of the pin appear to correspond. Other cap styles, such as those on the opposite page, are plainer, perhaps more practical, but still decorative.

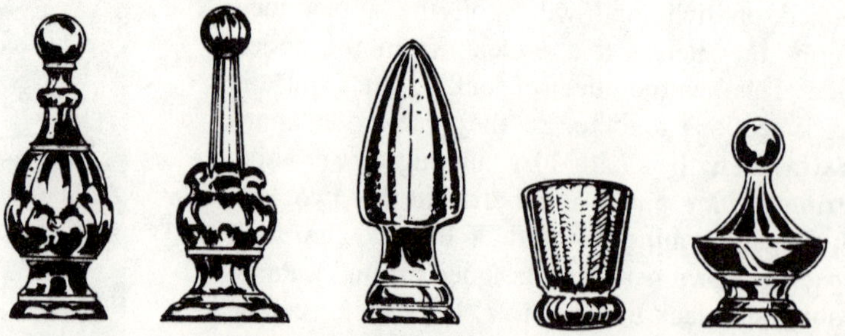

SEE ALSO

Bolts . . . Chests . . . Doors . . . Fasteners . . . Locks, door . . . Lubrication, home . . . Nails . . . Screws . . . Storm doors and windows

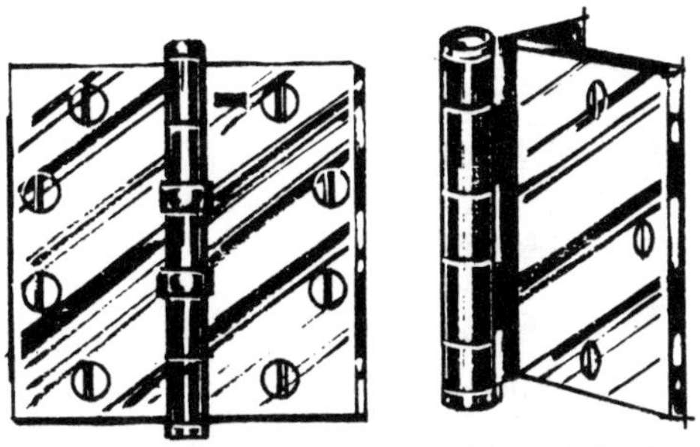

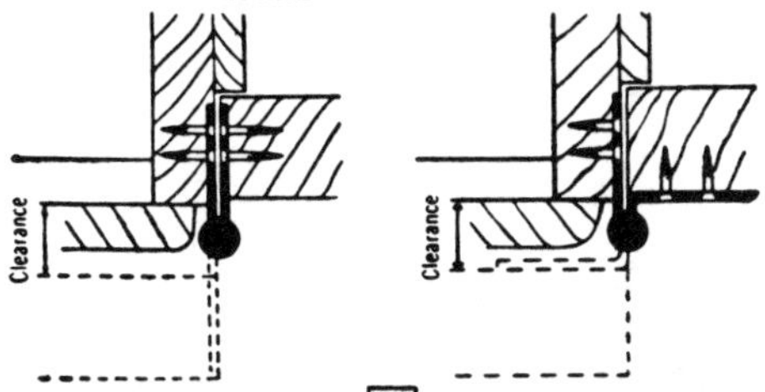

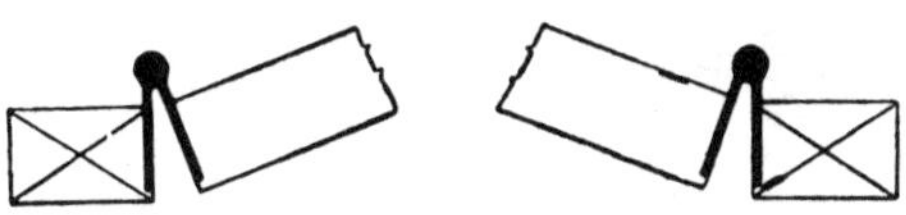

Notice that on doors opening out, the left-hand door takes a left-hand hinge and the right a right-hand hinge. On doors opening in, the hand is reversed

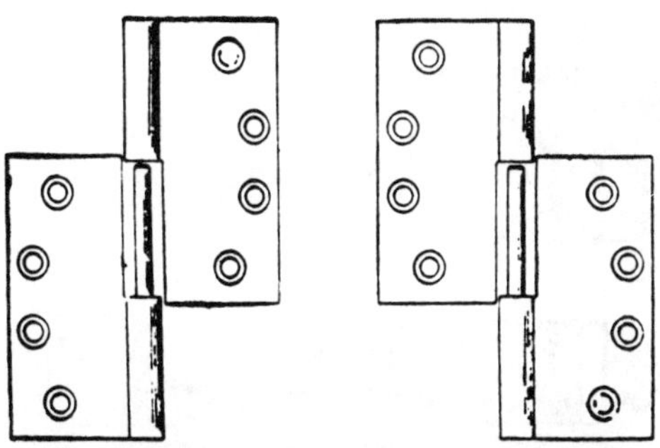

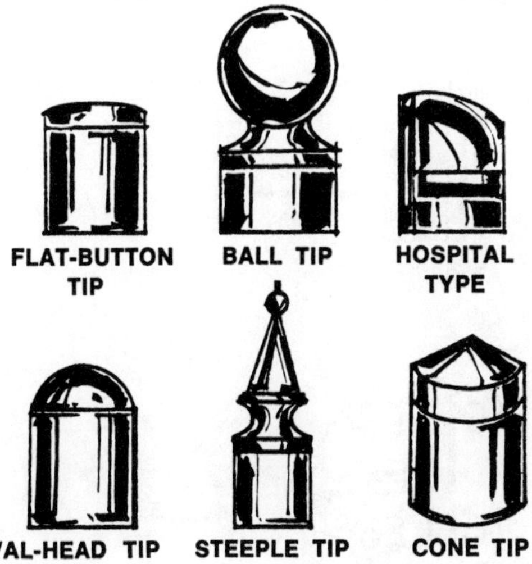

1. The type of hinge required.
2. The type of metal required or desired.
3. The finish desired.
4. The hinge weight and bearing structure.
5. The size of the hinge required.
6. The pin style desired.
7. The "hand" of the hinge.

This list is not as imposing as it may appear. In general, common door hinges are of four types: the full-mortise, half mortise, half surface and full surface. Again, in general, you have a choice of three groups of hinge weights and bearing structures; regular weight with plain bearing; extra heavy with plain bearing; and regular weight with ball bearings—that's right, ball bearings.

As a rule, the full-mortise hinge with plain bearing is perhaps the most commonly installed on entrance doors. If yours is an average family, your entrance door—the one you use mostly going and coming, front or back—swings on its hinges 40 times daily, or roughly 15,000 times a year. This classes it as a "medium-frequency" door. But 15,000 openings a year add up to a lot of punishment on the wear surfaces of the hinges, which are generally lubricated less frequently than they should be.

Such doors, if they are of average height and width and 1¾ in. or more in thickness, should normally swing either on three extra-heavy, plain-bearing, full-mortise hinges, or three regular-weight, ball-bearing hinges for maximum hinge life. Lower-frequency doors are usually hung on hinges of regular weights. It's generally recommended that doors fitted with closers be hung on ball-bearing hinges for maximum service.

Half-surface hinges are often used on the lighter screen and storm doors. One leaf is screwed to the door stile; the other is mortised into the jamb. The half-mortise hinge is the reverse—mortised into the door and applied to the surface of the jamb. The full-surface hinge is screwed to both door and jamb (or trim) surfaces. Of course, the full-mortise hinge is mortised into both door and jamb.

The hand of a butt hinge is determined from the outside of the door. How? Just stand inside the doorway with your back to the hinge side of the jamb. If the door is to swing to your right, it takes a right-hand hinge; if to the left a left-hand hinge. The outside of a cupboard, bookcase, cabinet or closet door is the room side, of course.

In cabinet hinges you can just about write

BUTT HINGES

Full mortise, regular weight, nontemplate, nonrising pin, five knuckles, button tips. For doors of residences and apartment houses and other medium-weight wood doors receiving infrequent service. This butt is used where a high grade of hardware is desired. Used on wood doors with wood jambs. Size open: 2″ x 2″, 2½″ x 2½″, 3″ x 3″, 3½″ x 3½″, 4″ x 4″, 4½″ x 4½″, 5″ x 5″, 6″ x 6″

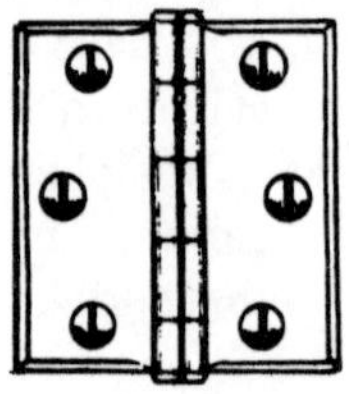

Full surface, regular weight, nontemplate, five knuckles, button tips, flat back. For folding doors. Smaller sizes are recommended for cabinet doors. Used on wood doors. Size open: 2″ x 2″, 2½″ x 2½″, 3″ x 3″, 3½″ x 3½″, 4″ x 4″

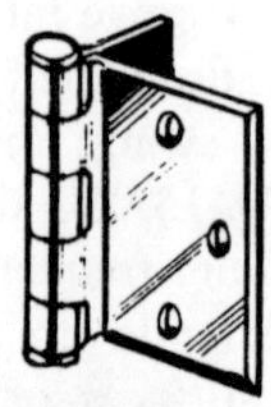

Half surface, regular weight, nontemplate. For doors of residences or combination screen and sash doors. Smaller sizes recommended for cabinets only. Used on wood doors with wood jambs. Size in length of joint: 2″, 2½″, 3″, 3¼″, 4″, 4½″, 5″

Half mortise, regular weight, template, nonrising pin, five knuckles, button tips, two ball bearings. For medium-weight hollow-metal doors receiving average frequency service. Used on hollow-metal doors with channel-iron jambs. Size: 4½″, 5″

Ball tips furnished in place of button tips on above hinges on order

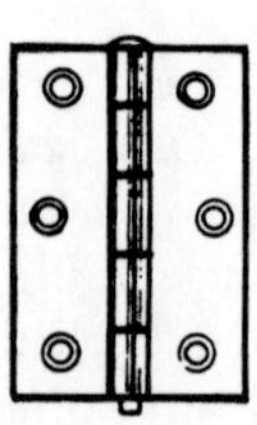

Narrow, lightweight, wrought steel, loose oval-head pin.

Joint size	Width open size
1″	1″
1½″	1⅜″
2″	1⁹⁄₁₆″
2½″	1¹¹⁄₁₆″
3″	2″
3½″	2¼″
4″	1⅞″
4½″	3″
5″	3³⁄₁₆″
6″	3¹⁵⁄₁₆″

OLIVE-KNUCKLE HINGE

Right hand

Full mortise, regular weight, nontemplate. For medium-weight doors receiving average frequency service. This hinge is equipped with a ball bearing. The pins in the brass and bronze are stainless steel. Loose joint. Specify hand. Good on wood doors with wood jambs. Size open: 5″, 6″

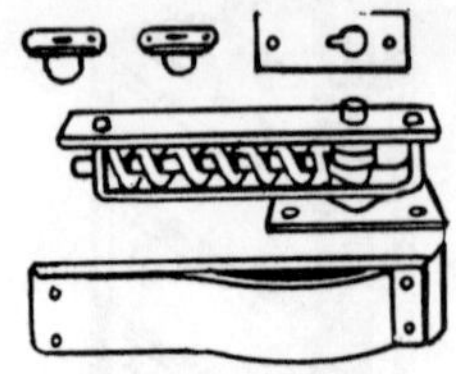

Ball bearing. Holds the door open at 96 deg. For 1¼ to 1¾″ doors. Beveled edge. Reversible side. Plate, 9 ½″ x 2 ⅜″. Floor plate, 3¼″ x 2¾″

CONTINUOUS HINGE

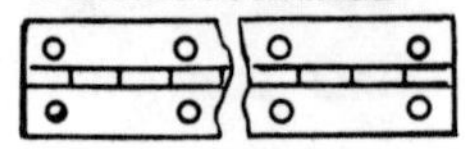

Wrought steel and wrought brass

STRAP HINGE

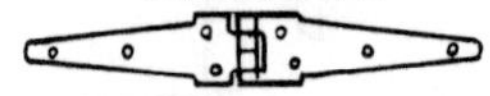

Wrought steel. Size (length each leaf): 2″, 3″, 4″, 5″, 6″, 8″, 10″, 12″

T-HINGE

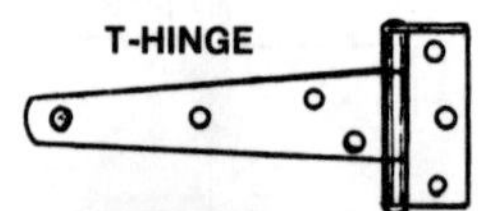

Size (length of strap): 4″, 5″, 6″, 8″, 10″, 12″, 14″

ADJUSTABLE-TENSION SPRING HINGE

Full surface. The spring tension may be adjusted for any weight door by moving adjusting peg. Furnished with loose reversible pin. Size open: 2¾″ x 2¾″

SCREW HOOK AND STRAP HINGE

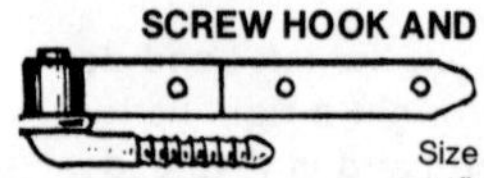

Size (length of strap): 6″, 8″, 10″, 12″, 14″, 16″, 18″, 20″, 22″, 24″, 30″, 36″

CABINET HINGES

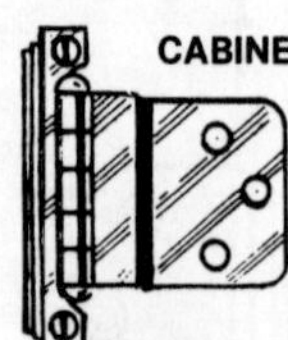

For lipped doors (⅜″ lip) Offset, ⅜″, ½″, ¾″. Jamb-leaf length, 2 ½″

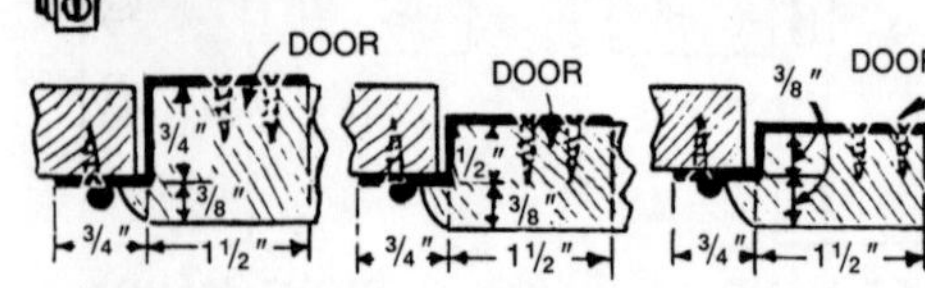

Offset, ⅜″. Jamb-leaf length, 2½″

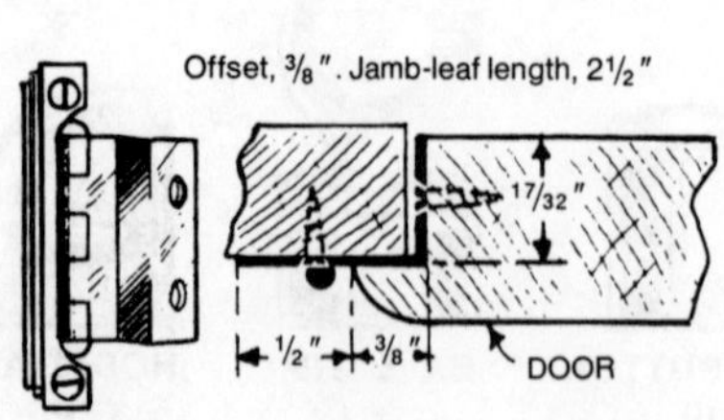

Offset, ⅜″. Joint, 1¼″

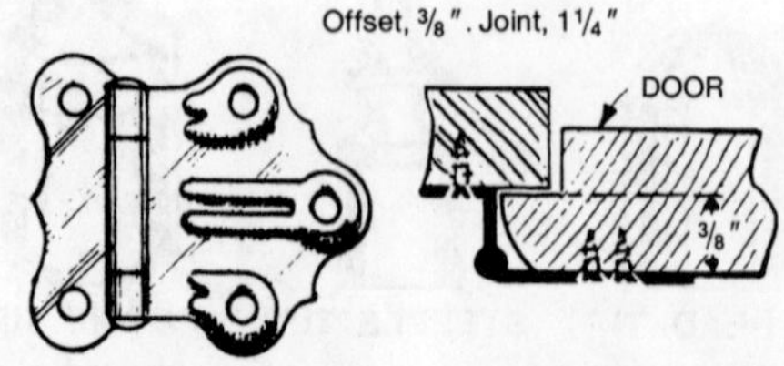

your own ticket. You can buy a hinge to swing almost anything you're of a mind to hang—lipped doors, flush doors, slab or overlay doors, with hinges either concealed, visible or partly visible.

Hinges commonly come in five metals: steel, stainless steel, brass, bronze and aluminum. The latter four are rustproof and corrosion-resistant. Hinges of ordinary steel, a ferrous metal, are not corrosion-resistant or rustproof but have greatest strength and wearability. Hinges of steel should be protected with paint if exposed to weathering. Common cabinet and door hinges are also supplied plated.

There are also special-purpose hinges, such as two-way door and panel hinges, spring-actuated hinges that close the door when you release it, and hinges that hold the door open until released.

It's a common practice (and generally recommended) that all outside doors of 1¾-in. thickness be hung on three hinges rather than a pair.

Of course it's important that the pins of the three hinges be in precise alignment. Most hardware dealers will give you a simple template with which you mark the location of the hinge leaves on both the door and jamb. You also punch-mark the location of the screws with the same template. There also are special tools available for marking and locating hinge mortises and screw holes on both door and jamb.

Contractors and others with a number of doors to hang generally speed up the job by using a special adjustable template that clamps on the edge of the door. Sliding members of the template are then arranged to locate the mortises. A router with a special guide is used to cut the mortises, each to exact size to take the leaves of the hinges being used. The whole operation takes only a minute or two per door.

But as a do-it-yourselfer you rely on the simple template and careful workmanship. Good fitting calls for neatly cut mortises in both door and jamb. That means you work with a razor-sharp chisel and a light hand on the hammer; and you take special care to locate screw holes exactly on center. It'll take you more time "by hand" but if you watch each step of procedure you can hang any door as neatly as the pros.

Hinges (except exterior steel ones) should not be painted, and they should be lubricated occasionally. Lift the pin slightly and run a single drop of light oil around it. Then tap it lightly back in place.

DETERMINING PROPER HINGE LENGTHS

Thickness of doors (in inches)	Width of doors or height of transoms (in inches)	Height of butt hinges (length of joint) (in inches)
¾ and ⅞ cupboard doors	To 24	2½
⅞ and 1⅛ screen doors	To 36	3
1⅛ doors	To 36	3½
1¼ and 1⅜ doors	To 32	3½
1¼ and 1⅜ doors	Over 32 to 37	4
1⁹⁄₁₆, 1¾ and 1⅞ doors	To 32	4½
1⁹⁄₁₆, 1¾ and 1⅞ doors	Over 32 to 37	5
1⁹⁄₁₆, 1¾ and 1⅞ doors	Over 37 to 43	5 extra heavy
1⁹⁄₁₆, 1¾ and 1⅞ doors	Over 43 to 50	6 extra heavy
2, 2¼ and 2½ doors	To 43	5 extra heavy
2, 2¼ and 2½ doors	Over 43 to 50	6 extra heavy
1¼ and 1⅜ transoms	To 20	2½
1¼ and 1⅜ transoms	Over 20 to 36	3
1½, 1⁹⁄₁₆, 1¾ and 1⅞ transoms	To 20	3
1½, 1⁹⁄₁₆, 1¾ and 1⅞ transoms	Over 20 to 36	3½
2, 2¼ and 2½ transoms	To 20	3½
2, 2¼ and 2½ transoms	Over 20 to 36	4

Number of hinges required

Doors 60" high and under	2 butt hinges
Doors over 60" high and not over 90" high	3 butt hinges
Doors over 90" high and not over 120" high	4 butt hinges
Transoms 48" wide and under	2 butt hinges
Transoms over 48" wide and not over 84" wide	3 butt hinges

Build a foldaway hobby center

By HANK CLARK

This compact wall cabinet serves both father and son in providing the best in a place to tinker or get lost in a hobby

SEE ALSO
Airplane models . . . Cannon models . . . Drawers . . . Modelmaking . . . Ship models . . . Storage ideas . . . Workbenches . . . Workshops

ANY HOBBY can be twice the fun when you have a place all your own to work. A place that's off limits to other members of the family, that has everything within easy reach and can be closed up for safekeeping when you walk away.

Whatever your hobby—model building, slot cars, electronics, trains or just plain tinkering—this hobby center is the ultimate in a place to work. You can come and go without having to clean up each time; there are shelves, drawers and tool panels galore, and it all folds up into a compact wall cabinet that's only 18 in. deep.

The center is unique in the way it unfolds for

work. It has a 24 x 48-in. "workbench" that lets down like a drawing board, nesting tool-panels that swing out and a bank of drawers that swing with a door to reveal inner shelves for paints, airplane dope and parts. A sound-absorbing pinup board of acoustical tile across the back lets you stick up what you can't hang up. There's a nook for books and room to display your "works of art." What's more, there's a tray under the hinged drawing-board workbench for storing drawing paper, plans and other drafting essentials, and when the workbench swings up, you have a second pinup board on the underside. A strip line outlet across the back of the work center provides convenient plug-ins for a hand grinder, soldering iron and glue gun.

A handy lamp on an adjustable swiveling arm is attached to the upper shelf so it can be aimed right down on your work. The lids of baby-food jars screwed to the underside of the upper shelf let you store countless small parts in glass jars.

A SHALLOW TRAY hinged to the underside of the drawing-board workbench provides plenty of handy storage for plans and papers. Light flips out of way.

a catch holds it vertical

The slanting workbench is supported by two drawers which have turnbutton legs attached to the inside. The legs swing down inside the drawers to let you close them. To clear the workbench for swinging it up, materials and work can be pushed back under the 12-in. bottom shelf. A cupboard catch screwed to the upper shelf holds the workbench in a vertical position.

Your hobby center should be a minimum of 6 ft. long to accommodate a 48-in. long workbench. The end pieces of the cabinet are 18-in.-wide plywood and cut back to 11½ in. at a point 29 in. from the lower end. The ends are joined with a 1 x 12 shelf placed 11 in. down from the top and with an 18-in. wide counter. Then a second 1 x 12 shelf is placed between the ends, 5 in. above the counter. Next, a 1 x 6 is placed vertically between the two 1 x 12 shelves 16 in. in from the right-hand end and flush with the back of the cabinet. Four short shelves are fitted between the 1 x 6 and the cabinet end. A second 1 x 6 is installed vertically at the opposite end of the center tool panel and another shelf is placed between the 1 x 6s, 5 in. up from the lower 1 x 12. The area above this shelf is filled with a Celotex or cork pinup board.

The slanting workbench is hinged to the edge of the 1 x 12. When it swings up it laps the two swing-out doors.

Basic stock for this project is ¾-in. A-D (good one side) fir plywood. However, hardwood-faced plywood (¾-in.) in walnut, oak,

THIS IS HOW the center looks when it's closed. The Celotex bottom in the tray provides a pinup board for your clippings. Basic unit is plywood.

continued

maple, etc., can be used for a "furniture finish."

If you use fir plywood, be sure to smooth the surfaces that will show with fine sandpaper on a block. Then prime the surface with a plywood paint and sand it again to remove the "tooth" of the grain. Two coats of enamel provides the best finish; lightly sand the surfaces between coats and wipe with a tack cloth.

BASIC CONSTRUCTION DETAILS

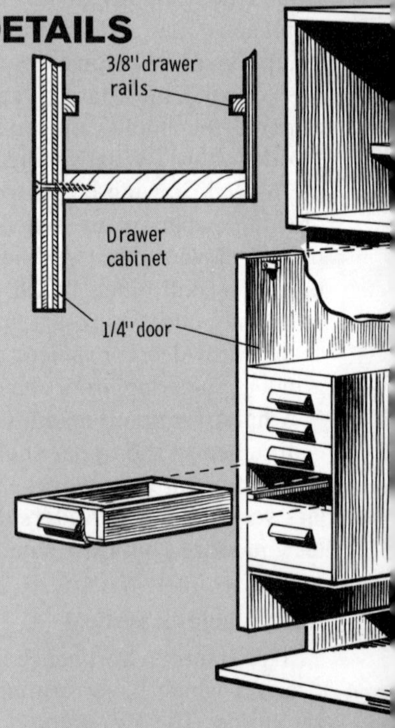

Your basic material is ¾-inch plywood, simple to work with. But hardwood-faced plywood will make a "furniture finish" piece to grace your home as well as give you a place to work. Complicated cuts, curves and angles, are avoided. You'll find that a table saw and a drill do everything that's required. Repeated use of simple butt hinges allows the 18 inches of depth to open out until you get almost another room.

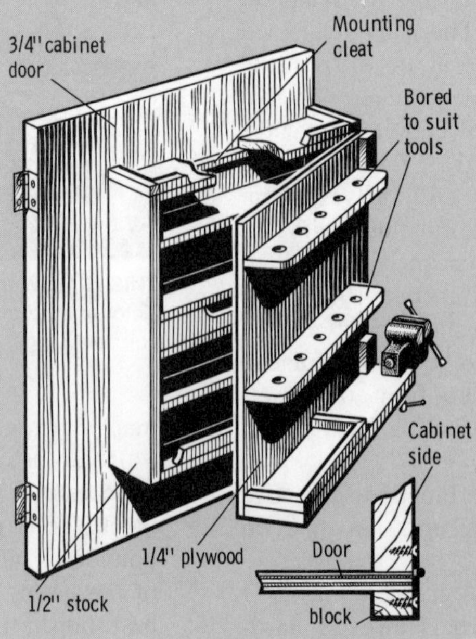

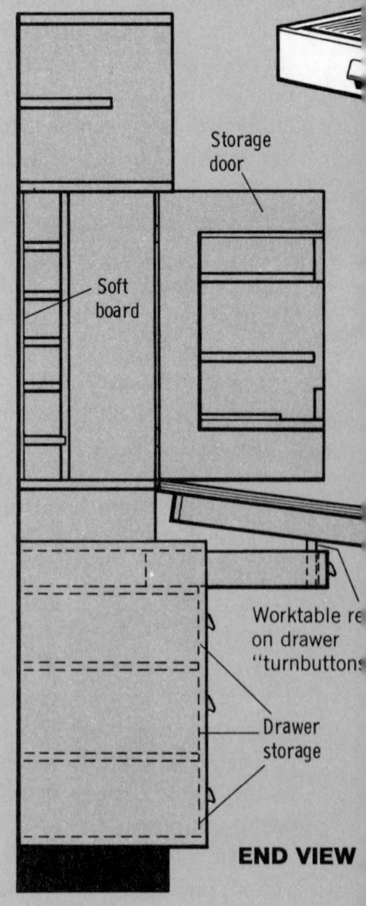

Worktable
1/2" soft-board bottom
3/4 x 3"
DRAWING-STORAGE TRAY
Work-table
Tray
Upsom board
T-hinge
3" butts

ONE BIG skylight turned this enclosed porch into a solarium that is bright on the dreariest days. At night you can stay warm while you count the stars

Let the sun shine in

By MIKE MCCLINTOCK

■ AS A BUILDER I've installed many different skylights in many different locations. I'm still amazed at the difference one can make in a room. The enclosed porch in these pictures was added onto the house, and although there are windows all along the outside wall, little light was transmitted across the porch into the adjacent living room. And dark wood on walls and ceilings made the porch seem smaller than it really was.

A dormer might have worked here, or a raised roof. But of all possibilities, the easiest and least expensive was also the best. A neighbor and I opened the ceiling with the largest skylight available, a 46-inch-square unit from Ventarama Corp., 40 Haven Ave., Port Washington, NY. I think they're the best units going and have never had a callback on a job where I've used them. They're fully assembled and framed, use integral copper flashing and have a screen and an operator mechanism to lift the bubble for summer venting. I recommend this type instead of a fixed unit because it is less susceptible to condensation caused by hot, humid air collecting near the ceiling. For a vaulted ceiling or crawlspace over a flat ceiling, the roof installation is the same. A dropped ceiling needs more framing to close off the crawlspace.

To start, we located the skylight area inside and made corresponding measurements to get the exact location on the roof. On a vaulted ceiling, after cutting away the Sheetrock, drive a

RAIN, ICE and snow don't bother the Ventarama unit shown above. You can leave it open for ventilation and not run home to close it if it starts to rain. A curved flange at the base keeps water from dripping into the opening. The hardware is strong enough to break through a crust of ice after a storm (left). Check your job with a hose test (right)

10d nail up through the roof at each corner of the opening to mark the cutout. With the area outlined, we pulled off shingles and felt paper and cut through the roof deck with a sabre saw (drawing 1). Then we cut away the center rafter. Be sure to cut an extra 3 inches at each end to allow for double headers that frame the opening and carry the load from the interrupted rafter (draw-

TOOLS OF THE TRADE

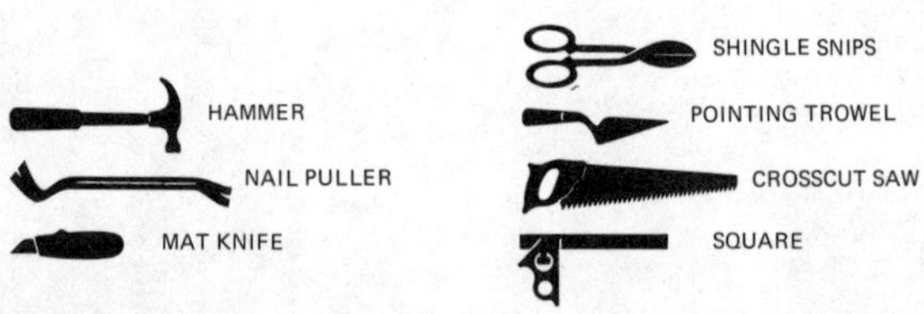

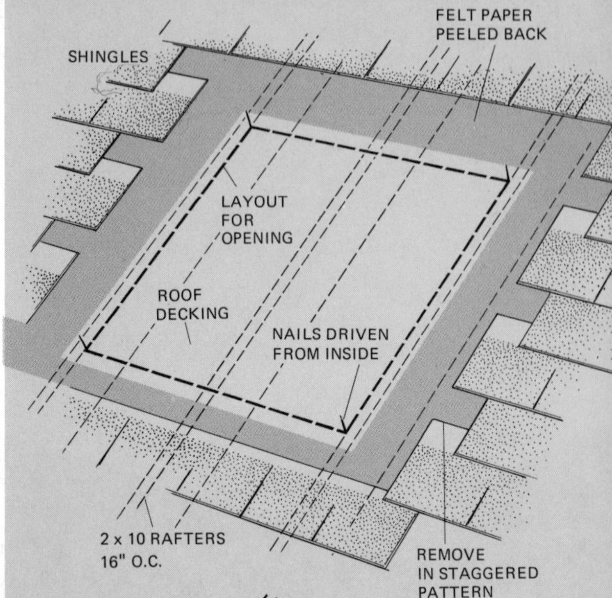

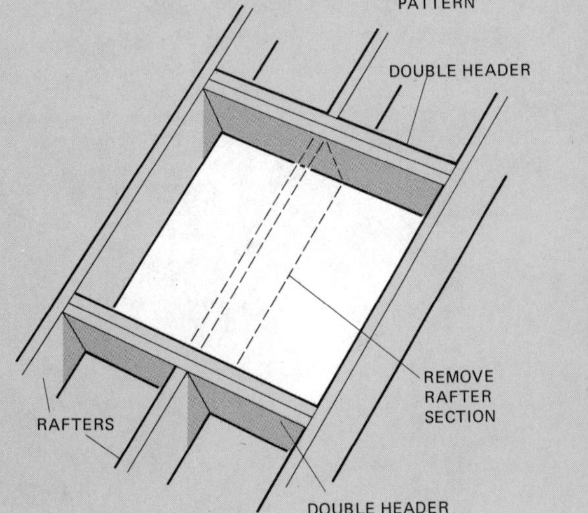

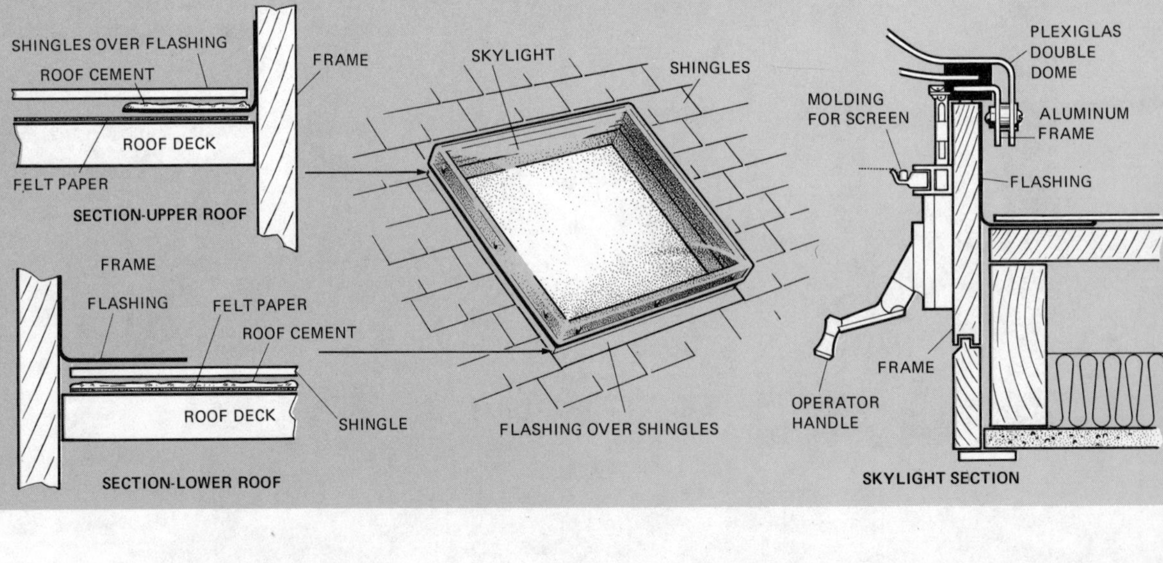

THE ROOF window shown above is made in Denmark. It's from Velux-American, 80 Cummings Park, Woburn MA

ing 2). We repeated this cut in the wooden ceiling below but increased the depth of the opening to let in more light. We then nailed 2x4 uprights along edges of the two openings to frame the short tunnel between outer and inner roofs.

For a more waterproof condition, we set flashing around the unit in a bed of roof cement and secured the bubble with nails through the frame into the adjacent rafters (drawing 3). The final step outside is to lace the shingles (use the ones you removed) back into the roofing pattern and cut them to fit the flashing. Above the unit we set the shingles in a second bed of cement over the copper flange to prevent water from backing up underneath. Along sides, shingles should run 2 to 3 in. past the lip of the flashing that is secured to the roof with copper clips. On the lower edge, the flashing sits in a bed of roof cement spread on top of the shingles so all water will run onto the roof surface. While the frame is open, check the installation for leaks by simulating a downpour with a garden hose.

We used ¼-inch A-C plywood over the tunnel frame and painted it white to reflect as much light as possible. Molding strips along edges of the ceiling cutout gave a final finishing touch. You can treat the interior many ways (even with mirrors) but you must make the exterior waterproof. Follow the maker's instructions and the steps outlined. Pinpointing the source of a leak later on is, at best, a guessing game; you may have to redo all the flashing. On our job we angled the back wall of the tunnel to let the sun's rays stream directly through double glass doors into the living room. The porch is now so bright that we converted it into a solarium with plants.

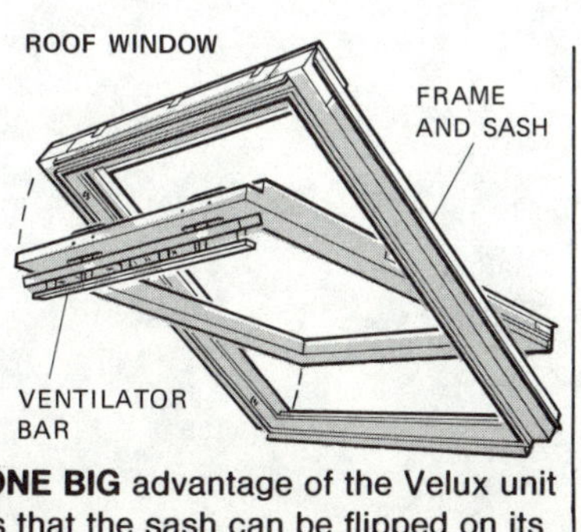

ONE BIG advantage of the Velux unit is that the sash can be flipped on its pivot hinge for easy cleaning, inside or out

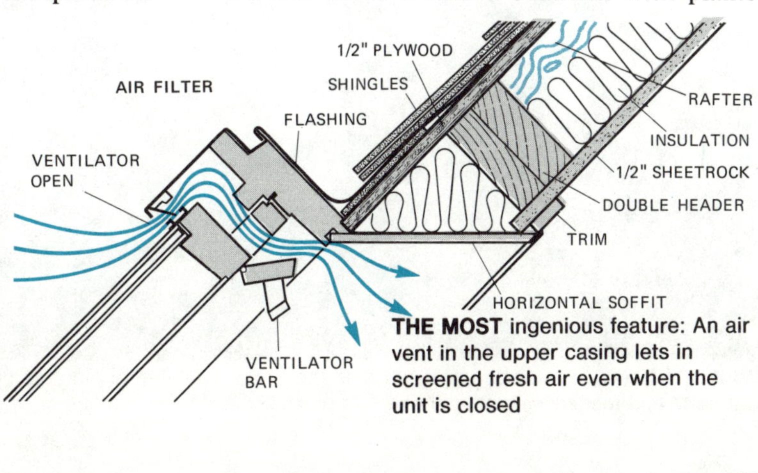

THE MOST ingenious feature: An air vent in the upper casing lets in screened fresh air even when the unit is closed

WHILE THIS coffee table can be sized to fit the space you plan to put it in, construction method remains the same. Cut parts and test-assemble them, then disassemble and paint. Lattice on walls can be screwed or nailed.

Create an unusual room with strips of wood

■ INSTALLING LATTICE STRIPS over a painted wall is one quick way to give a room a new feeling. And, if you can apply strips to one or more pieces of furniture at the same time, you will give the room a custom look.

In the room on the facing page, strips of 1½-in.-wide lattice are applied diagonally to the wall at 45° angles. The vertical and horizontal strips that box in the diagonals simplify the installation considerably.

The coffee table is a shop project that requires one sheet of ½-in. plywood and about a weekend of your time. You can use interior-grade, A-D plywood for the table and not worry about the edges because they will be covered with lattice.

All four sides are exactly the same size. Cut these pieces first when building the table; then carefully stack them to make sure they are identical.

On the D side of the plywood, install the glue cleats at one end of each side as shown—set back ½ in. to receive the joining side. The cleats can be fastened using either 1¼-in. ringed nails or 1-in. flathead screws (turned into countersunk holes.) If you opt for the nails, use your diagonal cutter to nip off the tip of each nail before driving (or the points will come through the plywood). Next, install the cleats upon which the top will rest. With sides completed, the case can be assembled. When all four sides are assembled, check with a square to make certain corners are exactly 90°. *Before the glue has a chance to dry,* measure for, and cut, the top piece. Install the top using glue and flathead screws in *deep* countersunk holes. If you have cut the top perfectly square and with a neat fit, it will hold the case square while the glue dries. When dry, the screw holes on top can be filled.

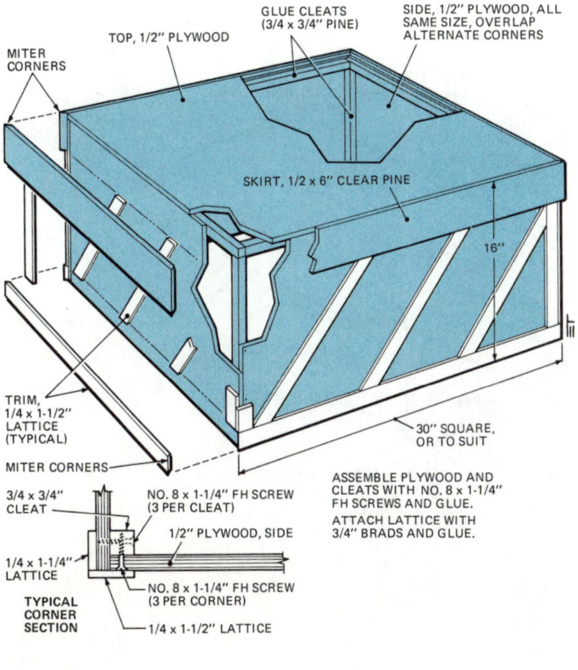

ASSEMBLE PLYWOOD AND CLEATS WITH NO. 8 x 1-1/4" FH SCREWS AND GLUE. ATTACH LATTICE WITH 3/4" BRADS AND GLUE.

Lay out the lattice and cut all strips and assemble without glue to check for layout and fit. When satisfied, remove the lattice and apply a finish before final assembly.

For a proper finish, sand all surfaces of the table with a belt sander; first use an 80-grit paper, then 120-grit. Dust off and apply a coat of a pigmented shellac, such as Bin. Repeat the steps for the lattice.

Next, sand all painted surfaces lightly with 150-grit abrasive paper; dust and wipe with a tack cloth. Apply the finish color of your choice to the table and white semigloss paint to the lattice.

Lattice for the walls should also be painted before application. It can be secured to the wall using flathead wood screws into wall studs or white glue and 6d finishing nails. No matter which fastener you use, be sure to predrill holes to avoid splitting.

SEE ALSO

Basement remodeling . . . Brick, simulated . . . Family rooms . . . Painting, interior . . . Paneling, hardboard . . . Paneling, plywood . . . Paneling, wood . . . Remodeling

Six low-cost home improvements

- Decorative planter for the bath
- Laundry center for compacts
- Charming door chime
- Away-from-home security
- Attractive new yard light
- A dimmer for mood dining

By WAYNE C. LECKEY

DECORATIVE PLANTER

Greenery does wonders in adding a glamorous look to a bathroom. If you are looking for an attractive way to display plants, here's how it can be done cleverly with a cantilevered planter that actually does double duty in supporting the sink.

Securely lagscrewed to studs in both back and end walls, an open frame as shown at left will give ample support for the lavatory while providing flanking twin planters for live or artificial greens. If artificial, omit the metal liners and use 2-inch-thick slabs of green Styrofoam to hold your greenery. In each case, the planters are fitted with wood bottoms. You can make the boxlike frame from common ¾-in. fir plywood and give it a rich, expensive look by covering it with wood-grain plastic laminate such as Formica. Use glue and flathead wood screws to assemble the frame. Fancy towel rings add to the overall good looks. The original planter was made to support American-Standard's 20 x 30-in. Ultra lavatory in marble china finish.

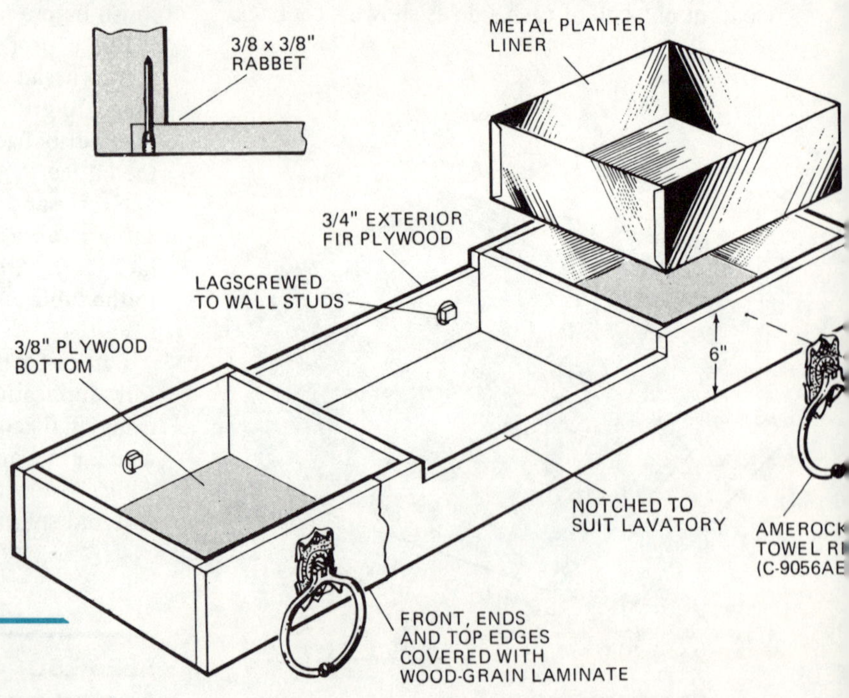

SEE ALSO
Bathrooms . . . Checkers, outlet . . . Clothes dryers . . . Doorbells . . . Electrical wiring . . . Planters . . . Security, home . . . Washing machines . . . Wiring, electrical . . . Yard lighting

LAUNDRY CENTER

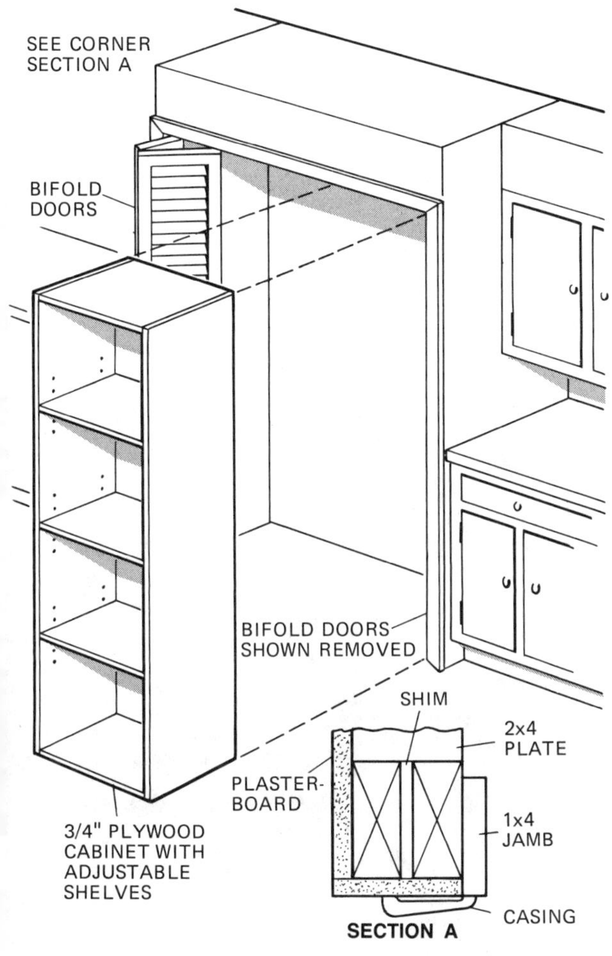

When the wash is done and you'd like to park your rollabout compact washer out of sight, you can do it in this kitchen "garage." The built-in not only accommodates the washer and companion dryer but provides four roomy shelves for storage. When closed, good-looking bifold doors hide it all from view. A space-saver stack rack lets you roll and store the washer under the dryer in a 21-in. space. The floor-to-ceiling, closet-like enclosure is framed with 2 x 4 studs and ⅜-in. plasterboard, and the freestanding shelf unit is a simple plywood box open front and back. Compact appliances are by Westinghouse.

DIMMER SWITCH

If dining by soft, simulated candlelight is not reason enough to install a dimmer control in place of the conventional toggle switch, maybe a lower electric bill is. Keeping lights in the TV room, baby's room and halls at a low level will save energy and money, even extend bulb life.

Some dimmers control light intensity by a knob you turn, others like this solid-state Glyder by Lutron which has a knob you slide up and down. It's simple to install a dimmer switch. Turn off the electricity, then remove screws holding the wall plate, back out the screws that hold the old switch in the outlet box and disconnect wires. Then you reverse the steps to connect the new switch, press a fingertip control button in place over the end and turn the electricity back on.

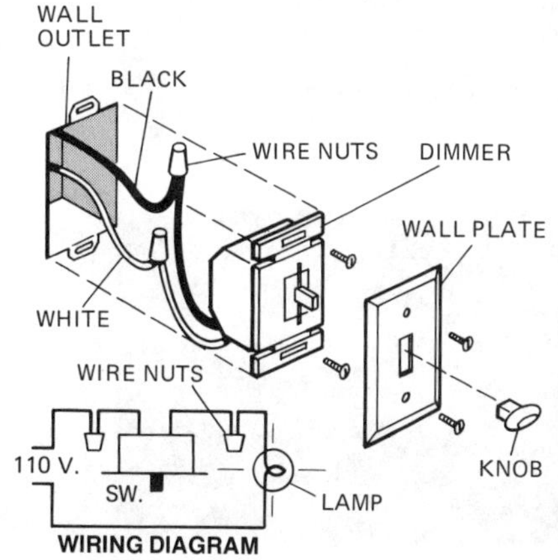

DOOR CHIME

If you have been wanting to update that raucous door buzzer with a new melodious chime but haven't done so because the thought of electricity bothers you, there's no need to worry. In making the switch from old to new, you are actually dealing with low-voltage wiring that's safe and easy to handle. The job requires little more than unhooking the existing wires and attaching your new chime. The diagram shows how wires from the front and back-door buttons go.

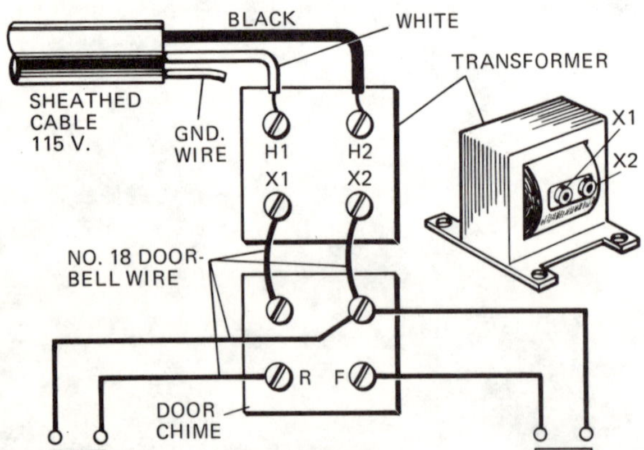

TWO-DOOR SYSTEM

DOOR CHIMES can be contemporary works of art and striking wall accents. This is the Sculpture model by Nutone.

HOME SECURITY

10:00 P.M. Kids in bed. Mom and Dad watch late movie in family room. Rest of house is dark.

12:30 A.M. Movie is over, lights go out in family room, on in kitchen where Dad has midnight snack.

12:55 P.M. Snack's over, lights go out in kitchen, on in bedroom. Mom and Dad are retiring.

1:30 P.M. Junior awakens, makes trip to bathroom, leaves light on for Dad to turn out later.

LAMPPOST FOR YOUR YARD

A yard light does many things. It bids welcome. It discourages prowlers. It adds nighttime beauty to the yard and lights the way to your door.

Before installing a yard light, check your local building department on electrical code compliance. Then dig a posthole (below the area's frostline) and a narrow trench to the power source. Once the cable is laid in the trench and up through the post, place the post in the hole, plumb and brace it in both planes with stakes. Fill the hole with concrete mix to about 6 in. below ground level. Let the concrete set 24 to 48 hours, then mount the lamp fixture. Attach the black cable wire to the black fixture wire, the white cable wire to the white fixture wire and the green cable wire to a ground connection on the fixture. If power is from a surface outlet on the house exterior, turn off the current and attach an L-shaped conduit to the outlet. Pull cable through the conduit and connect it. If no outside outlet is available, run conduit through the basement wall.

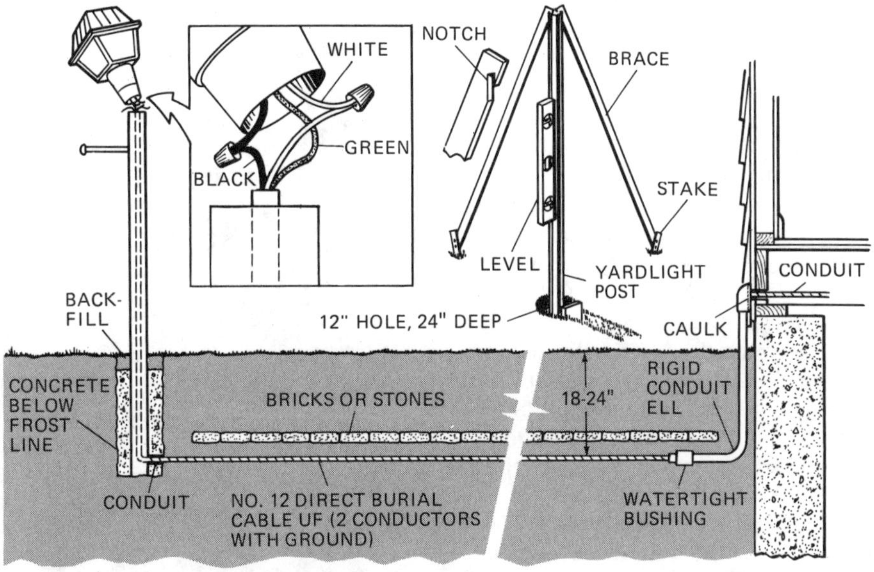

Whether you're away on vacation or just out for the evening, lamps plugged into several automatic timers to go on and off at varying intervals in different rooms will give your home that "someone's-at-home" look and keep would-be intruders guessing. The price of three or four low-cost timers is a small investment toward safeguarding your home. Set to provide a normal lighting pattern around the clock, such timers will help make your home look occupied when it isn't. You can buy automatic timers where appliances are sold.

CONTROL TIMER plugs into wall outlet, lamp into timer. GE unit turns lamp on/off at preset times on 24-hr. repeat cycle.

Give your fireplace a custom look

IF YOU'RE GOING to install one of the new prefab, zero-clearance fireplaces in your home, consider facing the front of it with ceramic tile. We chose American Olean's Renaissance Copper style for its beauty, as well as its utility. Glazed tiles are durable and ideally suited for surfaces that tend to collect soot or dirt, since they wipe clean with a damp sponge. A specially formulated flameproof wall-tile adhesive (AO-1700 by American Olean) makes it easy for the do-it-yourselfer to tackle the job.

After framing out the enclosure for your unit, sheath it with gypsum board and begin to lay out for the courses to be centered above the fireplace opening. Spread the wall tile adhesive with a notched trowel and then set the tiles, leaving a ⅛- or ¼-in. space between them. Next, lay out and set the tiles at the sides of the firebox opening. A rubber mallet can position and level the tiles.

The border tiles can be cut by scoring and breaking with a hand cutter, or by using a power saw and carbide blade.

The hearth tiles are set in a 2-in.-thick bed of mortar while it's still wet. Adhesive is not necessary on horizontal surfaces. Our mortar bed was laid out to accommodate three full courses of tile, plus the trim tiles at the edge. Plan full courses wherever possible—the less tile cutting, the better.

A rubber-faced trowel is used to force grout into joints because it won't scratch the glazed tiles.

SEE ALSO

Energy, saving . . . Fireplaces . . . Firewood . . . Heaters, space . . . Tile, wall . . . Wall tile . . . Winterizing, homes

1 Spread wall tile adhesive over drywall. Level line (arrow) guides courses.

2 Set tiles over fireplace, draw vertical line for setting tiles below.

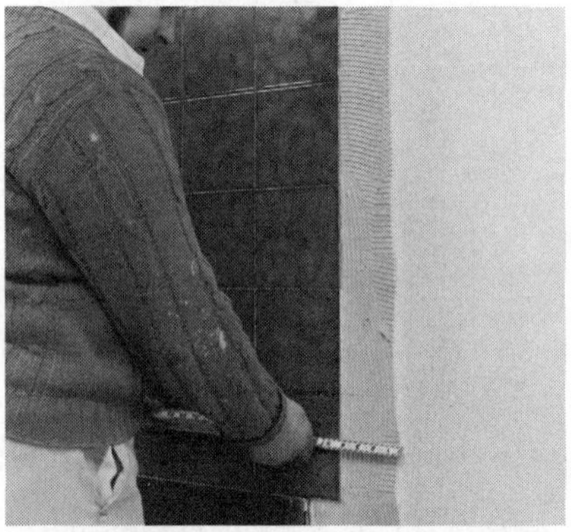

3 Next, measure for the width of border tiles which must be cut.

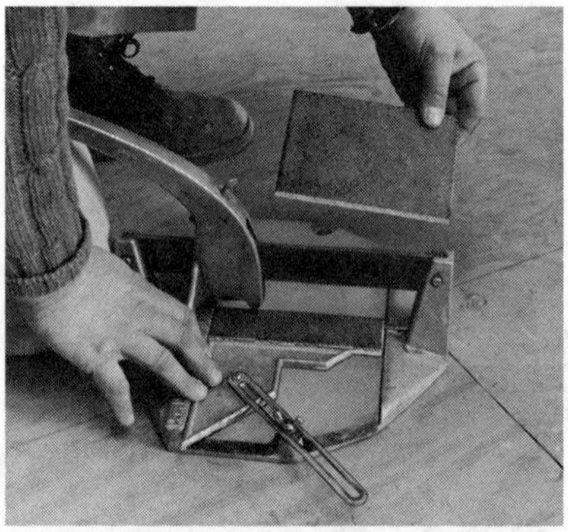

4 Cut border tiles with power saw or with hand-operated cutter (shown).

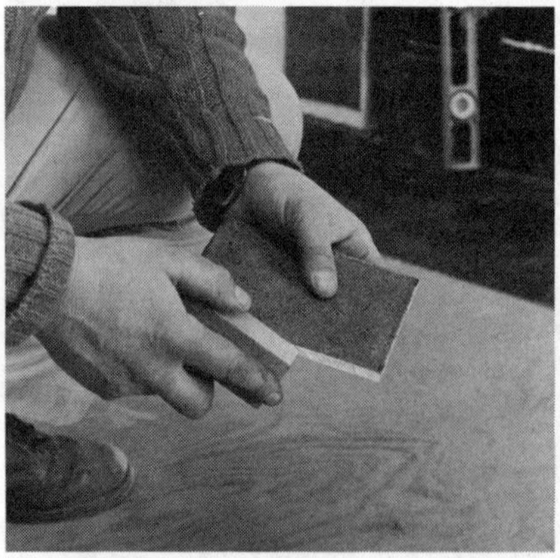

5 Use a carborundum stone to smooth cut edge of each tile.

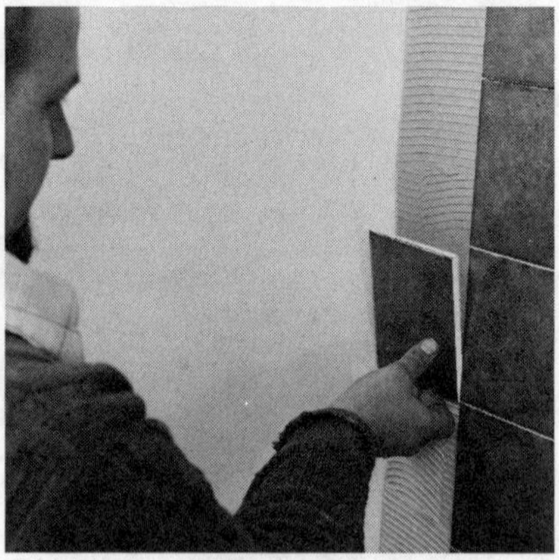

6 Make certain the border tile joints line up with the full tiles.

7 Wire lath is nailed to plywood to anchor mortar bed for raised hearth.

8 Trowel concrete 2 in. thick over wire lath, using a mortar mix.

9 Screed mortar bed with a straight board; check with a spirit level.

10 Hearth should extend 18 in. from opening at front, 12 in. at sides.

TIRED of a plain-looking fireplace? Consider a face lift with variegated copper-colored tile and brown grout for a look of understated elegance.

11 Draw line (arrow) where full tiles start. Apply skim coat of mortar.

12 Level and seat tiles in mortar by tapping the board with a hammer.

13 Position edge tiles carefully so the joints line up properly.

14 Corner tiles must be mitered using a power saw with carbide blade.

15 Force grout into joints with rubber-faced trowel; protect adjoining wall.

16 When grout starts to set, wipe excess from tile face with sponge.

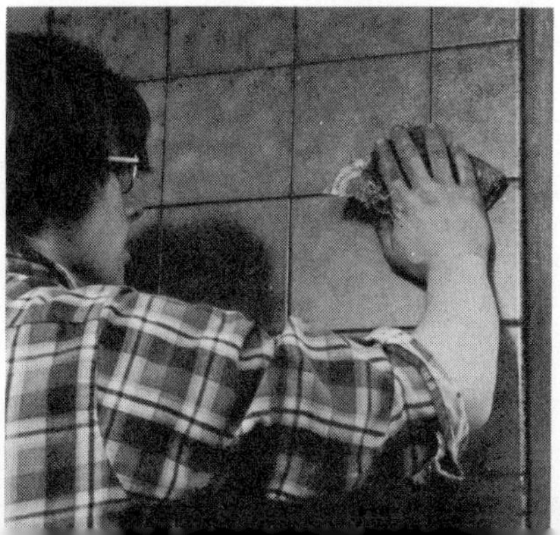

12 common fixups for your home

By STEPHEN WALTON

Certain minor repair problems are common to all homes These are the annoyances that don't cause great inconvenience, so they never seem to get fixed. Here's what to do about a dozen of them

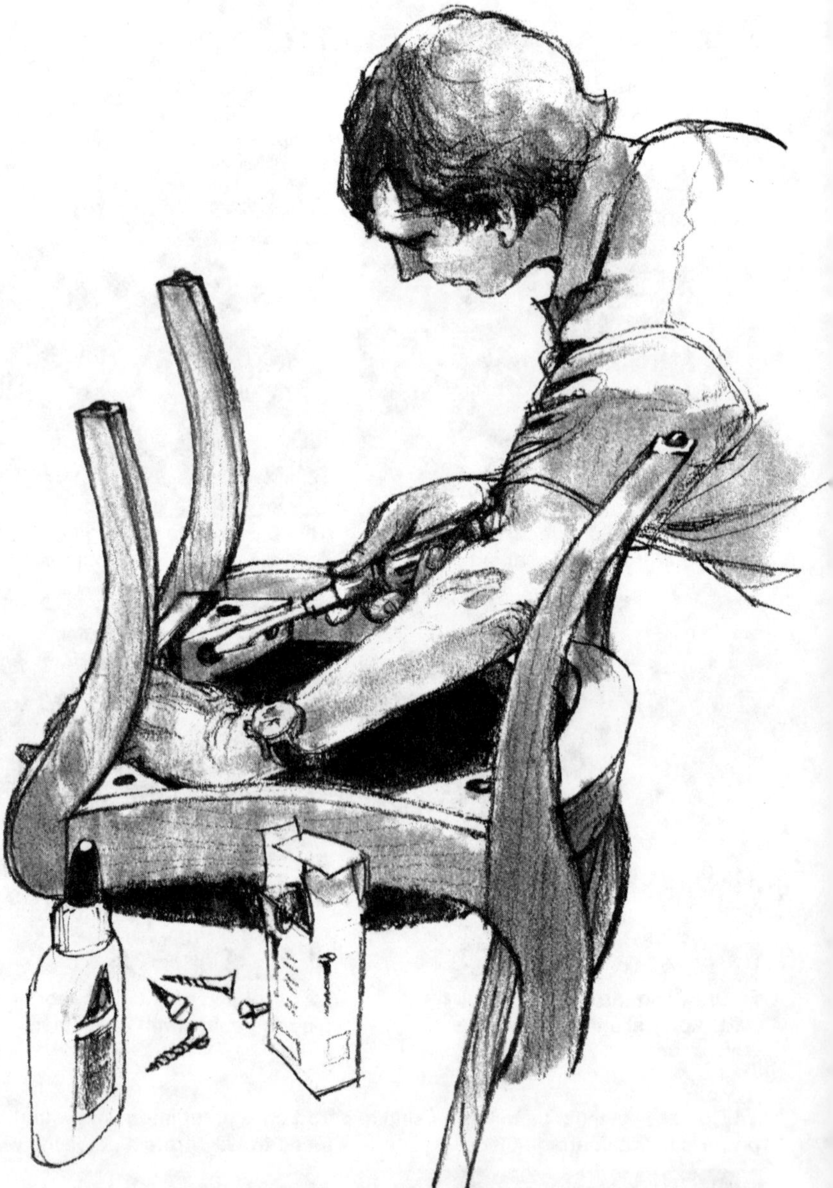

1 Tighten up wobbly furniture

You and your guests will want to sit comfortably—not in chairs that have the shakes. Chairs built with corner-block construction, like the one shown, may require no more than tightening the screws in the blocks. For other chairs, you can make corner blocks to hold those loose joints together—install them with white glue and screws. Note angled holes to let screws enter frame squarely. L-shaped or notched blocks can also be used.

SEE ALSO
Bathtubs . . . Caulking . . . Ceilings . . . Doors . . . Electrical wiring . . . Floors . . . Furniture, care of . . . Legs, furniture . . . Plumbing . . . Stains, removing . . . Tile, floor . . . Tile, wall

2 Fix sticking doors

Planing may be the only way to ease a binding door; clamping it to a wooden box is a good way to hold it—don't forget to cut hinge mortises back to original depth afterward. But you can try other remedies before you take the door down. If the bind is at the threshold, put coarse sandpaper there and swing the door over it. Loose hinges can make a door stick, so tighten hinge screws. If you find a free-turning screw in an enlarged hole, you can anchor it in a rolled-up scrap of metal toothpaste tube.

3 Put up a wainscot

Wainscoting is an attractive improvement—and a convenient coverup if the lower part of a wall is in bad shape. Kit type is easy to install with adhesive, nails, and clips between tongue-and-groove panels. The chair-rail molding at the top protects the wall from scrapes. For about $40, the kit will do a 13-ft., 4-in. run. Panels are prefinished, offer four color/texture choices. Made by Marlite Paneling, Dover, OH 44622.

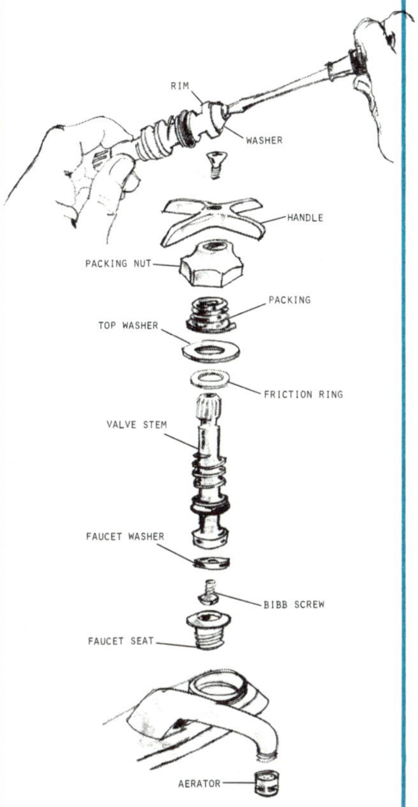

4 Stop that drip

Even if you're used to it, there's no reason to subject company to the torture of a dripping faucet, not when a new washer is usually all that's needed. A conventional compression-type faucet is easy enough to take apart—but don't use pliers on the ribbed upper end of the valve stem. Turn off the water supply to the faucet first, of course. If you damage that ribbing, you may later be able to turn the handle with no trouble at all, but it won't operate the faucet. If you hold the stem in a vise to remove the washer bibb screw, it should be a wood-padded type for the same reason. If you've replaced the washer and the faucet still leaks, the seat needs attention, since a rough or badly worn seat can let water past even a new washer. Your hardware store should have a valve-seat grinding tool—just follow the instructions that come with it. Don't overdo it, and remember to rinse the cuttings out before you reassemble the faucet. If the leak persists after you've dressed the seat this way, it's time for a new seat (if it's replaceable) or a new faucet. To replace a seat, use an inexpensive seat wrench and coat the new seat's thread with pipe compound.

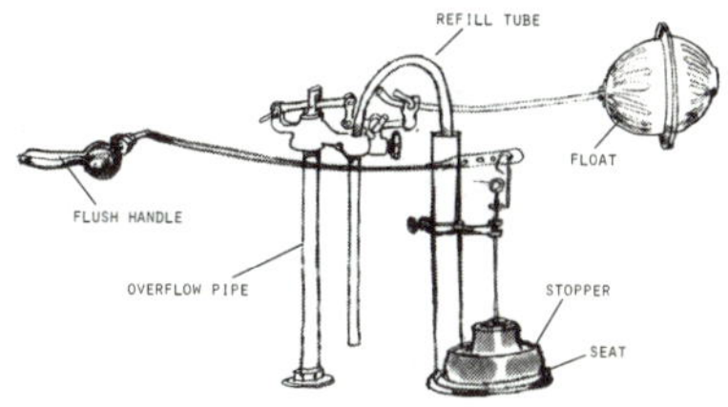

5 Tend to the toilet

If water continues to trickle into a toilet bowl after flushing, it probably means that the rubber stopper in the tank assembly has become hard with age and isn't making an effective seal. Shut off the water before making any toilet repairs. If the stopper is okay, or replacement doesn't help, the seat itself may be corroded, and cleaning it with emery cloth may be the answer.

Replacement of both stopper and seat with a modern flapper-type valve may be necessary, or you may have a worn washer in the float-valve assembly. With an old toilet, replacement of the entire float-and-valve assembly with a modern ballcock (without the float and arm) is a good idea. Kits for that purpose are made by Fluidmaster, Inc., 1800 Via Burton, Box 4264, Anaheim, CA 92803.

6 Hide scratches

Blemishes (that's the trade term) on furniture—those small nicks and scratches—are easily dealt with. Just using a tinted polish on them may be enough. If that won't do it, use a touchup stick from your paint or hardware store. If you can't find one that's an exact color match, get two or more and blend them. Fill the scratch and rub well, then apply wax and rub that.

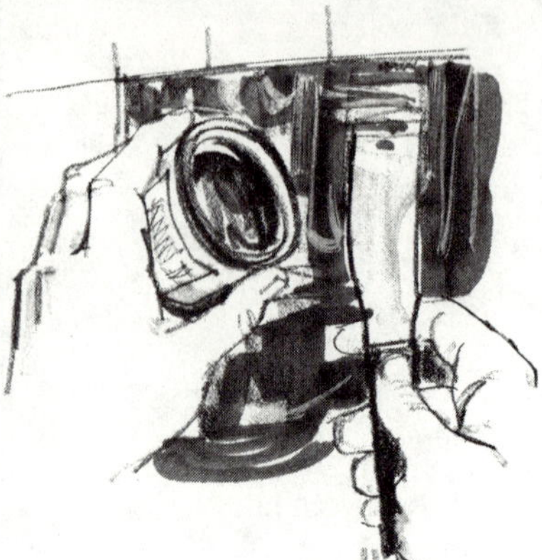

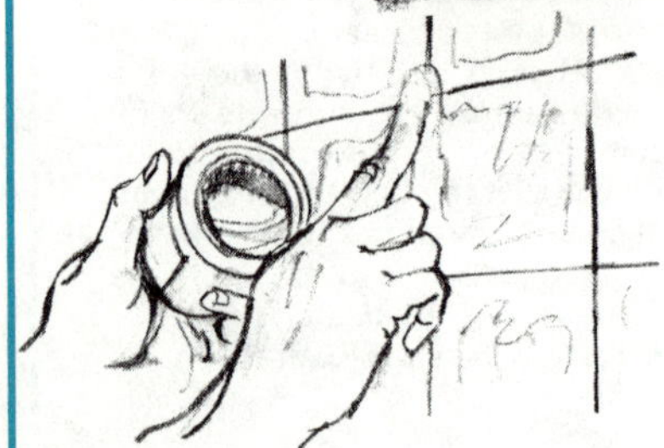

7 Fix ceramic tile

Loose ceramic tile in the bathroom doesn't just look bad—it can lead to water damage. First, be sure to find *all* the loose tiles or you won't really be doing the job—tap with your fist, but not too hard, since you want to be able to put the original tile back up. With the tile down, scrape the old mastic off with a putty knife; you may have to soften it with solvent. Get the old grout off the tile; most you can break away, some you may have to grind or file off. Then apply new adhesive to the wall—be sure it's dry—as in the top picture, and spread it out with a serrated trowel.

Press the tiles into place, aligning them with others and allowing for grout lines. Acrylic latex grout is easiest to use. Press it into joints with a fingertip. Wipe down gently with a barely dampened sponge, then let the grout dry overnight before you rub with a soft, dry towel to take the white film off tile surfaces. To make tile sparkle, use a good glass cleaner.

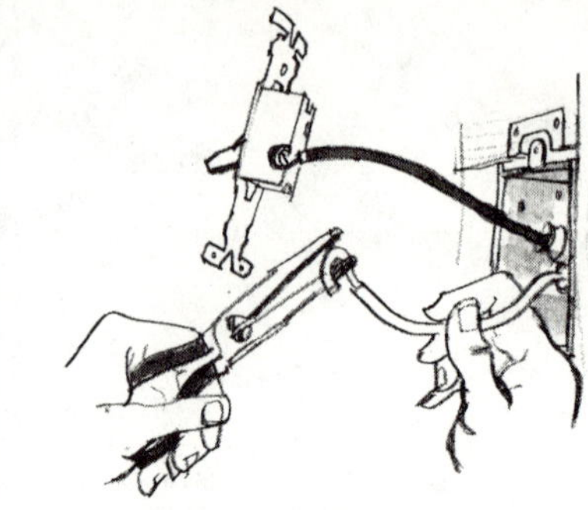

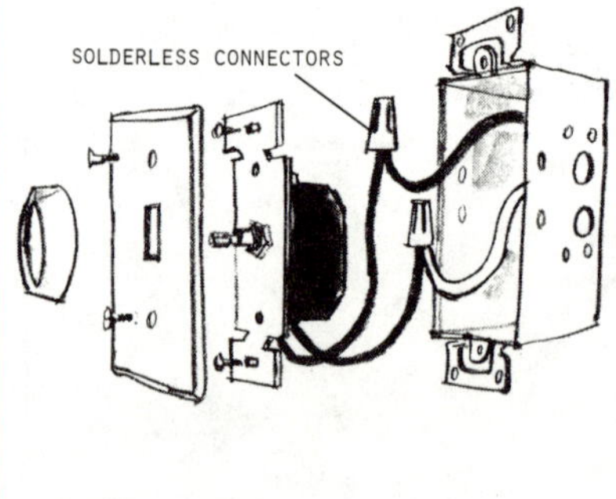

8 Replace light switches

Here's how to fix that light switch in the guest room that hasn't worked right in years. Turn off the circuit at the service panel by yanking the fuse or flipping the circuit breaker. Remove switchplate and the screws that hold the old switch. Then it's no more than a matter of loosening the terminal screws on the old switch to remove the wires and then connecting the new switch.

See that the bare wire ends have a curl that's clockwise when they're in place, so they'll remain secure as you tighten terminal screws. Coil the wires back into the box and screw the new switch into place, taking care to align it for free operation with the switchplate replaced. If this is a job you don't like to do too often, put in a mercury switch; besides the advantage of silence, they also offer a service life of many years.

If the switch is in living room, dining room or family room (or any room used for TV watching), a dimmer switch is perfect for creating lighting moods (and saves electricity and lengthens a bulb life as well). Installation of a typical dimmer (for incandescent lighting in permanent fixtures) is shown above. Dimmer wires and supply wires are twisted together and solderless connectors (often supplied with the dimmer) are twisted on tightly; the dimmer is fastened to the box like an ordinary switch and the original switchplate replaced. Just be sure not to exceed specified wattage.

9 Patch wall cracks

To assure a good bond between patching compound and wall, the crack should be first V-grooved (special tools are sold, but a can opener works perfectly well) then dusted so that no loose matter remains. Use a large sponge to dampen the crack thoroughly and then apply a first coat of the patching compound, forcing it into the crack with a 4-in. joint knife.

Press wallboard tape tightly into place, then press it into the compound with the knife, pressing hard enough to squeeze a little compound out at the edges. Cover tape

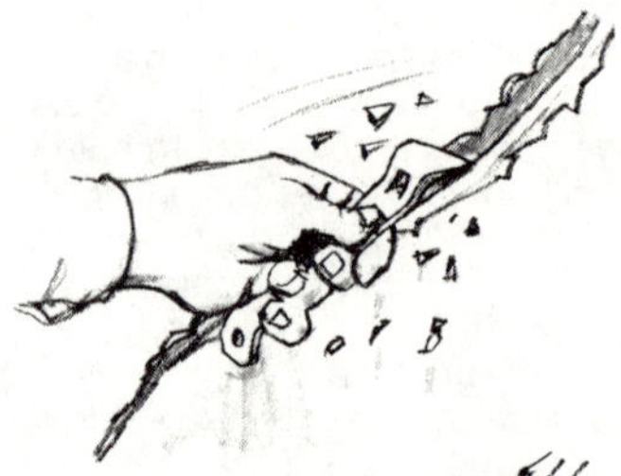

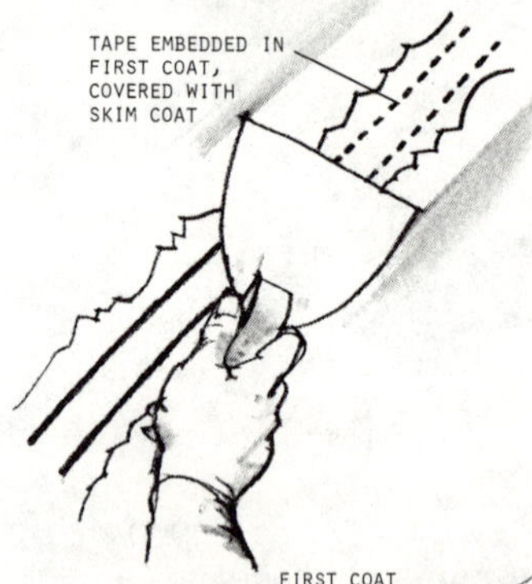

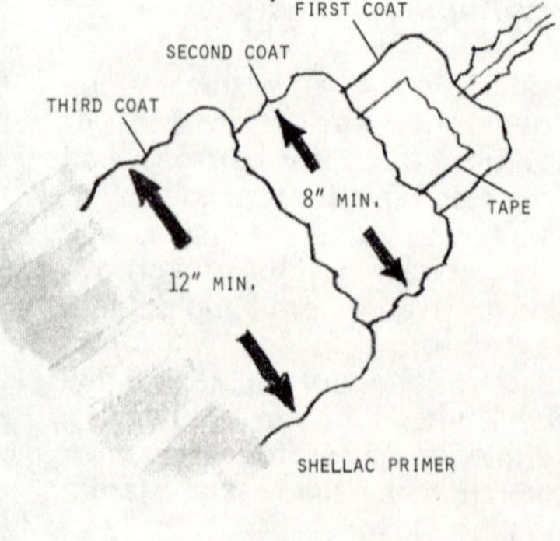

with a thin skim coat. Three coats in all are recommended. Let each dry thoroughly and sand high spots down between coats (sand with care on plasterboard or you may damage paper surface). When the top coat is dry (after at least 24 hours), it can be feathered into adjoining surfaces by rubbing with a slightly dampened sponge. Easy does it, though, or you'll be rubbing the water-soluble compound off.

After the patch has been sponge-sanded, it must be primed or it will show through paint. White shellac is commonly used, but vinyl and oil-base primer-sealers are also suitable. Paint or wallcovering can then follow.

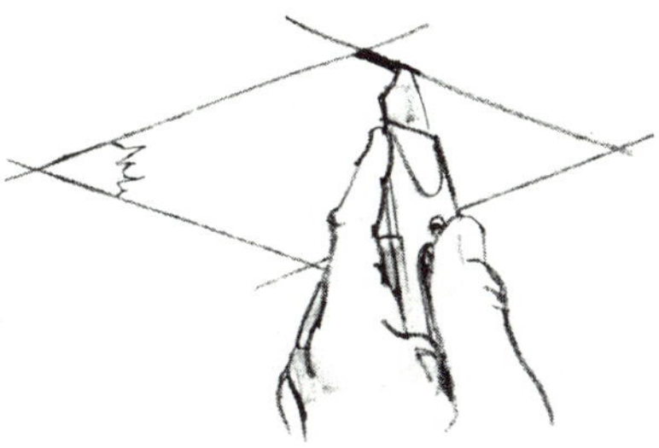

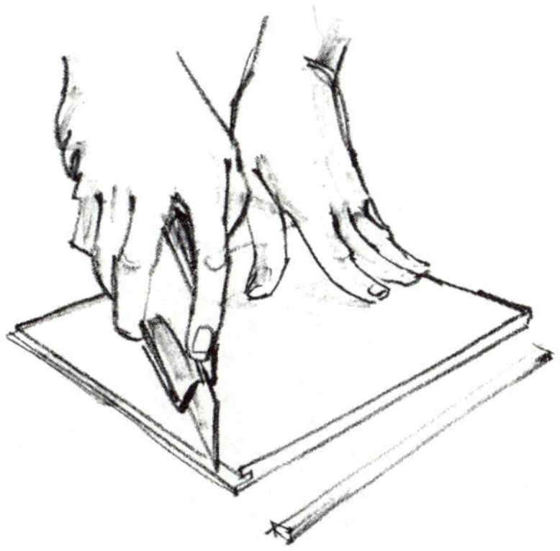

10 Replace ceiling tile

Ceiling tiles are up where you wouldn't expect them to get broken, but it does happen. You remove damaged tile by carefully cutting it out with a heavy utility knife, a jab saw (a short hacksaw blade with a handle at one end) or a keyhole saw. Clear the area in the frame of staples and bits of tile. To fit the hole, the replacement tile must be trimmed of protruding tongues—a utility knife should do the job. Apply adhesive (the type used with ceiling tile) to the back of the tile and press in into place, level with the surrounding tiles.

11 Resetting floor tile

Floor tiles that have lifted or curled up at edges or corners are a safety hazard as well as an eyesore. Apply a household iron, not to flatten them down, but to soften the old mastic below enough to let you lift each tile out. Then you scrape away as much as possible of the old adhesive and apply new. Press the tile back into place, wipe up excess mastic, and keep the tile under weights overnight.

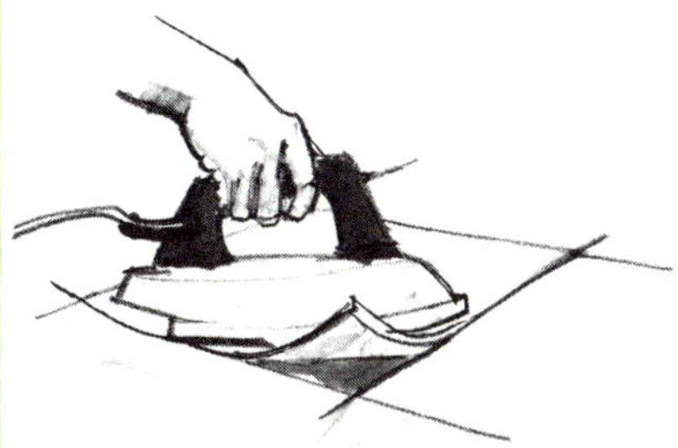

12 Caulking bathtub seam

The crack that develops along the rim of the tub is easy to fix with modern caulks. First, make sure you remove *all* the old caulking, gouging it out with a stiff putty knife but

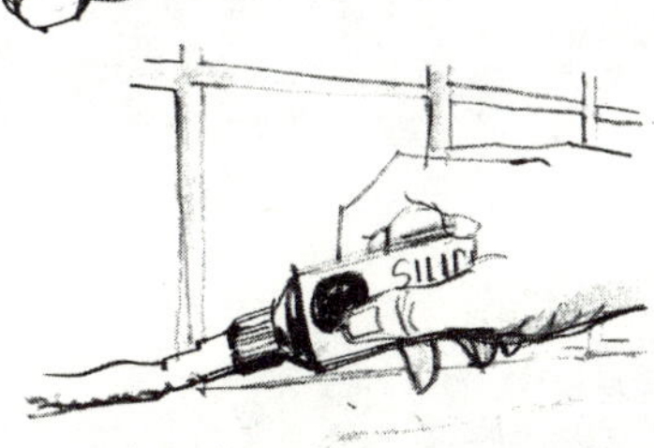

taking care not to damage either tub or wall tiles. After dusting the cleaned seam, wipe it with alcohol to remove residues that could keep the caulking from adhering. Caulking—a type specifically made for bath use—goes on in an unbroken bead just wider than the crack. Push it *into* the crack with a cloth or wet fingertip, forming a smooth, concave seam. A wet cloth will remove any excess caulking from the tile and tub.

. . . and other things

Naturally, you want your home to look attractive when you're having company—and you want it to be safe, too. Here's how to do a few other minor jobs that will add to the safety, appearance and convenience of your home.

■ Loose carpet—double-face tape will hold it down in most locations. Do the same thing with those throw rugs that are always sliding on bare floors.

■ Replace your jangling old doorbell chimes. They're easy to install following the makers' instructions.

■ Replace worn catches on kitchen cabinets with new magnetic ones.

■ Hide a house key in the yard—but *not* under the front door mat.

■ *Don't* prune evergreens on your property—save that for just before Christmas and you'll have the trimmings for decorative use.

Raise the roof to gain more space

This major remodeling job was done in several stages while the family actually lived in the house. First came the sliding doors and new siding and then the most important feature—a new raised mansard roof-line to give the family valuable living space

ORIGINAL STUCCO HOUSE (above) had A-line roof, small attic space and porch. Bottom: after the face-lift.

SEE ALSO

Remodeling . . . Remodeling, exterior . . . Roofs . . . Siding . . . Sliding glass doors . . . Windows

FRONT OF HOUSE (above) with third story and new mansard roof added. Family room, under construction at right, will have mansard roof to match. Rear view (below) shows recessed balcony in third story, new dining-room addition, sun deck and family room being added.

ITS PROXIMITY to downtown Minneapolis prompted Mr. and Mrs. Richard Prescott to buy the 1910-vintage house shown in the small photo on the opposite page. Living with a little sawdust and construction debris does not disturb them, so the Prescotts did their remodeling in several stages. First, they removed the front porch, installed sliding glass doors and applied Masonite's X-90 lap siding over the stucco. Then came the most ambitious phase of their work: Removing everything above the second-floor ceiling, adding a huge third-floor master bedroom and changing the roof line. The new addition has inset windows on three sides of an asphalt-shingled mansard and a charming balcony overlooking a large back yard with swimming pool.

Deciding to do more remodeling, the Prescotts added a dining room with lots of windows in back for easy viewing of the rear grounds.

When we photographed this handsome home, the current project was the addition of a family room which will lead out onto a sun deck.

We added on and saved—and so can you

By RICHARD F. DEMPEWOLFF

When we needed more space we had to decide whether to buy a new house or add on to our present one. We decided to add on ourselves and our house soon grew a new den, dining room, bath, entryway and two-car garage. It took me 54 weekends and a couple of vacations to do the job

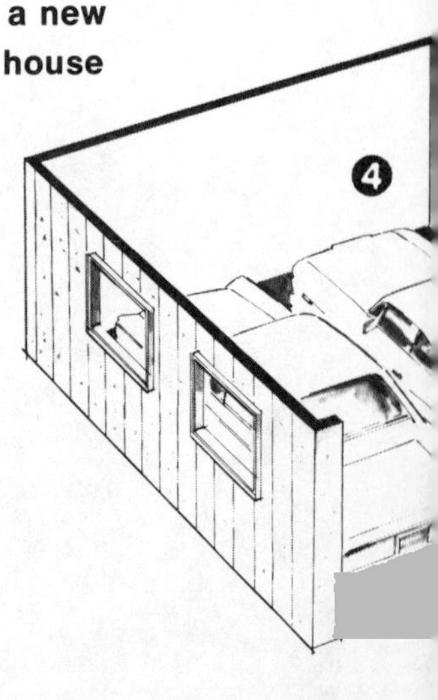

SEE ALSO
Gutters and downspouts . . . Lumber . . . Measurements . . . Nails . . . Remodeling . . . Roofs . . . Sheathing . . . Siding

A NUMBER OF YEARS ago I found a beautiful piece of land in the Pocono Mountains of Pennsylvania, and decided to build the vacation home I had been dreaming about for years. The home has served both friends and relatives well for over 15 years of weekends and holidays.

With four rooms and a bath it was adequate for us at first, but as our flow of guests grew through the years, the squeeze was on. We needed more space for sleeping and privacy, and a shelter for our cars. Storage space also would be a pleasant addition. In the original home there was only a fireplace, and since winter weekend visits be-

L-WING ADDITION (left, above) extends at a right angle from the porch end of original cottage. What it did for our living space is shown in diagram (below). The original house is above. New wing is from far end of porch.

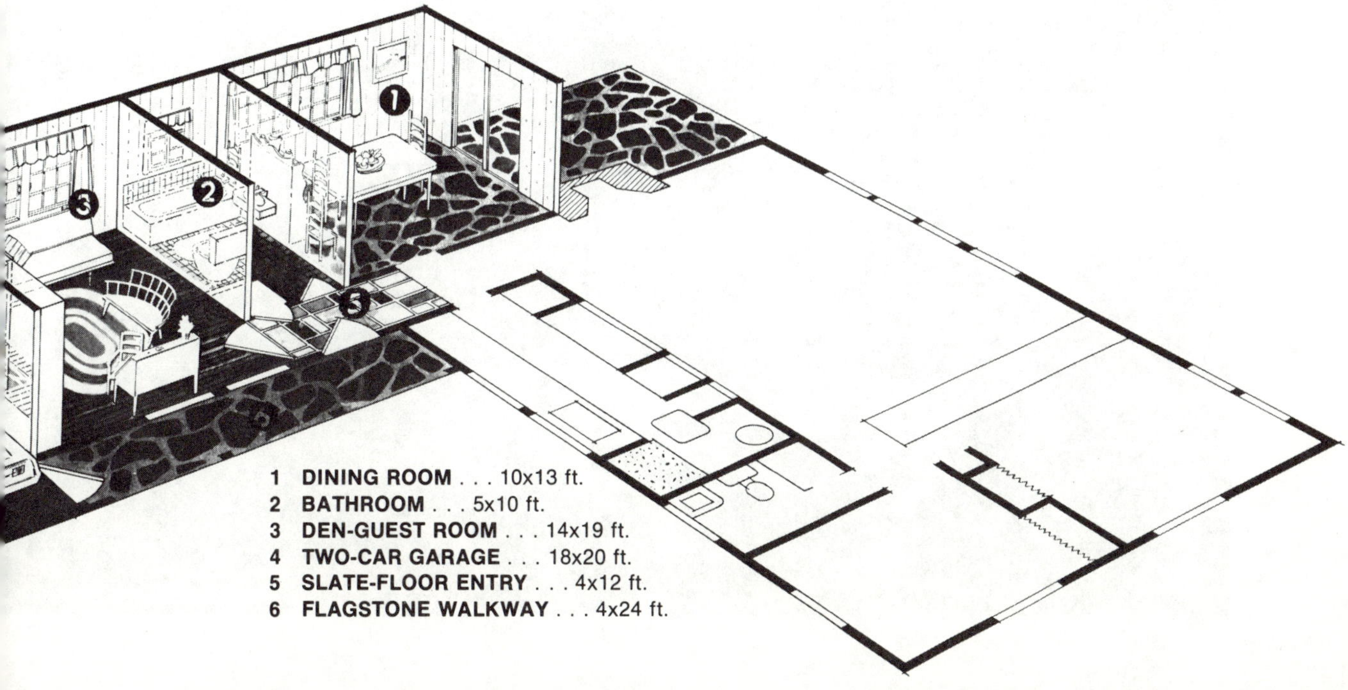

1 **DINING ROOM** . . . 10x13 ft.
2 **BATHROOM** . . . 5x10 ft.
3 **DEN-GUEST ROOM** . . . 14x19 ft.
4 **TWO-CAR GARAGE** . . . 18x20 ft.
5 **SLATE-FLOOR ENTRY** . . . 4x12 ft.
6 **FLAGSTONE WALKWAY** . . . 4x24 ft.

continued

FLOOR JOISTS ARE sunk into foundation wall and rest on a sill along the ledge formed by top course of 4-in. block. This, plus use of 7-ft. 9½-in. sidewalls, permits using 4x8-ft. panel siding.

WALL SECTIONS are assembled and joined on the subfloor decking, then tipped up into final position.

FIBERBOARD SHEATHING panels are snubbed right against the rafters and fastened with 2-in. nails.

GABLE END RAFTERS are cut and assembled on the ground, then lifted into place and braced. Care must be taken to insure peak is exactly same height from bottom cord as trusses. Studs can be cut to fit.

came more frequent, our hideaway needed central heat to make it more comfortable.

Thus, we were faced with the two choices that seem to face many homeowners: We could (1) sell the original house and build something more commodious elsewhere, or (2) find a way to add onto the existing house.

We sat down and carefully figured the finances. A breakdown of costs of each alternative revealed that an "L" wing would provide what we needed for approximately half the cost of a new home with the same facilities—*even allowing for the money we'd net after selling the old one*. This assumption was based on the fact that I'd build the wing by myself. A new house, on the other hand, would have to be largely contracted. Though I am skilled enough to do most of the work, I figured I couldn't run up 2000 sq. ft. of structure working alone in less than four or five years of weekends.

So the wing won—as it would for most people in these days of soaring costs of labor and material. The interesting thing to note here is that such an extension can be added to almost any house of one or two floors if the land to put it on is available and meets code requirements. The important factor is to take your time in planning the addition so that it looks like part of the original structure and not a "tack-on." Thus the roof design and pitch must be carefully considered to harmoniously fit in. If they follow the original, you're safe. On most homes, and especially those with shallow pitch or flat roofs, an "L" may even improve the building's appearance by spreading it out and blending with the landscape.

one-and-a-half-year project

The work started in earnest when the snow was gone in the spring. I worked on it strictly as a weekend, holiday, and vacation project. It was completed and the final bills paid one and a half years later in the fall. When it was done we had gained an additional 972 sq. ft. of enclosed space, including:

- *A cedar-paneled dining room* (page 1479, lower right) occupying half of a former patio in the original ranch-type house. The flagstone deck from the patio was left as a handsome floor. I filled it with sealer and polished it with Butcher's wax. A 6-ft.-wide sliding glass door faces the remaining half of the patio which overlooks a spectacular mountain view.
- *A full bath* lined with gray fiberglass barn siding. I installed white fixtures as a contrast. The

tub stall is walled in gray epoxy panels to shed water from the shower head.

• *A den-guest* room (pages 1478-1479) paneled in natural cedar. The room includes built-in shelves and cabinets which flank a packaged fireplace. The floor is waxed, random oak planking. A sofa-bed can turn the entire room into an extra bedroom to accommodate a weekend guest couple in roomy comfort. Now I am using the room as my "branch office" when we're alone. If we feel the need some day, it could become a luxurious master bedroom with very little additional work or expense.

a garage which could "grow"

• *A two-car garage* that could be stretched to 20x20 ft. by simply extending the rear wall out under the 2-ft. roof overhang. This might be a good idea if you're a "big car" fan, or want to install a workbench and work area.

• *A redwood-paneled entryway,* with random slate-flag floor. This is good-looking and practical for a vacation home where country mud and slush can readily be cleaned away. Backing into the bath area from this hall is a 26x34-in. coat closet with shelves and bins for boots, storm lamps and other useful items that are likely to be needed in a vacation home.

• *A 4-ft.-wide covered walk* outside, paved in random flagstone. This parallels the entry hall between the house entrance and a door leading into the garage. Since this is covered, it offers you the convenience of getting from the house to the car without getting soaked.

• *An oil-fired, hot-air heating system* that provides balanced heat throughout the new wing as well as the original part of the building. Since both original house and wing sit on shallow bedrock over a tight crawlspace, the problem of a proper furnace seemed like a rough one at first. Actually, the solution was easy. Most manufacturers, we discovered, produce "horizontal" furnaces designed to fit beneath floor joists where clearance is as little as 2 ft. Plenum and ductwork come off one end.

make original house match

How long did it take to put together everything listed above? Ground was broken in April of one year and the structure was finally finished by October of the following year. Two months of weekends were used, however, replacing windows in the original house to match those in the new wing. The original house also had to be resurfaced with the new fiberglass siding to match the new wing. Finally, the heating system had to be installed throughout both the new and the original part of the house.

Did I have help? Yes. You do need help with some things—handling heavy trusses, raising ceiling panels, closing in the roof before the rains come and so on. The foundation hole was contracted. A local electrical contractor relocated the primary electrical service box and Sears engineers contracted the entire heating system. Three husky sons of a neighbor were hired for a wide assortment of jobs from earthmoving to paneling, roofing and masonry. A brother (electrical engineer) helped with the wiring and building the new furnace chimney; a nephew helped with the framing, roofing, and substrates. And my wife, a genuine good sport and house enthusiast, was a willing painter and general helper. Friendly relatives, incidentally, who knew they'd be invited up later, made dandy volunteers. It all helped speed the project to completion.

54 weekends plus vacations

Including all help, however, paid and volunteer, 1428 man hours were spent on the wing alone. It involved 54 weekends (seven of them three-day affairs) and two three-week vacations.

The satisfaction of watching a house grow under your own hands can never be appreciated by anyone who hasn't built one, and it's not as hard as you may think. We learned many techniques that helped speed the work by learning as we went along and asking local professionals for hints and advice.

The framing in our wing is similar in design to the original house. We used a stepped foundation wall in which the last course of block is 4 in. wide. Joists rest on a sill behind the top row. This stunt lowers the house into the foundation wall, permitting the use of standard 4x8-ft. panels for sheathing and siding.

A single, 44-ft.-long, doubled-up 2x12 header supports the roof trusses across the long spans of garage doors and between the posts at the front.

Roof and sidewalls were tied into the existing house after erection—but before interior surfaces were covered. The critical task of making a waterproof joint where the roofs meet is all important if you want a dry home.

With the wing finally complete we are spending even more time at our vacation home and entertaining more guests. It took some careful planning and a lot of weekends, but it was worthwhile.

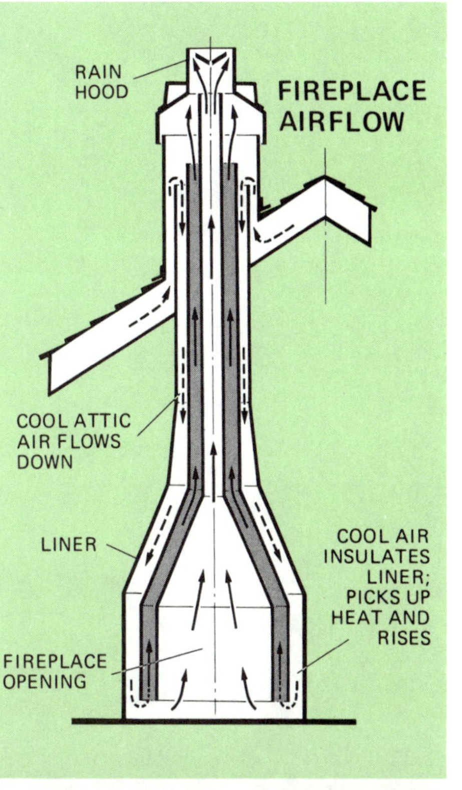

PACKAGED FIREPLACE (above) can be set on a wood floor, backed against a flammable wall with no fire hazard. Triple-pipe flue (right) is cooled by air. Cutaway of fireplace assembly (above, right) shows how the circulation of cool air between the two layers of steel provides insulation for outer surface.

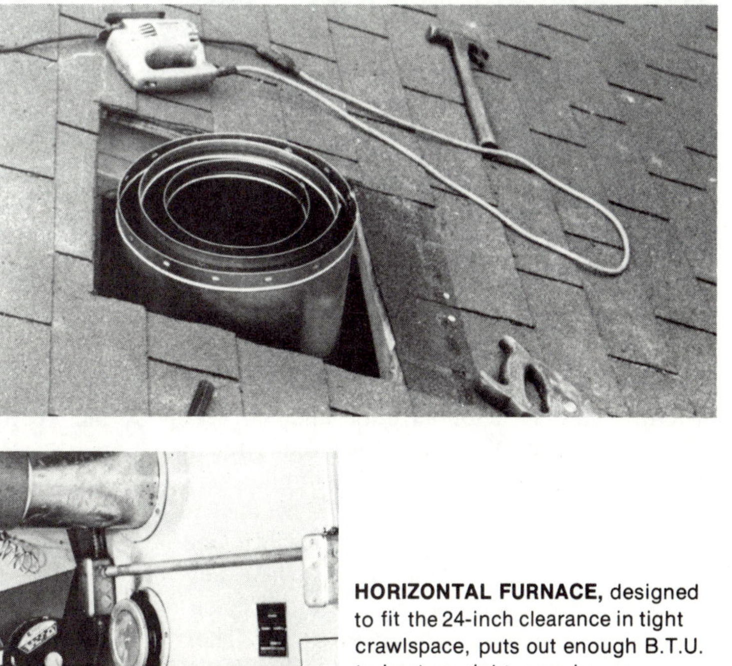

HORIZONTAL FURNACE, designed to fit the 24-inch clearance in tight crawlspace, puts out enough B.T.U. to heat an eight-room house.

Expand over an attached garage

WHEN YOU EXPAND over an existing structure, you save a lot of trouble and expense. The basic foundation is already there, and, in some cases, so is the floor. You simply build upward on top, avoiding many of the headaches of starting from scratch. This is what Mr. and Mrs. Larry LeJeune decided to do when their fifth child arrived and they needed more space. The starting point was an attached garage. They conferred with architect Gerald C. Luedke of Minneapolis, Minn., who conceived and designed a two-stage improvement:

SEE ALSO
Additions, house . . . Decks . . . Garage doors . . . Garage remodeling . . . Remodeling, exterior . . . Siding . . . Stairs

• The first was to add a family room, complete with woodburning fireplace, alongside the garage.

• The second was to build over the garage to gain a master bedroom that was away from the existing four bedrooms. The new wing, which permitted construction of a private bath and sitting room as well as bedroom, also has Pella sliding doors that give access to a deck over the new playroom.

Inside it was decided to create a cathedral ceiling of rough-hewn cedar so the rafters were left exposed and stained. The entire room is paneled to eliminate future painting.

Outside, the roof pitch follows the existing structure. The result is that the addition does not look tacked on but gives the appearance of having always been there. To keep costs down,

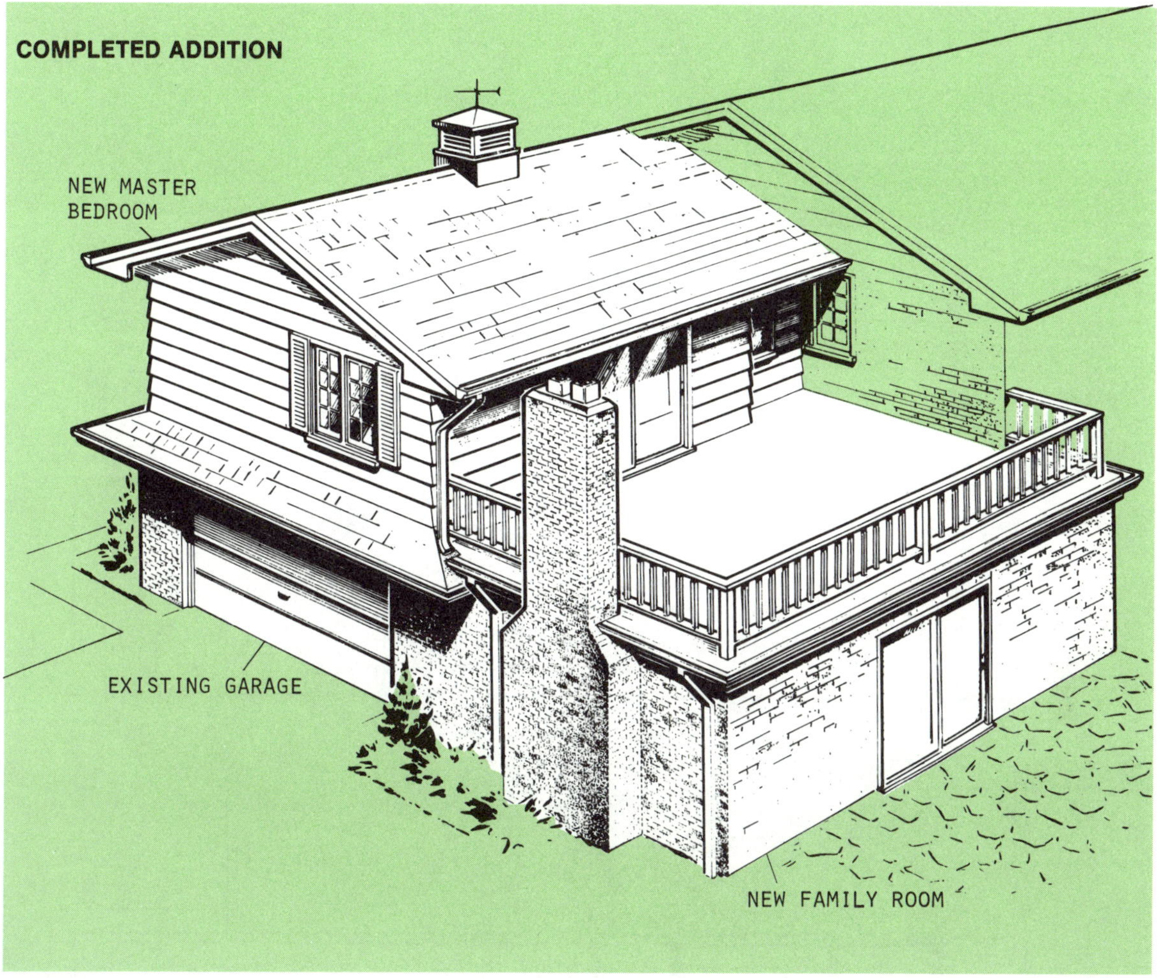

continued

aluminum siding, rather than brick veneer, was used.

Expanding up, when possible, rather than attaching a new structure is a practical approach to home improvement for several reasons. It is more economical because the footings under the garage are already there. Thus, excavation and concrete work are not required, and if desired, that money can be put toward interior luxuries or extras. And expanding up also leaves more yard area for outdoor activities.

Whether you decide to add both rooms in one project, one only, or one now and the second as time and money permit, the building concept the LeJeunes used is a sound one. Once either or both additions are closed to the weather, interior work can proceed as you—not the elements—dictate.

COLONIAL HOME (below) was adequate when the family first moved in. When more room was needed, a bedroom was added over the garage and a playroom alongside.

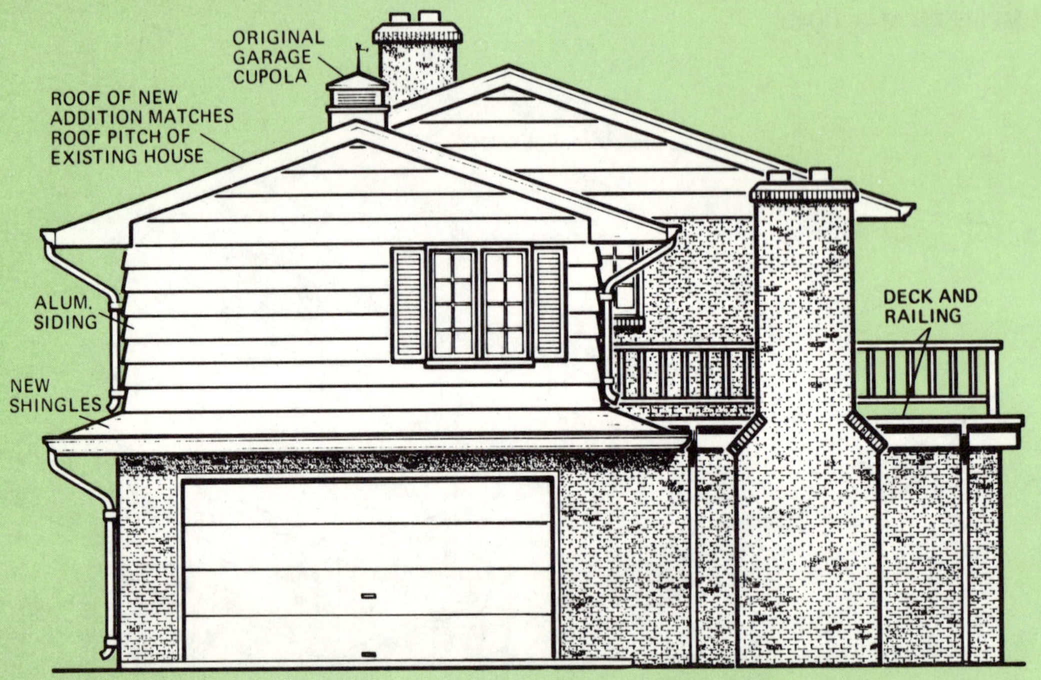

SOUTH ELEVATION

expansion over garage, continued

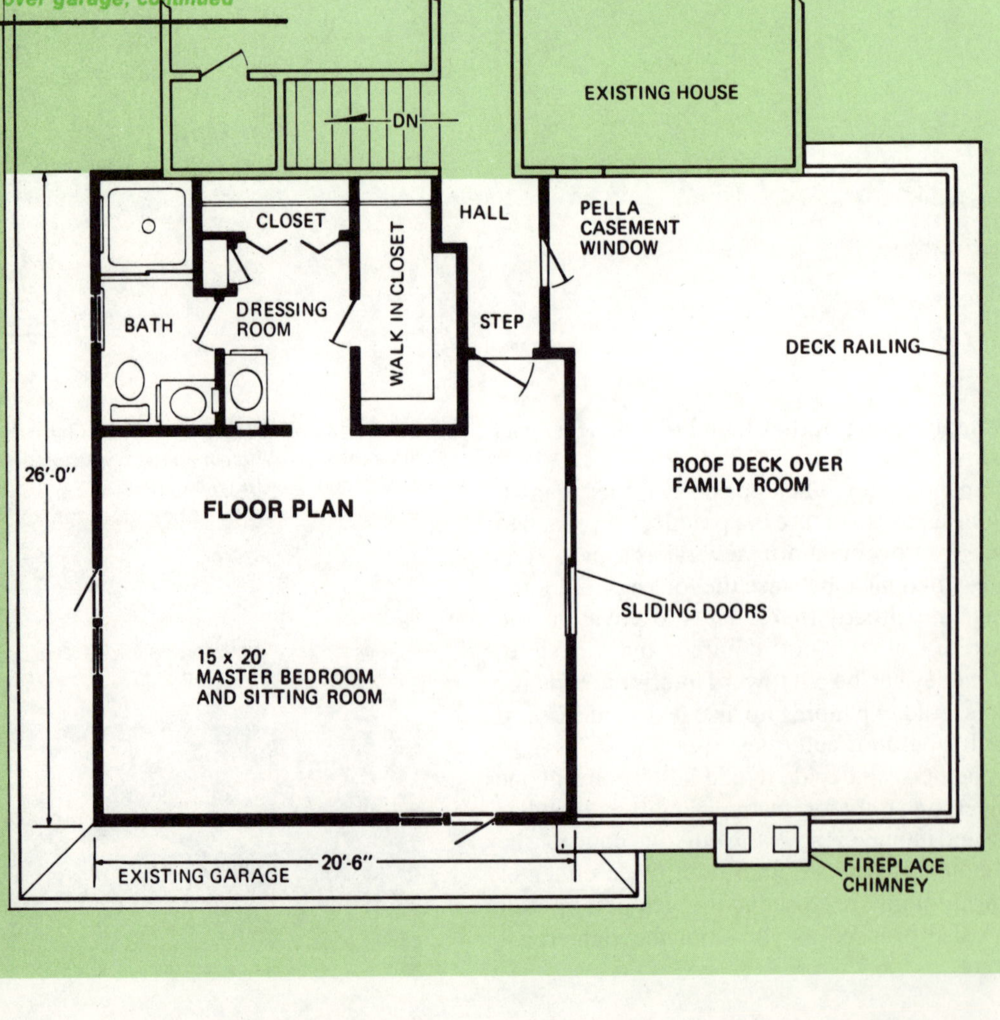

Your house number belongs in lights

By RUDOLPH F. GRAF and GEORGE J. WHALEN

Your guests will have no trouble finding your house after dark if you put the number up in lights. This scheme borrows power from your doorbell

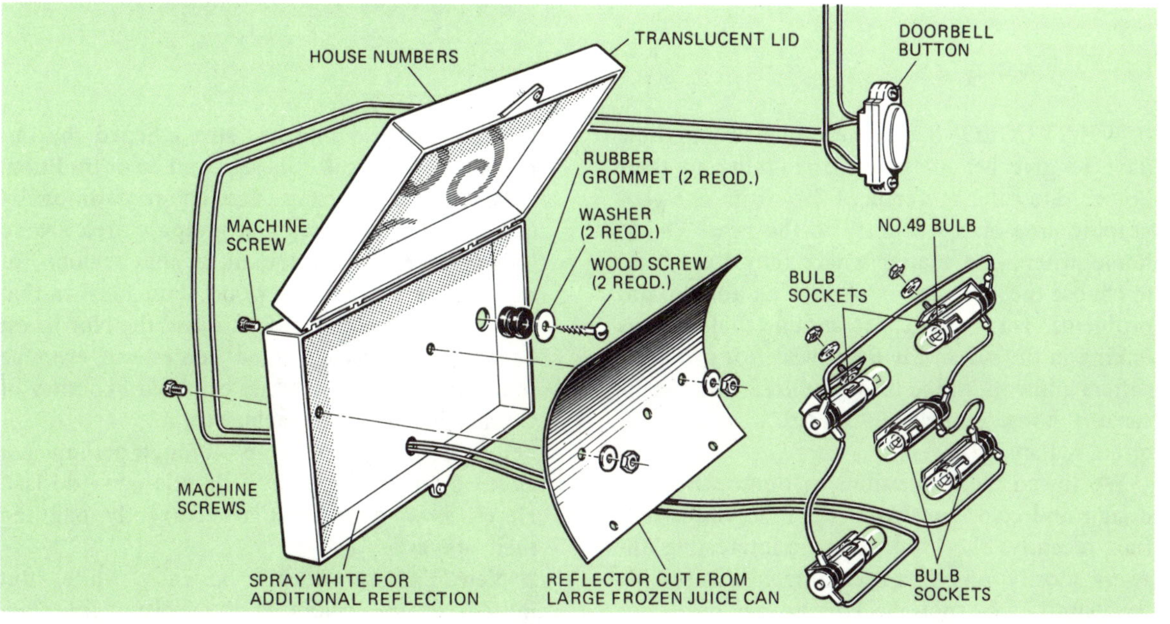

■ EVER WANDER DOWN a strange, dark street peering at invisible house numbers to find the address you're after? Your guests won't have that problem if you illuminate your house number—and you can do it without running new wiring.

The trick is a low-voltage lighting system that draws its power from your doorbell's transformer. This circuit is always on, and its wiring comes right out to the bell button, where it's easy to tap into. The bulbs are No. 49 "flea-power" types (Lafayette 32 F 66210) requiring only 60 thousandths of an ampere each, at two volts. Use five bulbs in series for a 10-volt bell circuit, eight in series for a 16-volt chime setup.

While the wiring to the doorbell button may appear to be only a switch loop, what you're actually doing is drawing power through the bell circuit—just enough to light the bulbs, but not enough to activate the bell. When the button is pressed, the light will momentarily go out and full power routed to the bell will ring it.

Choose a plastic box big enough to hold your house number. If its lid is transparent, make it translucent with a light spray of white acrylic paint to diffuse the light. The numbers can be plastic or metal.

The reflector assembly is cut from a 12-ounce, aluminized-cardboard frozen-juice can. The miniature bayonet sockets (Lafayette 32 F 28038) are bolted to the reflector as shown in the drawing.

Wire the bulbs in series and run the wire through a hole in the box; knot the wire inside so the connections won't loosen if the wire is yanked, and leave enough wire outside to reach the doorbell button.

The bolts that hold the reflector to the box, and the screws holding the box to the wall, should pass through washers and rubber grommets, so the box won't crack when you snug up the screws.

House painting with a regional flavor

Different parts of the country have distinct color preferences and special painting problems. Here's how to select the best color and paint for your area and apply it so it provides a durable finish no matter what the climate

By HARRY WICKS

WHAT COLORS are homeowners using these days to give beauty and individuality to their homes? Do color preferences vary from one geographic area of the country to the next? Or do homeowners—no matter where they live—tend to choose the same colors? And what about paint problems? Isn't it logical to assume that a home baking in the sun of the Southwest, for example, suffers ailments unlike those endured by a northeastern house subjected to cold weather and, often, sea spray?

We tossed these questions at Bonnie Bender, design and color consultant for PPG Industries, Inc., recently. She supplied some interesting answers, mostly from data accumulated in a round-the-country tour spot-checking houses.

"Initially," she said, "the tour was made to confirm previous studies on house color preferences."

The general trend—across the country—is to the use of a quiet palette of exterior colors by homeowners who are repainting or remodeling their homes. The palette includes rich historic colors—grayed blues, olive-to-deep greens, mustard yellows, charcoal and weathered grays. This range of colors applies to repaint work on both wood and masonry homes.

The color lines that have, in a real sense, divided the country into specific architectural types show signs of dissolving. This shouldn't mean that cities and towns steeped in history will lose their original flavor and inherent charm. In fact, the past Bicentennial has strengthened the importance of the role of design and color tradition.

What it does mean is that colors traditionally associated with a major geographic area are no longer the exclusive domain of that region. For example, the primarily wood stain finishes that are associated with California and the Northwest have moved East. Stained homes can even be found in the historic white clapboard country of Connecticut and Massachusetts.

But heritage impressions—though perhaps not as strong in character as a decade ago—do last. Here's how Americans are currently painting their homes:

- New England is still basically white. But muted historic colors of the coastal cities are moving inland. One paint dealer in Glastonbury, CT, estimates that 80 percent of his sales in exterior paints are now in historic colors.
- The South continues to use white and pastels. White, for instance, is still No. 1 choice for Florida's stuccoed homes. But, in Old Charleston, SC, neutrals and other pastels are judiciously mixed with white to reflect the primarily Georgian quality of architecture.
- Midwest. In this section of the country—the farm belt—rural colors persist. The Victorian farmhouse shown here typifies the current color preferences of this area.
- Southwesterners pick colors that relate to surrounding terrain. In Santa Fe, NM, much of the color character is related to tradition and maintaining architectural and design heritage. The colors, not so incidentally, are also functional—they resist dirt and provide good color retention in spite of harsh sun.
- West. In general, lifestyles on the West Coast are more informal than elsewhere and the color

SEE ALSO
Ladders . . . Masonry, painting . . . Paint rollers . . . Painting, exterior . . . Remodeling, exterior . . . Scaffolding

SOUTHWEST: Here, color it white and add adobe tones to those that relate to the surrounding terrain and blend with the landscape. Desert earth tones persist because they have functional purposes too—they resist dirt and have good color retention.

MIDWEST: White and traditional rural colors remain popular in the farm belt with expanded use of earthy browns and reds. The gingerbread farmhouse shown above is painted in a rich color called Rural Red while the trim details have been finished with contrasting white.

SOUTH: Pastels and whites continue to dominate. A major paint contractor in Old Charleston (where this house is located) claims that "colors are slow and easy, just as life in the city is—and we want to maintain that gracious character."

PAINT PROBLEMS—REGIONAL AND NATIONAL

Some paint problems are strictly regional but most of them occur all over the country. For example, in the North and Northeast, sleet, snow and gale-force winds are normal conditions. Ice and dust storms often plague the Midwest. Strong sunlight (with its ultraviolet rays) is characteristic of the Southwest or desert climates while fungus growth is associated with the humid climate of the South. Add the variables of a home's age, surface finish build-up, special deteriorating conditions and you realize how extensive the research and testing must be to produce quality house paint.

Typical paint problems include:

- ***Blistering*, the most common failure, occurs when moisture locked in siding is drawn from the wood by the sun's heat. Moisture under a tight paint film will also vaporize and expand to form blisters.**
- ***Peeling* occurs for several reasons. Most often it is caused by applying oil paint to a moist surface. It also occurs when new paint is applied over several thick coats.**
- ***Cracking* generally results from a paint that has aged to an excessively hard finish. Hairline surface cracks permit water to seep into the wood; this causes flaking.**
- ***Alligatoring* is caused by an improperly built-up paint film.**

Every home requires individual attention to repair deteriorating sections and to prepare surfaces properly for painting.

FAR WEST: Colorful Victorian house in San Francisco typifies the originality and individuality of city dwellers. Owner chose bright colors to give the house a jewel-like appearance. In the country, West Coasters opt for muted earth tones.

NEW ENGLAND: Most houses in New England remain white, but the latest survey shows muted colors moving inland. Many homes display the colors that echo back in history. Such historic colors now are available in both latex and oil-type paints.

preferences reflect that attitude. There is extensive use of cedar and redwood siding on low-slung homes that nestle into hillsides. Muted golds, avocado and earth tones prevail and blend handsomely with surrounding terrain. But homes in urban areas tend to be painted with bright colors that reflect a greater degree of individuality.

old favorites still prevail

Colors that have been regional favorites still are. The difference today—as compared to a decade ago—is that colors no longer seem to be confined to areas. In other words, people are using the colors they like—no matter where they live.

preparing your home for paint

Start by making a careful inspection of the entire house. It's a good idea to bring a pad and pencil along with you so you can write down any irregularities you spot or note any areas that need particular attention or prepainting preparation. Look for trouble spots where paint failures occur most often: at window and door frames, around steps, behind gutters and downspouts, and under eaves. Particularly check areas where moisture accumulates, for example, where a patio butts against house siding.

If you have an excessive amount of peeling, cracking or blistered paint, it will be necessary to remove the old paint before starting to repaint. Spot removal can be accomplished by using a hand scraper and then feathering the old paint—with a disc sander—for a smooth transition into raw wood. On heavy removal tasks, a belt sander can save a lot of back-breaking rubbing; use an open-coat paper, such as 40-grit, to start and work your way up to at least 100-grit. Sand the surface thoroughly before applying any paint.

Cracks, holes over nailheads and the like should be filled too. Fillers that are formulated for exterior use are available from your paint dealer.

If surface conditions are generally good, prepainting work is greatly simplified. Most professionals give siding a going-over with a wire brush to rid the surface of heavy dirt. If the house exterior is just plain dirty, it makes sense to wash it down with a solution of household detergent and water. Use the garden hose to give the surfaces a complete rinsing and make sure siding is absolutely dry before applying an oil base paint. If you are using latex paint, you can start to apply it immediately after the hosing-down job is finished.

PREPARING AND PAINTING SIDING

AFTER GIVING siding a careful visual check, sand rough areas smooth and dust.

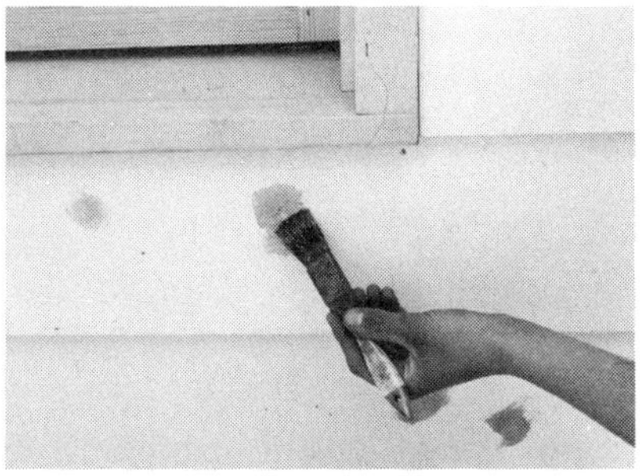

ON NEW bevel siding, seal all knots with dabs of primer or aluminum paint.

DIP BRISTLES halfway into paint, then tap brush against can to remove excess.

PAINT butt edges first on clapboard or shingles; do a 3-ft. run at a time.

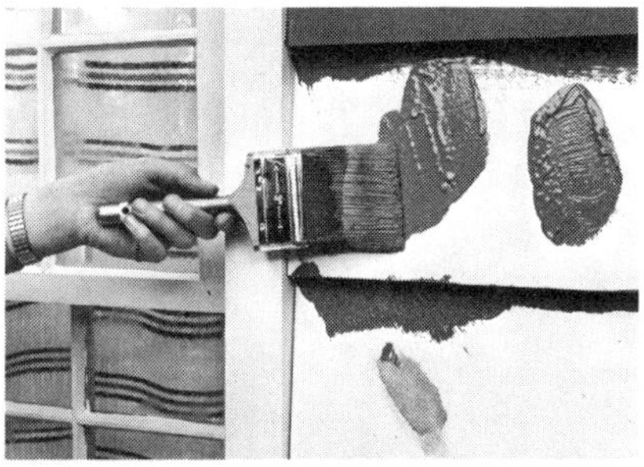

APPLY healthy paint blobs to weather face of siding, then brush smooth.

END PAINTING with smooth uniform strokes and cut-in around painted trim.

PAINTING WINDOWS

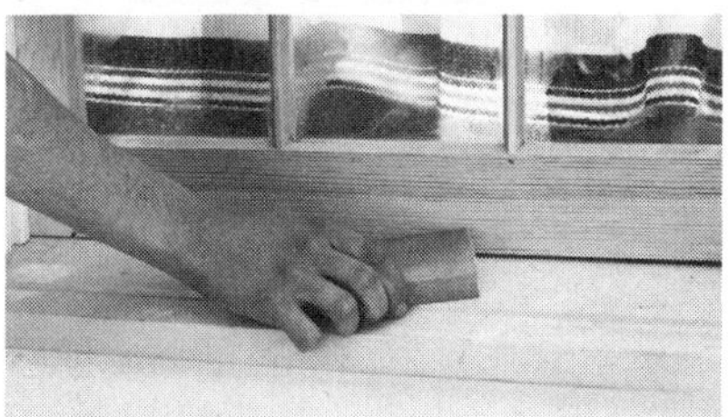

SAND ALL SURFACES of window and trim, and dust carefully.

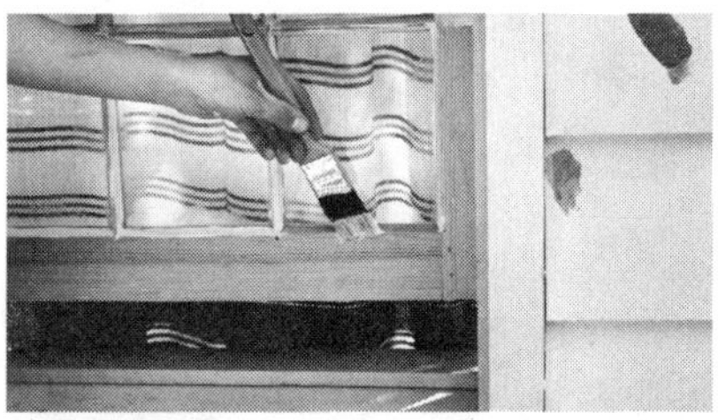

USE A SASH brush to cut in muntins. Apply primer before reglazing.

APPLY the finish coat; when dry, remove paint with a razor blade.

about burning off

Many homeowners are tempted to speed up paint removal by burning with either a blowtorch or propane torch. There's no doubt that this method does remove paint speedily, but it also brings with it the risk of serious fire damage. If you must use a torch, keep a garden hose at the ready on the ladder with you. To be safe, soak down each section as you finish flaming it.

To have paint flamed off by a professional is prohibitively expensive because of the soaring cost of insurance premiums.

painting basics

Start by getting your tools together: You will need the right-length ladders, dropcloths for protecting shrubbery, brushes, ladder hooks (for holding paint cans) and, of course, brushes. If you are using an oil-based paint, you will also need a solvent such as turpentine for clean-up. For water-based paints, brushes and tools can be cleaned with soap and water.

A 4- to 5-in. brush is best for painting the larger surfaces. Anything smaller doesn't transport enough paint from can to wall. A too-large brush will wear you out because of its weight. You should also buy a 1½- or 2-in. sash brush for cutting in—that tricky painting on windows.

In most cases, it is best to figure on a two-coat application—a prime coat and the finish coat. Start the job by priming and painting windows—so ladders won't be leaned against newly-painted siding. When windows are done, the siding can be painted.

Start at the top of your house and work your way down to ground level. If possible, try to work on relatively dry days when the temperature is above 50° F. If you can, work on the shady side of the house; that is, try to paint the west side during the morning and the east side in the afternoon.

A lush greenhouse in your window

By JOHN GAYNOR and HARRY WICKS

Add a touch of year-round beauty to your home by converting a window into a lush greenhouse. Decorative plants of different varieties will provide a display that can be enjoyed from the inside—and outside—your home. If there's a gardener in the family, the window can double as a "hothouse" for propagating plants well in advance of the outdoor gardening season. You can pick an easy-to-install commercial unit or you can build the greenhouse detailed on these pages

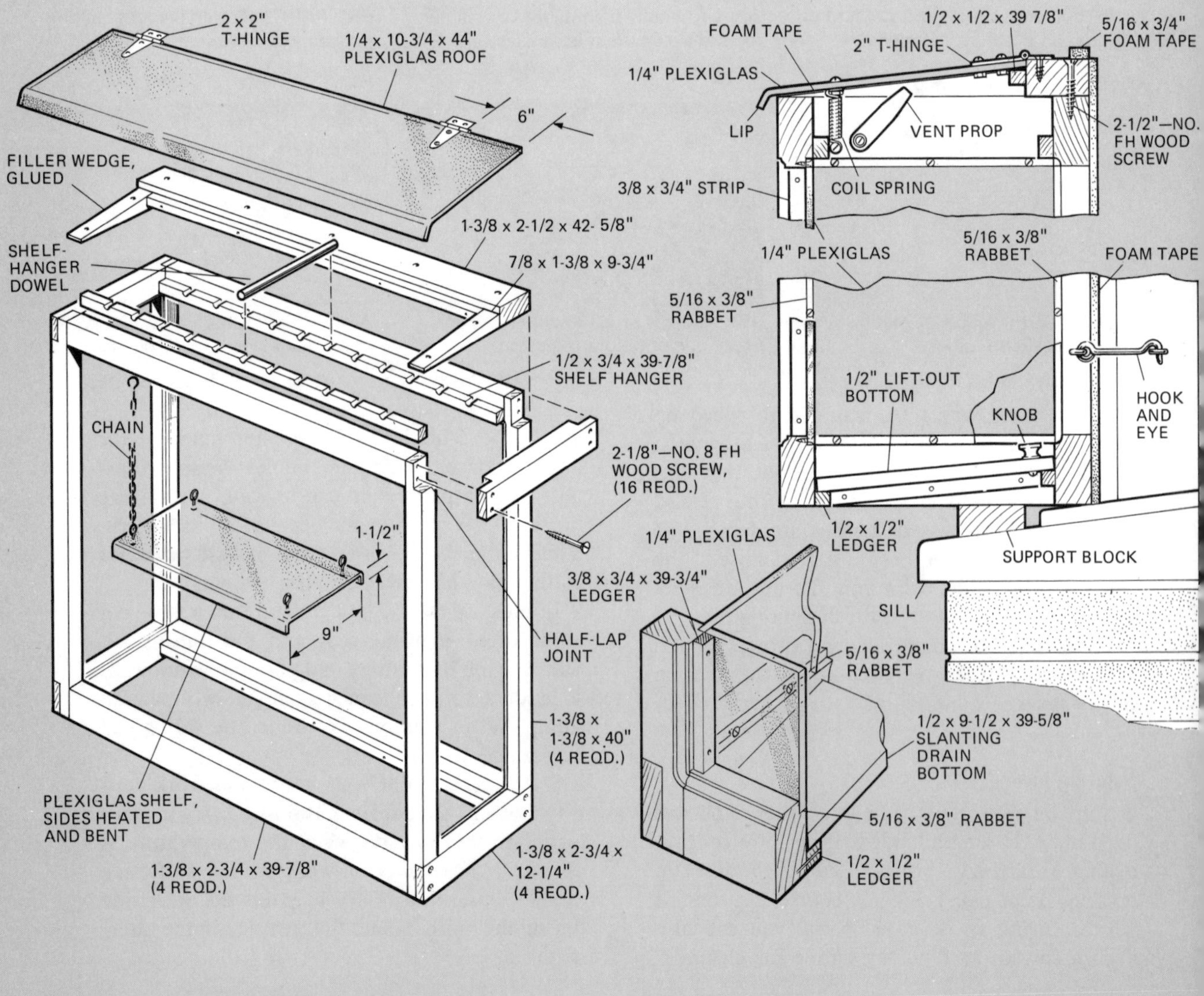

OUR WINDOW GREENHOUSE lets you add heat, supplemental light, and complete climate control.

continued

TO FINISH the greenhouse, apply two coats of exterior varnish to the redwood frame.

Ideas that make this greenhouse great

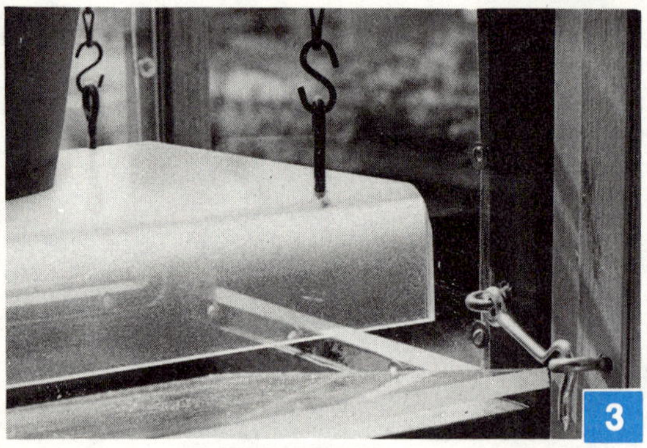

1. PLANT HANGERS are cut from ⅜-in. steel rods that, like all metal parts, are sprayed with flat black Rustoleum. **2.** Shelves of ¼-in. Plexiglas are cut to length and 12 in. wide. When a 1½-in. flange is bent along each side a shelf width of 9 in. is left. **3.** The unit shown is held in position with four screw eyes and hooks. Foam tape keeps out any drafts and water from entering. **4.** The plastic top is held in open position with one wood hinge at each end. A spring prevents the top from chattering in stiff breezes.

WHETHER YOU PLAN to use your window greenhouse for plant propagation or just plain enjoyment of flowers, certain features must be incorporated in order for the unit to be a true greenhouse.

- Provision for ventilating is necessary. Our version with operable top and bottom gives good air flow even with sash closed.
- If the climate and your growing plans dictate, you must have provisions for heating. On this model it's a simple matter to install a commercial electric heater.
- As in full-scale greenhouses, moisture must also be contained. Here, because window sash remains in place, you assure the greenhouse climate being independent of house climate.
- You must also be able to install supplementary plant lights if needed. On this model it is simply a matter of running in the electric wire.
- While a southern exposure is ideal because of its sun and warmth, other window locations can be used so long as they receive at least some direct sunlight during part of the day, especially in winter months.

Because the unit attaches with just four hooks and eyes, fastening in the window opening is easy. And the unit is self-contained; you don't have to remove the window sash. This means no drafts in the winter and no need for caulking or waterproofing.

good construction features

Fashioned of ¼-in. Plexiglas and redwood, the box is designed so that the inside plane of the Plexiglas and frame are flush. As a result, all condensation collects on the bottom (which, in turn, is pitched forward toward the front) on a water-impervious material where it can be removed by sliding back the bottom. Additionally, the bottom is easily removed for cleaning out any dirt or leaves that may collect.

To finish the greenhouse, apply two coats of exterior varnish to the redwood frame.

'bubble' greenhouse

A plastic window garden, called Nature Bubble by its maker, Feather Hill Industries, Box 41, Zenda, WI 53195, fits inside a window like an airconditioner. The unit is ideal for those who are interested in getting the jump on spring by starting garden plants inside and moving them outdoors when weather permits. Instructions for mounting the bubble are packed in the carton. Installation time is about one hour. A tray for germinating seeds is included. If desired, it can be used instead to hold potted plants.

EVERYONE HAS A FAVORITE WAY to store small parts and tools. Mine is in refrigerator ice-cube trays obtained cheaply at a discount store. They are kept in a rack I made from scrap ¾-in. plywood. The rack sides were grooved to take the tray lips. With some tray types, dividers can remain in place to make compartments for small parts.—*Arthur L. Ramos, San Anselmo, CA.*

RECLAIMED CINDER BLOCKS can be made into a serviceable drainage pipe. Dig a trench 3 or 4 ft. deep and at least 1 ft. wide, pitched toward a dry well or stream. Hold blocks in position with stones wedged between them and the trench walls. Place plastic or 15-lb. felt over joints to keep dirt out of water passage. Refill the trench and grade.—*Tony Sgro, Newburgh, NY.*

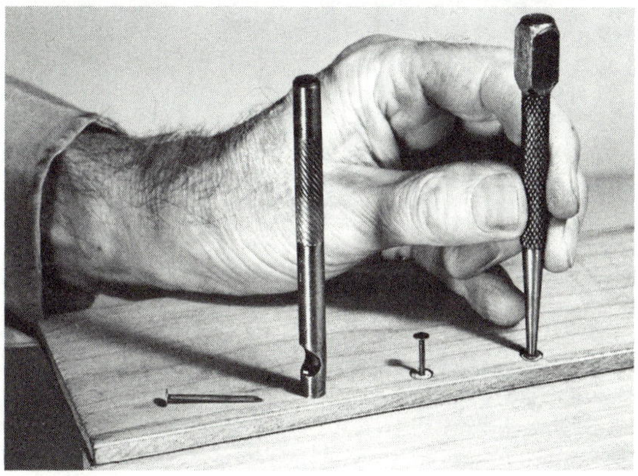

COMMON NAILS, superior to finishing nails in holding strength, are difficult to countersink without raising splinters. But not if you first use a hollow leather punch to mark their locations. Use a punch diameter that roughly matches nailhead size. You can then drive and set the nails as though they were the finishing type.—*Harry J. Skelton, Eugene, OR.*

A SLIP-ON EXTENSION which seats and "locks" itself over the shouldered end of the tap is made by cross-drilling the extension at base of its axial hole. The latter is made about 1/16 in. smaller in diameter than the tap, after which the cross hole is filed, top and bottom, to produce two flats. All but ¼ in. of the axial hole is rebored to accept the tap's shank.—*E. B. Walters, Chicago.*

Grow a graceful indoor garden

■ AN INDIVIDUAL POTTED PLANT adds an attractive touch to a room. But when you group several plants in an indoor garden, you'll create a luxuriant display of foliage that hints of spring—even when snowdrifts are piled outside the window.

The arrangements shown are both practical and good-looking. They're designed to simplify daily plant care. And construction (detailed on pages 1607 and 1608) has been kept simple. In addition, the structures protect the floor beneath the plants.

Place your indoor garden so plants get best exposure to light. If artificial light is needed, you can use a type specially designed for horticultural purposes. (Vita-Lite by Duro-Test Corp., North Bergen, N.J. is such a light; it emits the full spectrum of natural light plus the benefits of the ultraviolet spectrum.)

Contemporary plant stand. Simplicity is the word here. The unit consists of short lengths of 2 x 10 redwood fastened to a pair of 2 x 3s. The trickiest part is maintaining the angle for the holes which receive the dowel legs. If you lack

SEE ALSO
Benches, potting . . . Cold frames . . . Garden shelters . . . Gardening . . . Planters . . . Strawberry barrels . . . Terrariums

HERE ARE TWO lush indoor gardens—a contemporary plant stand (opposite page) and a living wall that blends with colonial decor (left). You can build either in just a single weekend.

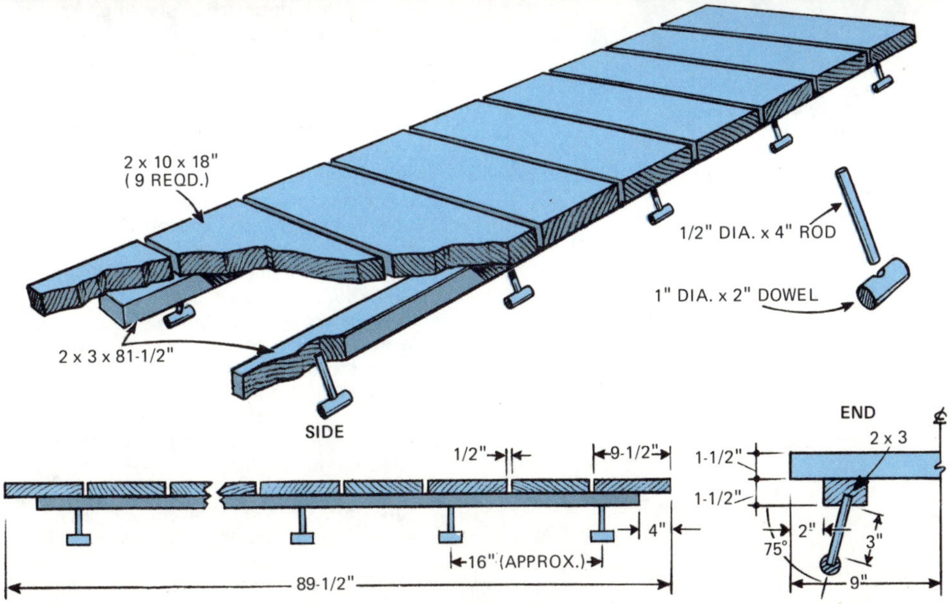

know-how for setting up a drilling jig, simply make the legs vertical.

Finish the stand using clear waterproof sealer on the redwood.

Living wall. Constructed of ¾-in. plywood with a 2 x 4 grid, this garden requires no elaborate joinery—all pieces are simply butt-joined.

Start by measuring the wall area and if necessary, adjust drawing dimensions. The unit's height is critical so make certain you measure carefully. The top can be flush with, or just a shade lower than, the window stool. If you build a taller unit make certain you will be able to operate the windows.

Assemble the wall unit using waterproof glue and screws since dampness is sure to get onto the wood areas. The wall unit is freestanding—unless the floor it rests on is badly out-of-level. If so, shim the unit plumb with wood shingles and use several screws through the unit's back into the wall studs. The floor grid is of 2 x 4 stock. Each well is fitted with a sheet-metal box. The joints of the box are soldered to protect the floor below.

To finish, apply a coat of primer, allow to dry and paint with colors to suit the decor of the room. For looks, paint the grid interior black and use wall color on the face to coordinate with the wall unit.

Tips for starting an indoor garden

Which plants to grow is basically a question of light source. Actually, you can grow practically any plant indoors, from roses and foliage to lush tropical varieties and cactus. It all depends on the quality of light. Do you have direct sunlight all day? Or is it partial or filtered sunlight? Or northern light? Or artificial light? Once you know the location of your indoor garden, you can select your plants using any good plant book giving a full list of light and temperature requirements.

Pots. Most indoor gardeners prefer clay pots, but you may want to pick up several ceramic jardinieres for use as color and shape accents in your planting setup.

It's a good idea to buy correct-size clay saucers to go with the pots. Pick those that have a protective coating to prevent water from seeping through to plant stand or furniture.

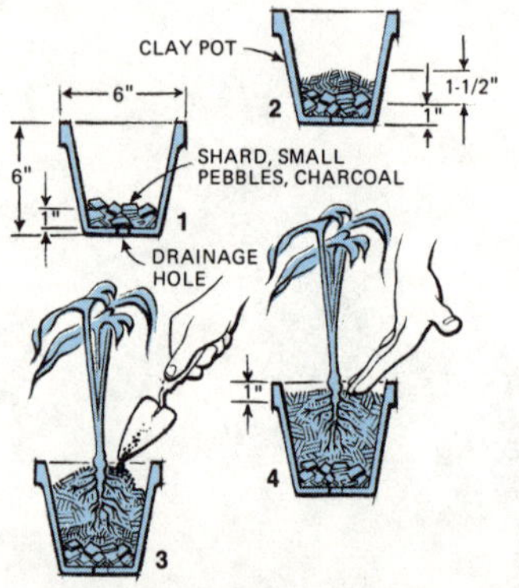

Potting a plant. Use only a clean container to pot a plant. And a new clay pot should be soaked overnight in water to minimize the amount of moisture it will draw from planting. The sketch illustrates the four basic steps of potting: 1. Fit a piece of shard (broken pot) over the drainage hole then add some porous stones. Toss in some pieces of charcoal, too, to keep the soil sweet. 2. Add a small mound of soil—about 1½ in. deep. 3. Holding the plant in place, fill around it with soil. 4. Firm the soil around the stem, then eliminate any air spaces by striking the pot on the bench several times. Soil should be about 1 in. from top so there is room for watering.

Watering and feeding. When you water, do it thoroughly—add water until excess runs from the drainage hole. Water your plants in the morning because moisture lingering at night invites fungus disease.

Humidity. Since plants release moisture through their leaves, an occasional spraying with a fine water mist is helpful.

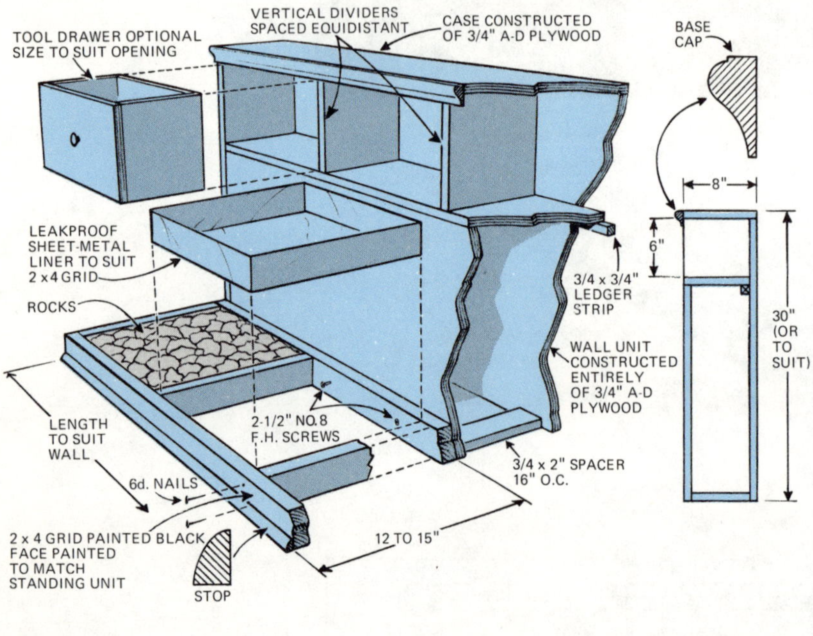

A COUPLE OF RUBBER GROMMETS pushed into the holes in your can-opener handle, will make this kitchen utensil a lot easier on your hand each time you use it. The grommets should be of a tight press-fit so there will be no chance of their dislodging and causing problems when the opener is placed in your dishwasher.—*Ken Patterson, Regina, Sask.*

CLEANING HARD-TO-REACH PLACES inside electrical equipment is easier with the aid of a slender, flexible tube coupled to a vacuum-cleaner hose. Here, a plastic bottle is used as an improvised step-down coupling between the hose and the rubber tube. The bottle fits snugly over the hose nipple; a glue nozzle with the tip removed subs for a bottle cap.—*Walter E. Burton, Akron, OH.*

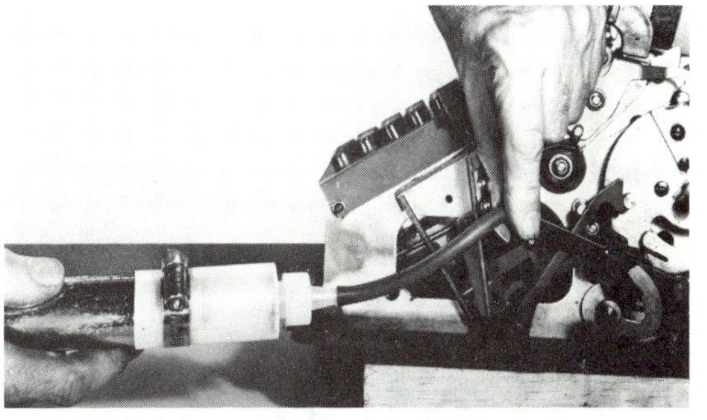

A LATHE TAILSTOCK CHUCK having a taper shank can slip when a large bit is taking a sizable bite. To reduce the chuck's tendency to rotate, clamp on a lock pliers—near the chuck base—positioning its handle so it will bear against a toolholder clamped in the toolpost parallel to the drill. This trick has worked for me every time.—*B. W. Ervin, Kent, OH.*

GLUING PICTURE FRAMES and other right-angle objects calls for a high degree of accuracy. Here's a foolproof method. Simply use two large corner brackets and a C-clamp as shown. After fitting the joint, apply glue and fasten the clamp and brackets until excess glue oozes out. Wipe off excess glue and set the piece aside on your bench to dry.—*Kent Peterson, Philadelphia.*

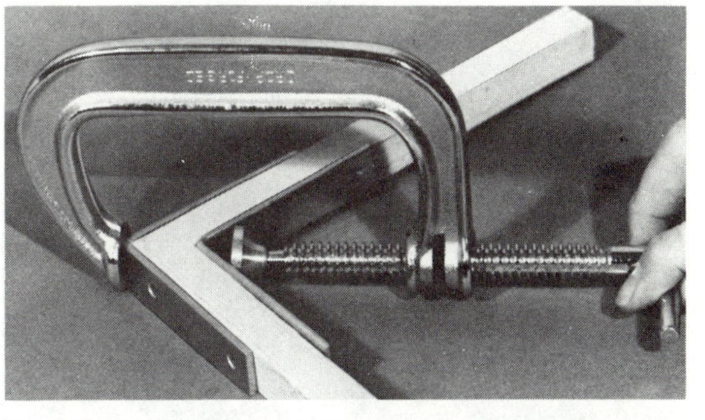

A LARGE STEEL ANGLE BRACKET works better than a try square, you may find, when used as a guide in helping you saw a 90° cut with a handsaw. The flat side of the bracket offers more bearing surface for the saw than the thin blade of a square, and it may be somewhat easier for you to hold it against the board.—*Pat Kendall, Chicago.*

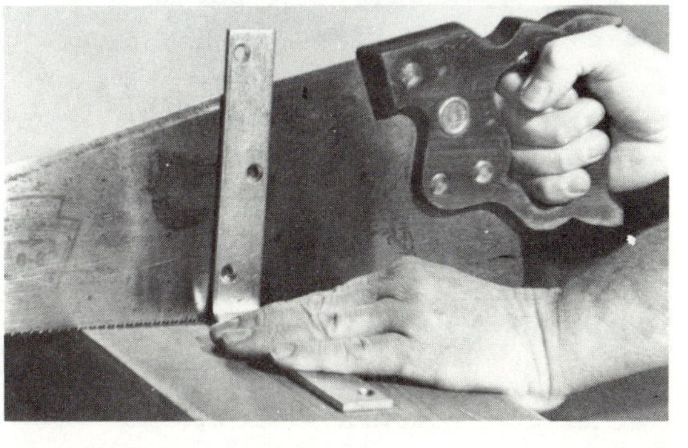

How to spot a good house

Learn how to be a sharp shopper before setting out to buy a new home. By knowing what to look for, you can get more house for your money and cut the risk of buying a lemon. Here are the steps to follow in learning how to judge a house

By LEN HILTS

SPOTTING a good house begins with a check of nearby lots, to see that there is favorable water drainage. Next, look at the design of the house and how it relates to the lot. Then inspect the exterior. If you are satisfied up to this point, then start an investigation of the interior layout and condition.

SEE ALSO

Home improvement . . . Insulation . . . Painting, exterior . . . Remodeling, exterior . . . Roofs . . . Vacation homes

WHEN BUYING a new house, visit other homes being constructed by the builder, where you can see how they are built.

■ WHEN YOU BUY A HOUSE, you make the single largest purchase of your lifetime—so in this, of all purchases, you should be a wise buyer. Yet too many people buy a house with less investigation than if they were buying a new TV or a used car.

How does one become a good house buyer? The average family buys from one to three homes in a lifetime, not enough to become experienced house hunters. Furthermore, home purchases often are made under pressure. Buyers may have only a few weeks to shop because of a transfer, or because they sold a house they must vacate by a specified date.

And there are so many considerations beyond the condition of their new house: neighborhood, proximity to shopping, transportation and schools.

Most people worry about price when buying a house, yet price is one of the easier problems to solve. You know how much money you have for a down payment. You soon learn how much mortgagors will loan on a house, and how much the monthly payments will be. These factors set the limits on your purchase. The real problem is one of finding a good house that fits your family's lifestyle within the boundaries set by money.

No matter how much you have to spend, you should be able to get a good house for your dollars by knowing what to look for and what to avoid.

A GOOD FLOOR PLAN is as important as good construction because it affects your daily life. Look for good separation of living, working and sleeping areas. Bedrooms should be shielded from entertaining areas. You should be able to go from one room to another without passing through a third room. The plan at the near right is poor because all traffic must criss-cross through the living room. Both plans at the far right work well because they permit good traffic flow and there is separation between the living and sleeping areas. Other items to check: The kitchen should be near the garage; some type of entrance hall should be provided; bathroom should be located near bedrooms; and there should be easy access to the house from the front.

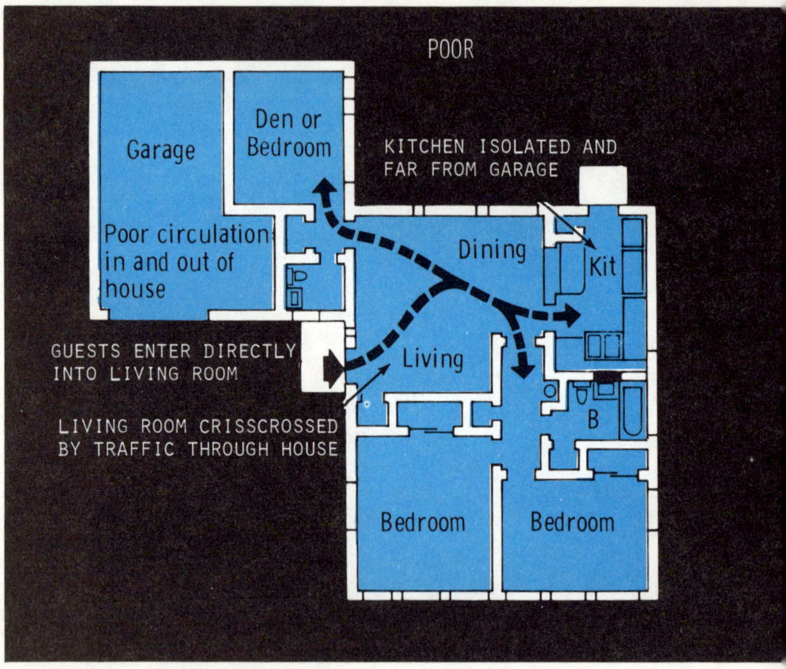

Ask yourself these questions when buying a house, old or new:

1. Does the house have an attractive appearance? Is it well-situated on the lot, with a good house-to-site relationship?

2. Does it have a livable floor plan? Does traffic move through it sensibly, and are the different living areas well separated?

3. How good are the major appliances, including the furnace, water heater, sump pump, and laundry and kitchen appliances? How old are they? Are they reliable units with recognized brand names?

4. What type of electrical service is supplied, and how good is the wiring?

5. How well is the house constructed?

6. Has the basement (if any) ever flooded?

If you know the answers to these questions, the chances of buying a bad house are cut considerably.

Appearance. A good house is set on the lot to take advantage of the best view or best exposure

IMPORTANCE OF A SOUTHERN exposure for main living areas is shown below. With sun low in winter, you take advantage of its light and heat. In summer, sun is high and is usually blocked by roof overhang.

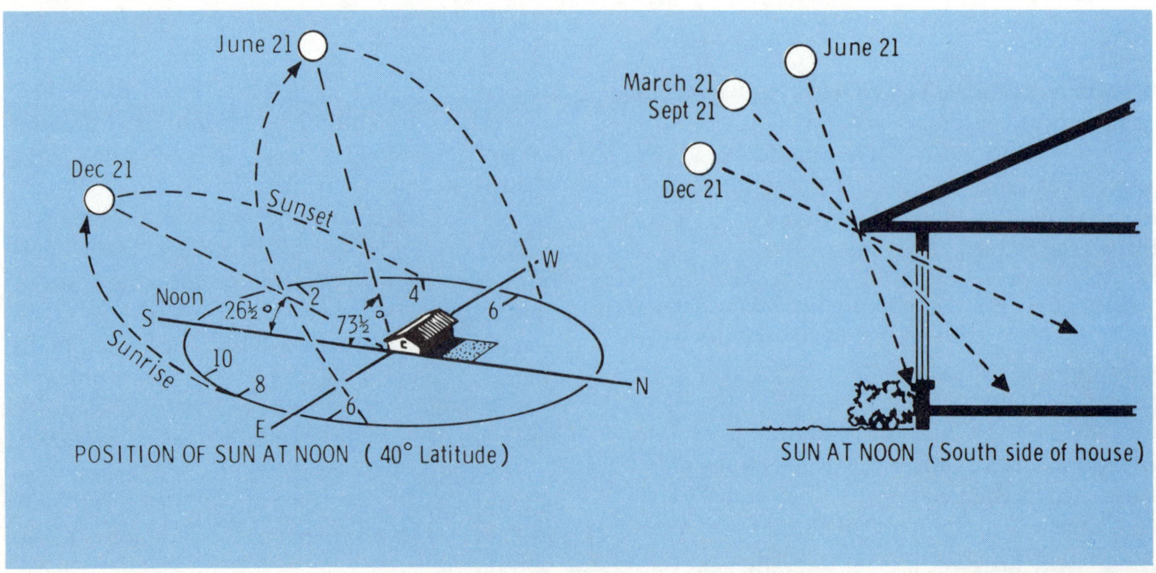

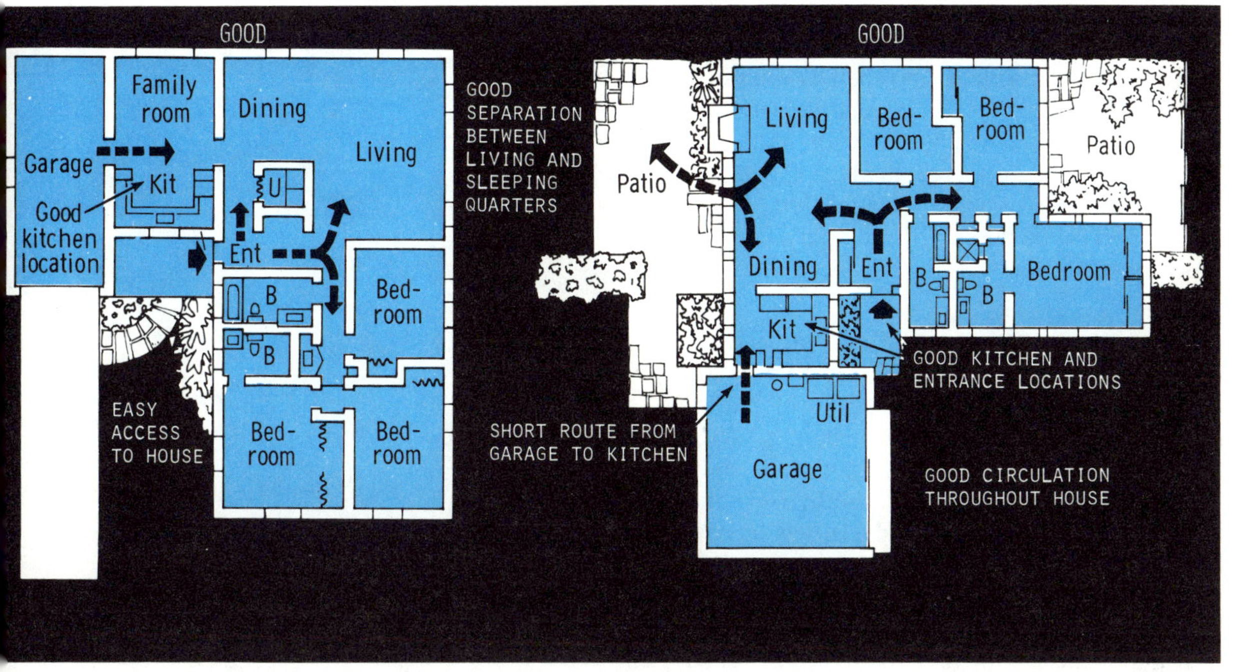

in relation to the sun and prevailing winds. A southern exposure usually is best. It is the only one that lets warm sunshine into your house all winter. This means bright, pleasant rooms and lower heating bills.

South windows are easy to shade with deciduous trees, which lose their leaves in the winter to let the sun through; by awnings; or by deep roof overhangs, which allow the lower-angled winter sun in when you need it.

Not all houses, of course, can face south. This is where the design of the house becomes important. Though it may face a street to the east or west, the house can be designed with big windows in the side with the best view, and it can be oriented to the south side. A poorly designed house, for example, might have many windows in the north side and few on the south.

Stand outside and visualize the effect of the sun on the house, keeping in mind windows and placement of trees. How will the sun affect the house in the summer? In the winter? The side of the house facing the prevailing wind and storm track will take the brunt of driving rains and winter winds. Is it sheltered by trees? Does it have too many windows? Are there storm windows? If there is an entrance on this side, is it sheltered in some way?

Ordinarily, a house should be set forward on its lot to give you the most land at the back for your private use. As you look at a house and lot, mentally divide the grounds into three main areas: public, private and service.

The *public* area is the front lawn. The *private* area, screened from public view by the house and landscaping, is the part for outdoor living. The *service* zone consists of the driveway, and areas for trash cans and outdoor equipment storage.

A large public area is a disadvantage because you must maintain it for the sake of appearance, yet you get very little practical use from it. At the same time, this area is vital to the overall appearance of the house, for a skimpy public area reduces the apparent size of the house.

A large private area means you can do more outdoor living. Look for patios, screened porches, cookout and garden areas on the private side of the house.

When looking at service areas, look for adequacy and convenience. The service areas should be screened from those areas used for outdoor living.

Finally, consider water drainage around the house. Can storm water drain away from the house? The natural slope of the lot and nearby land should carry rain water away from the foundation. Be wary of homes in low spots which receive drainage from adjacent areas. The best house location is one which is higher than other nearby land, and which is graded for good water runoff.

House-to-site relationship. Look at the house from the front. Does it seem to stick up out of the ground? Or does it blend into the lot—part of a unified whole? Part of this is good landscaping and part is the way the house is built on the lot. Decide whether improved landscaping might improve the house-to-site relationship. If so, don't forget to add the cost of new landscaping to your house budget.

Types of houses. You'll find single-story homes; the story-and-a-half house; the two and three-story house; and the split-level house. Each has advantages and disadvantages.

You won't have stairs to climb in the one-story house. It is easier to maintain, both inside and out, and items like painting and roof repairs cost less.

The one-story house allows the most flexible floor planning, but not all one-story houses are well planned. Look for good room zoning—good separation between the living, working and sleeping zones.

The story-and-a-half house isn't often built today, but thousands have been put up over the years. The house is basically designed for living on the first floor, with the attic space sometimes finished to provide additional bedrooms.

Check the attic in these. If unfinished, you should see good insulation under the roof. If finished, find out how well it was insulated during finishing. These houses can get extremely hot under the roof because ventilation is usually provided only by small dormer windows.

A two-story house gives a feeling of size and permanence. You get the most house on the least land for the least cost per square foot. It offers natural separation between downstairs living activities and upstairs sleeping areas.

Two-story houses are easier to heat than spread-out ranch homes because heat rises. Downstairs rooms are cooler in the summer, while upstairs rooms may be quite hot. Check the insulation of the roof and mark it as a plus if the house has a ventilating fan in the ceiling of the second-floor hall (even if the house is centrally air-conditioned).

Maintenance of a two-story house is difficult. Exterior painting requires long ladders and some spots near the top may be hard to reach. Roof and gutter repairs can be difficult, even hazardous.

The split-level house combines some of the advantages of one and two-story houses. It offers a natural division of living zones, but it also

KEEP A SHARP EYE out for the use of top-grade materials in a house. Here, you can see good hardwood parquet flooring, an indication of quality construction. Don't be misled, however, by eye-catching features such as luminous ceiling or kitchen pass-throughs which may divert your attention from poor materials.

has stairs. However, you won't do as much stair climbing as in a two-story. Check these houses for good insulation in the lowest and highest levels. The lowest levels are partially below grade, and therefore may be subject to flooding and moisture problems. If the foundation was sealed and the walls were insulated, these problems are minimized. But rainwater drainage could be a problem.

As you examine the house (or any house), look for evidence of flooding: high-water marks on basement walls; equipment such as washers on platforms off the floor; and non-use of the basement for storage. If the basement is freshly painted, be wary. The paint may hide high-water marks.

The split-level house is best on a sloping lot, where it fits into the contours of the land. Sometimes, split-level homes are stuck on dead-level lots. Unless earth has been brought in to grade these places, they look like displaced persons on the land.

Floor plans. The keys to any floor plan are easy access to all rooms, good separation of the living zones, and a traffic pattern that is easy to live with.

When you enter a house, ideally you should be able to go straight to every room without passing through another room. If you must pass through a room, count it as one demerit. If you must go through the living room to get to the kitchen or to a stairway, score a double demerit.

Does the back door enter directly into the kitchen, or into a utility or mud room? Entry through a utility room will save a lot of kitchen clean-up.

One way to evaluate a house is to think of day and night areas. A house with four bedrooms may sleep your family comfortably—but what happens when everyone is up and active? Look over the house to see how many separate day-time activity areas there are.

A combined living room and dining room counts as one daytime space. A family room is one space. A combined kitchen-family room may be one space or two, depending on the lay-out.

How many daytime living areas do you need? This depends on your family. The lady of the house needs a kitchen, a laundry area, and perhaps a sewing area. The man may need a work or hobby area. Children of different age groups may have to be divided for afternoon play, and this calls for separate areas. Count up the areas you need, then see that your new house fits. Don't just buy on bedroom space alone.

The kitchen deserves critical attention. Look for a good "work triangle"—the arrangement of the refrigerator, sink and range. Measure the distance from the work spot in front of the range to the refrigerator door, and from the refrigerator door to the sink, and then back to the range. Add up the total running feet. According to research at Cornell University's Kitchen Laboratory, the minimum footage should be 12 to 15, the maximum 22. Anything less than 12 feet will be crowded; more than 22 feet will require too much walking.

Look for plenty of countertop space. The University of Illinois Small Homes Council recommends at least 4½ ft. of countertop on the open side of the refrigerator door, between the refrigerator and the sink; 3½ to 4 ft. between the sink and the range; and at least 2 ft. on the other side of the range. These are minimums. The Council also suggests a minimum of 8½ running feet of wall cabinets, plus at least 20 cu. ft. of storage under the counters.

Grade a house, too, on the location of its bathrooms. There should be a full bath near the bedrooms, and for greatest convenience, a full bath for each two bedrooms. Look for a powder room in the living area of a ranch house, or on the first floor of a multi-storied house.

Appliances. Are the range, oven, dishwasher and disposal unit built in? Find out how old they are and how well they work. You may face repair bills in the near future. Don't pass up a house when everything is good but the appliances are old. Just add the cost of possible appliance replacement to the cost of the house.

The same is true of the furnace, air-conditioning equipment, hot water heater, and the laundry units. All can be replaced, and indeed someday must be replaced. The real question is how much use you will get out of them before replacement. You don't want to face a large replacement expense on top of a new mortgage unless you are prepared for it.

Brand-name appliances are important because you have a better chance of getting service and replacement parts.

Electric power. This is a major consideration. Our use of electrical appliances has increased by astounding leaps in recent years. Homes which were adequately wired 10 years ago often can't handle the load of appliances a family puts to use today.

Ask the following questions about electric power service:

1. Is it two-wire or three-wire? (It should be three-wire.)

2. Is it 60-ampere service, 100-ampere service, 150-ampere service? At one time, 3-wire 60-amp service was considered adequate. Today, 3-wire 100-amp service is a bare minimum. If you have a workshop, look to 150-amp service as adequate. Get the answers to these questions from the power company, and if power is inadequate, find how much it will cost to increase the service. Do this now, before you buy the house.

3. How many circuits? You should have one lighting circuit employing a 15-amp fuse for each 500 sq. ft. of living area. In addition, you should have two 20-amp appliance circuits in the kitchen, breakfast area and dining room. Laundry equipment, the garbage disposer and the electric range should be on their own separate circuits.

Look at the main electric service box and count the number of fuses or circuit breakers. The use of fuses indicates older wiring. If you see circuit breakers, the work was done more recently—but still may not be adequate.

Check gas and electric bills. These tell you much about how well the house is insulated and the annual upkeep costs. If the electric bill is lower than your present bill, think again about the wiring of the house. You apparently need more electricity than the present occupants.

House construction and condition. If you are buying a new house, you may see it under construction, or see what the contractor is building into nearby houses. If you are considering an older house, you'll have to hunt for clues to good construction. Here are some features to look for:

1. *Foundation walls* of poured concrete usually are better than cinder or concrete-block walls. Block walls should be plastered with ½-in. of cement mortar on the outside. In high-quality construction they are reinforced with steel.

2. *Troweled-on waterproofing* is better than the brushed or sprayed-on type.

3. *Drain tile* installed at the base of the foundation walls gets rid of ground water that otherwise may get into the basement.

4. *Exterior walls* on a new house should have a primer and two finish coats of top-quality paint. If you are looking at an old house, find out when it was last painted. Depending on weather, paint quality and other factors, you'll have to paint every three to six years.

5. *Interior walls* may be lath-and-plaster or gypsum wallboard. As the house settles, lath-and-plaster is more subject to cracking. On the other hand, in skimpy construction thin ⅜-in. wallboard is too often used. This damages easily and allows transmission of noise. Wallboard should be at least ½-in. thick, and preferably ⅝-in. The best wallboard construction consists of two layers of board, the first nailed to the studs and the second cemented to the first.

6. *Flooring*, if it will be seen, should be hardwood, preferably oak, smoothly installed. Often, in kitchens and in rooms which will be carpeted, no hardwood is installed. Instead, a subfloor of plywood is put down, and the floor covering laid over it. There is no point in paying for hardwood you will never see.

The floor of the kitchen gets a lot of wear, and present-day kitchen floor coverings are both durable and beautiful, and offer easy care. If the floor is relatively new, count it as a plus. If it is quite old, figure on replacing it.

7. *Windows and doors,* in more severe climates, should be weatherstripped and have storm installations. In older houses, check for looseness and for windows which won't open.

8. *Kitchen counters* should have a durable surface, preferably a plastic laminate or ceramic tile.

9. *Electric outlets* should be well distributed throughout the house. The National Electric Code calls for an outlet every 12 feet of wall space, and a switched light, operated from a switch near the door, for every room. Check the kitchen for two separate 20-amp circuits strictly for appliance use.

10. *Bathrooms* should have waterproof walls and floors. The best are finished in ceramic tile. Plastic tile and hardboard tile panels also are used. Areas around the sink and tub should be tiled. Look for good quality electric and plumbing fixtures, with recognized brand names on them. An enameled cast-iron tub is considered top quality, preferably with a shower enclosure. Avoid plastic tubs.

Bathroom faucets should be made of brass coated in chrome or nickel. Look to see that they don't drip or leak, that they turn easily, and that sink and tub drains work properly. Flush the toilets to check the noise and the flushing action.

Plumbing is difficult to check. Turn on a water faucet to check pressure and rate of flow. If it is slow, be wary. The town may have low water pressure. More likely, the water pipes are too small or they are becoming clogged with lime deposits.

There should be a shutoff valve for every water fixture in the house. Listen for "water hammer" as you turn the faucets on and off. This banging noise is easily cured by installing standpipes in the system, but you have to pay the plumber. Add another cost item to the price of the house.

11. *The water heater* must be large enough for your family. Thirty-gallon types are seldom sufficient. Look for 40 gallons or more in gas-heated units, and 80 gallons in electric units. Good water heaters are guaranteed for 10 years or more. Ask when this water heater was installed.

12. *Asphalt shingles* on the roof should be of the 235-lb. type and should be sealed down with glue tabs to prevent wind damage. Look the present roof over for signs of wear—thin spots in the surface coating, crumbling edges, broken shingles. If wood shakes or other roofing was used, inspect to see that none are missing and that all are well-anchored.

Many people have decided to buy old houses with the idea of updating them. They feel they can get a good buy because of the condition of the house.

Under the right circumstances, this can be a good way to get a good house—but not cheap. If the house is basically sound, but needs such things as a new heating plant, new electric wiring, or new plumbing, you can expect a very hefty expense. If you are tempted to follow this route, pay an electrician, a plumber or a heating contractor to give you an estimate on the new work *before* you decide to buy. Your mind may suddenly be changed.

Also, in looking at very old houses, remember that in the old days, bathrooms were few and kitchens came equipped with a sink—period. Putting in new bathrooms and bringing an old kitchen up to date are expensive chores.

Many people hope to offset the cost by doing the work themselves. Experience shows that in very old houses, much of the work is so difficult that you end up with professional crews.

Things to look for in a very old house. These include wet basements, no drains in basement floors, doors and windows which stick because of excessive settling, ancient electric wiring, old and clogged plumbing, a tired heating system, absolute lack of insulation, signs of termites or termite damage, worn-out gutters, worn-out roof, worn-out water heater, and a general sagging of the house.

Be cautious of a house which has settled too much and sags. Restructuring a place like this is very expensive. If you see evidence of termites, find out how much damage has been done before you buy. You could be facing a large rebuilding bill.

Check the tilt of floors, the leans and curves of walls. These often mean that the house is in real trouble.

The right way to go after an old, old house is to check it for basic soundness. When satisfied that it sits well on its foundation and has no major problems, make a list of essential remodeling, including wiring, heating, plumbing, insulation, etc. Don't kid yourself as you compile the list. If the place needs the work, put it on the list—and don't assume you can do it all yourself.

Now get good estimates of the work, and then add this total to the price asked for the house. The new figure is the real price you may be paying for the house, even though it may take you a couple of years to pay it all out.

Does the house still look like a good buy? Make one other check. Find out what other houses in the neighborhood are selling for. Get some idea of what your house would be worth after the remodeling was done. You may find that you won't ever be able to get your money out of the place.

On the other hand, you may find that it's a great buy!

BY THE TIME you see the termite tunnels such as these, hidden damage is terribly extensive. The insects were at work a long time here.

THIS BATHROOM looks great, but poor workmanship can cost you plenty. The pipes here leaked, and the whole floor had to be replaced.

All about humidifiers

■ NO NEED TO WAKE UP on winter mornings with itchy skin or dried-out throat because your house air is too dry. A humidifier can add moisture that will help you feel—and your plants look—better during the dry heating season.

Adding a humidifier will also return much needed moisture to parched wood furniture and wallcoverings. One also helps cut down or eliminate static electric shocks when you touch a doorknob or light switch after walking on carpeting.

how a humidifier functions

Simply stated, a humidifier puts moisture into the air. It can do this in one of three ways: *evaporation, atomization* and *vaporization.* Evaporator units pass air over a moistened medium, such as a rotating pad or disc. Atomizer units spray water droplets into the air. Vaporizing units use a heat source to vaporize water into steam.

There are also three styles of humidifiers: tabletop units, console units that look like cabinets and built-in units that are installed out of view. In forced-air heating systems, built-in units are placed on a furnace plenum or duct. In hot-water heating systems, built-ins fit behind a baseboard. Generally, built-in humidifiers deliver the greatest moisture evenly through a house, while tabletop and console units humidify one or two rooms.

why heated air becomes dry

Indoor air becomes dryer in winter when cold air is brought into the home and heated. When warmed, this air is capable of holding more water vapor than it can when cold. But the amount of water vapor actually stays the same, so the relative humidity drops. Since this heated air can hold more moisture, but the moisture amount remains constant, the relative humidity goes down.

Experiments have shown that a person is most comfortable at temperatures of 70° to 72°F. when the relative humidity is between 30 and 40 percent. Without a humidifier, the relative humidity of heated air can drop to as low as 13 percent.

not all homes can be humidified

Before you buy a humidifier, inspect to make certain your house is both insulated and has a protective vapor barrier. Humidifying an uninsulated house is a waste of time and money, because the water vapor will go directly outdoors before the house air is adequately moistened.

Moisture added to the atmosphere of an insulated house that doesn't have a vapor barrier enters the insulation and condenses on it and the cold outer wall. This water makes insulation less effective and may cause rot in the wall.

selecting a humidifier

Whether you select a built-in, console or tabletop humidifier, choose one with a capacity to fit your needs. To make a wise decision, you must know the square footage of your house and its basic construction. The more loosely a house is constructed, the greater the amount of parched, cold air it lets in and the more moisture is needed.

The Air-Conditioning and Refrigeration Institute chart below gives humidity requirements in gallons per day based on an 8-ft. ceiling height:

House Construction	Building Size (Sq. ft.)		
	1000	1500	2500
Tight	4.2	6.4	10.6
Average	6.5	9.8	16.3
Loose	9.2	13.8	23.0

A humidifier you select should have its capacity rating clearly noted. After you've determined the needed capacity, other factors differ depending on whether you select a portable or built-in unit.

If your heating system won't accept a built-in humidifier, or if you want to humidify only part of your house, you can use a tabletop or console model.

Tabletops have the advantage of being light

SEE ALSO
Appliance repair . . . Appliances . . .
Energy, saving . . . Furnaces . . .
Heating systems, home . . . Radiator covers . . .
Stoves, wood-burning . . . Winterizing, homes

INSTALLING A HUMIDIFIER BETWEEN PLENUMS

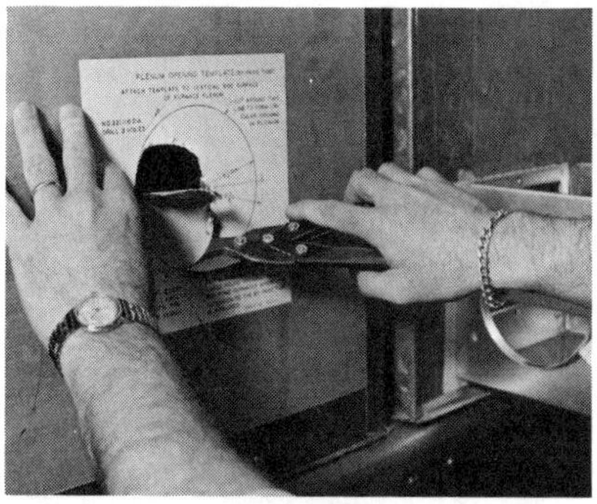

1. MOUNT TEMPLATES that come with this Skuttle kit and cut plenum openings. Note cabinet, in place at right.

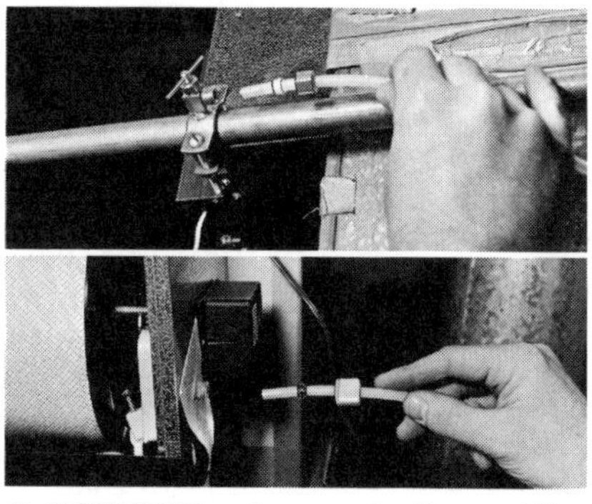

2. CONNECT water supply. Use saddle connector valve on water line. Attach tubing to it (top) and humidifier.

3. MOUNT humidistat; plug into 115-volt outlet (not to light switch). Motor over 3 watts may need grounding.

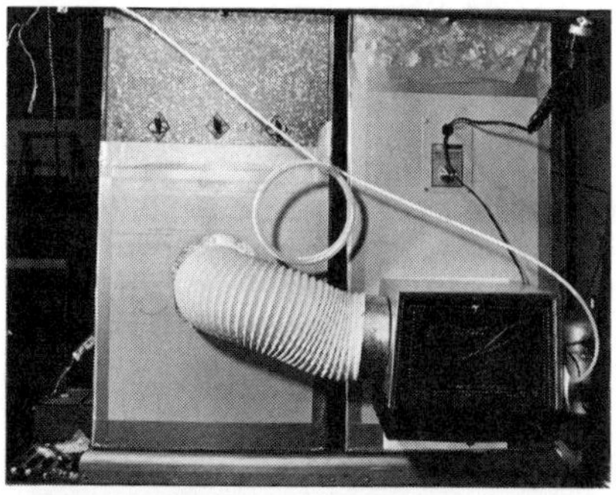

4. WHEN INSTALLATION is done, run water to check for leaks, energize electrical system, and set humidistat.

TYPICAL MOUNTING LOCATIONS

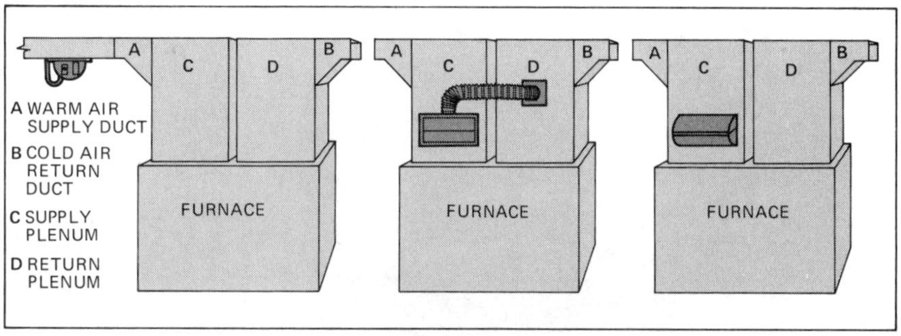

and easy to carry to a water source for filling. However, their capacity usually is limited to eight to 10 hours per fill.

Console humidifiers basically are a reservoir with a pad that passes through it. A fan forces air through the moistened pad, evaporating water and sending moist air into the room. The pad is on a revolving drum or is a belt on rollers. These units plug into standard outlets.

It's somewhat difficult to compare output capacities of consoles because makers specify output in a variety of ways. Some manufacturers talk about gallon capacity of their water reservoirs. Others give the square footage that the unit can humidify, or the gallons of water it releases a day.

But you can compare other features, such as ease of filling, moving, emptying, cleaning and servicing. Some units have a hose for filling at the sink. Look for a model that has a chute or funnel to guide the water during filling.

You'll need to clean the humidifier one or more times a season, depending on how fast mineral deposits collect. This is when a removable water reservoir is a great help—a reservoir with a drain is also handy, since there is usually leftover water. Also, check to see that the belt or drum is easy to remove for cleaning. Make sure parts are accessible for servicing.

Cost for console units is in the $65 to $165 range. Tablets that dissolve in the water reservoirs are designed to cut down on mineral build-up.

Built-in humidifiers can be powered or non-powered units. Powered ones deliver the greatest amount of moisture to your house. These are typically installed on a plenum or under a warm-air duct of a furnace in forced-air heating systems. They work by spraying a fine mist or exposing wetted pads to the air flowing through your heating system. The furnace fan then circulates the humidified air through the house. A humidistat can control the level of humidity.

The advantage of a built-in humidifier, besides its ability to humidify the entire house, is that it stops and starts automatically as directed by the humidistat. Some units can be installed so they run only when the furnace is working.

Powered built-in humidifiers range in evaporative capacity from ¾ to 8¼ lbs. of water per hour. (A gallon of water weighs approximately 8.45 lbs. Thus, to convert pounds into gallons, divide by 8.45.) Units cost from $65 to over $200, not including installation charge.

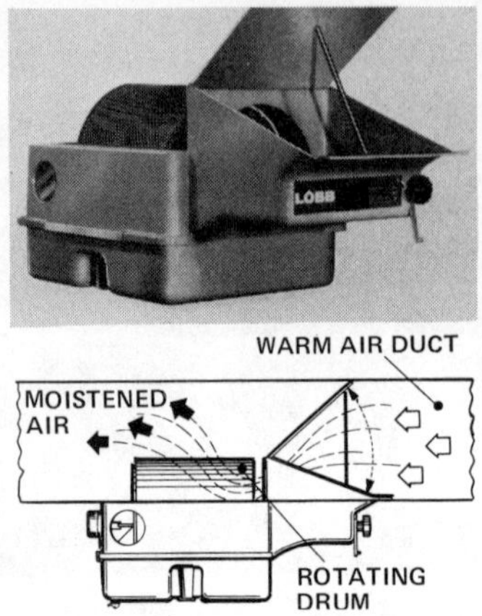

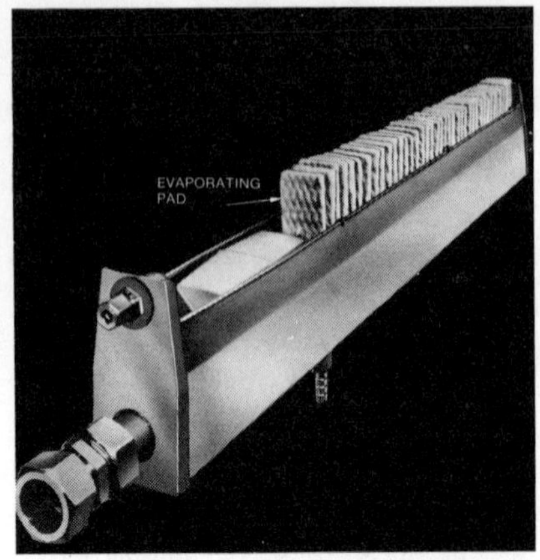

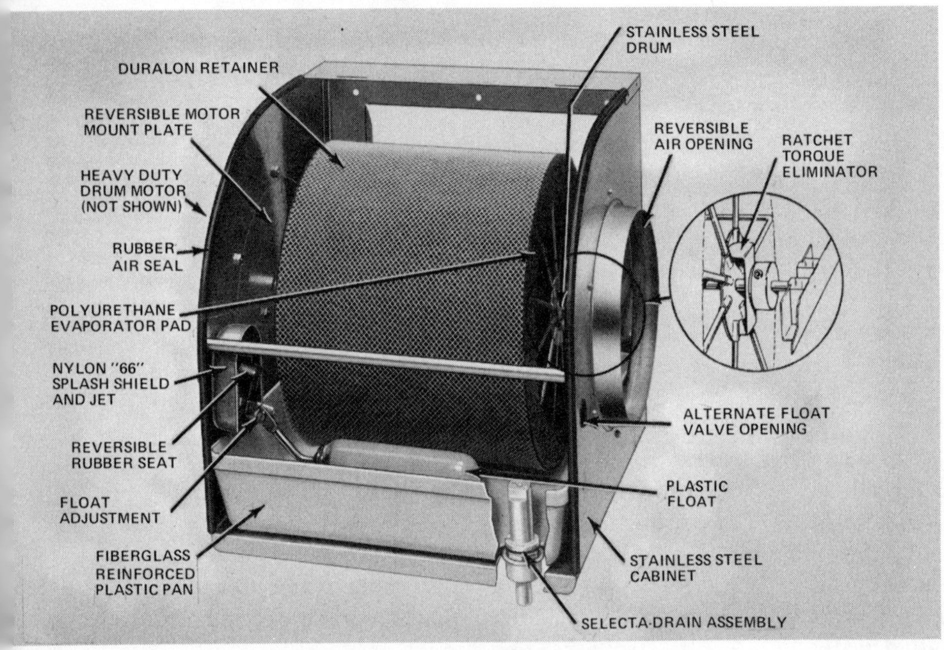

THE HYDRONIC humidifier, designed for hot-water systems, fits behind a baseboard. Water feeds into it, is absorbed by pads, transferred to air. Pennco, Box 223, Clarendon, PA 16313.

THIS HUMIDIFIER kit from Skuttle (top, left) has all parts for installation on a warm or cold furnace plenum of a forced-air heating system. The air is forced through a revolving pad.

THE AD 1 DUCT unit by Lobb (top, center) is installed as shown below it. Air in warm-air duct enters the unit via an adjustable manual baffle, passes the pad, is moistened and flows out.

INNER WORKINGS of a humidifier are shown (left). Motor-driven drum passes through a pan and picks up water to moisten air entering the unit.

Before you shop for a unit, check the dimensions of possible humidifier mounting locations on your heating system. As you shop, look for these features: ease of installation, inspection and cleaning. Any unit you plan to install yourself should come with complete directions. Prewired units are often the surest route. Units that have a window showing the machine's interior are the simplest to inspect. Models with removable components are the least trouble to clean.

The only tools you need to install a powered built-in humidifier are a hand drill, screwdriver, tin snips and pliers. It takes little more than an hour to complete most installations. Here's how you proceed:

1. Turn off the heat and electricity before installing the unit.

2. **Humidifier case.** With tin snips, cut an opening in the plenum or duct where you plan to make the installation. Attach the stiffener plate for the humidifier case with screws, then hang the box.

3. **Water supply.** Hook up the water supply to the humidifier by drilling a hole in the nearest cold-water line (if the saddle valve that comes with your humidifier isn't self-piercing). Attach the saddle valve. Run copper tubing between the valve and the float valve on the humidifier.

4. **Humidistat.** Cut an opening in the return duct or wherever you will place the humidistat according to the maker's directions. Mount the humidistat and connect it to the humidifier and power supply.

5. **Energize it.** Open the saddle valve to let the humidifier reservoir fill. Turn on the switch and set the humidistat at the level you wish.

INSTALLING AN UNDER-THE-DUCT HUMIDIFIER

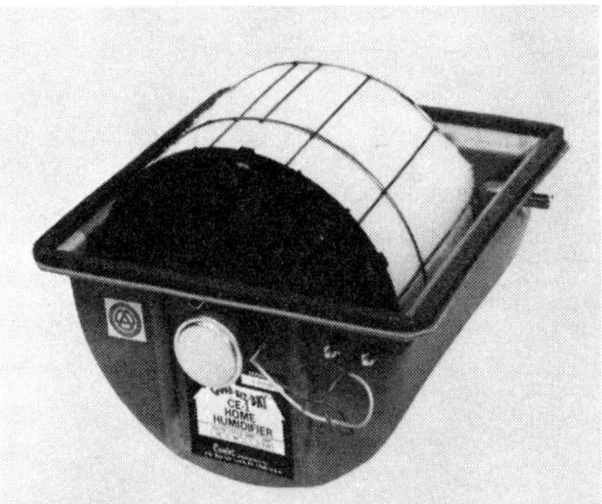

1. THE GOOD-BYE-DRY humidifier comes complete in a lightweight carton.

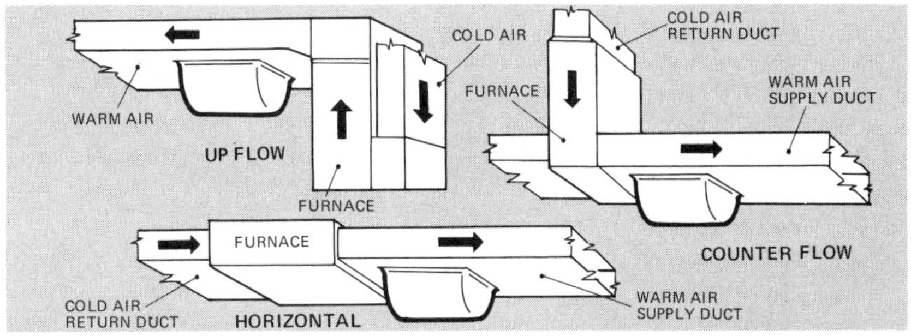

2. THE UNIT is designed for mounting under the warm-air supply duct of a furnace. Determine which type of furnace system in the drawings most resembles yours to see how you would install such a unit. If there is more than one supply duct from the plenum, use the duct that services the largest area of the house.

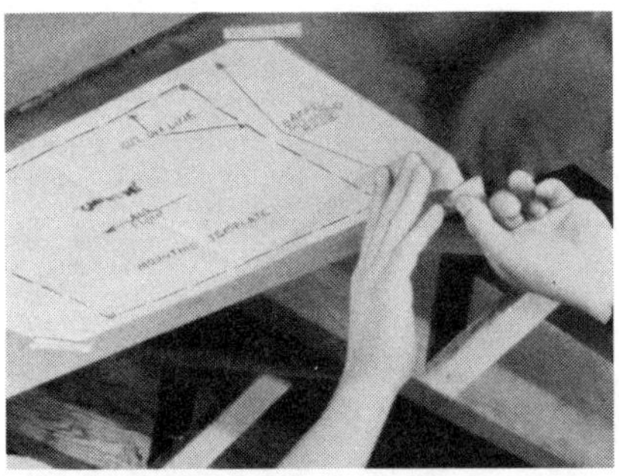

3. AFTER SELECTING A suitable location to install the humidifier, use adhesive strips to center the mounting templates on the underside of duct.

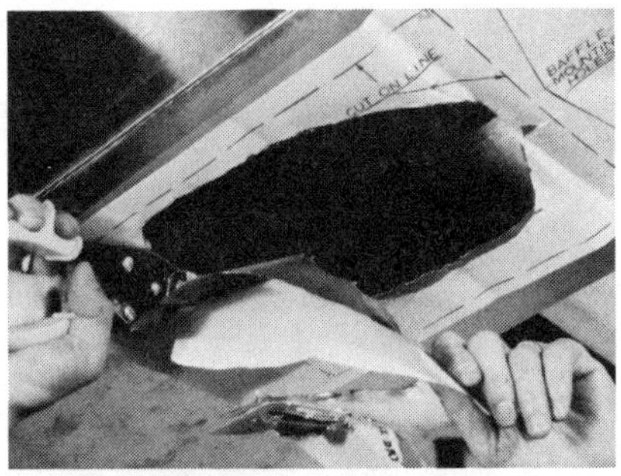

4. DRILL BAFFLE mounting holes marked on template. Using snips, cut through template and duct in spiral pattern until you reach dotted line.

5. ATTACH BAFFLE to its supports. Position it in duct with baffle underside facing airflow. It directs air to increase efficiency.

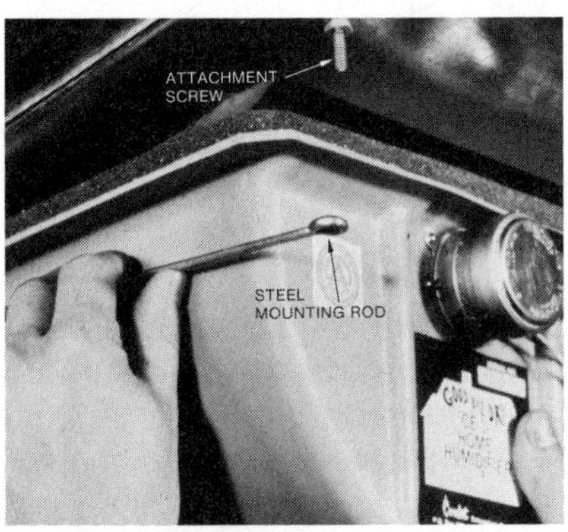

6. STEEL MOUNTING rods fit under edges of both sides of unit for support. Attach rods with screws, slide unit in place and tighten knobs.

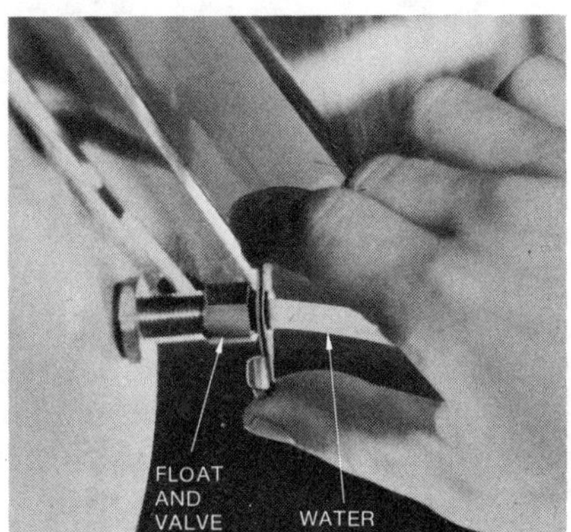

7. SECURE THE WATER tubing in thread of unit's float and valve assembly.

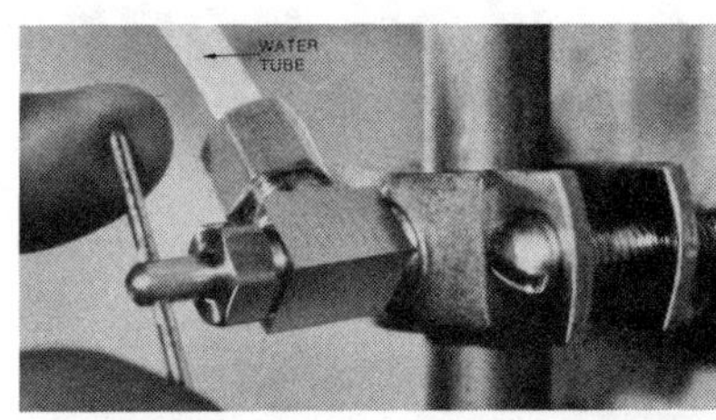

8. EXTEND TUBE to nearest copper cold-water pipe. (Steel or brass pipes need drilling.) Attach self-tapping valve and saddle bracket assembly at end of tube onto water pipe. Turn valve handle clockwise to pierce water pipe. To open valve, turn handle counterclockwise (as with an ordinary faucet). Water will enter the unit and be maintained at the proper level by a float valve.

9. TO MAKE the electrical connection, fasten prespliced wires to each terminal by tightening thumb nuts.

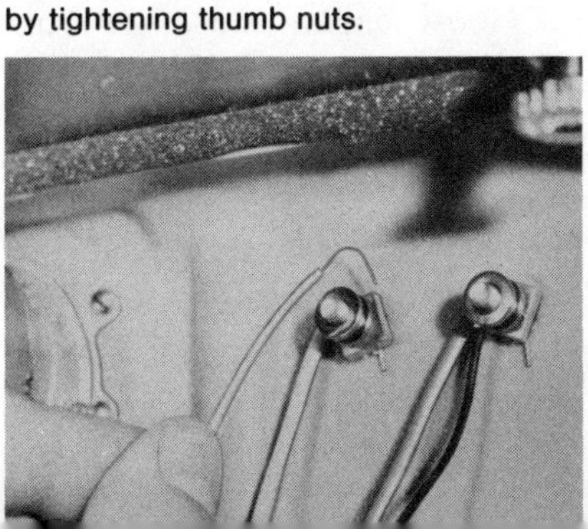

10. KIT COMES with 20 ft. of wire. Plug in the transformer to the nearest 110/115-volt electrical outlet.

11. ONCE INSTALLED, the unit will operate automatically with heating system to provide total house humidity.

Call your game from the wild

By ROGER LATHAM

An expert hunter tells you how game calls work and why you should use them

■ CALLING WILD ANIMALS is by no means unique to the modern-day hunter—even though he has the advantage of some mighty sophisticated equipment.

Centuries ago, the American Indian and the Eskimo learned that they could imitate the voice or sounds of various kinds of wild game and bring them within bow and arrow or harpoon range. To them, it was a matter of survival. You either called successfully or you didn't eat!

SEE ALSO
Backpacking . . . Binoculars . . . Boat camping . . . Camping . . . Knives, hunting . . . Map reading . . . Marksmanship . . . Shooting . . . Shotguns

But today, modern, efficient instruments are made to call just about anything. You can even get portable record players for attracting predators.

Among upland game there are callers for wild turkeys, bobwhite quail, mourning doves, pheasants (in a sense), Hungarian partridges and squirrels.

The duck callers include quackers (black and mallards) and whistlers (pintails, wood ducks and widgeon). Goose callers are made from Canadas, blues, snows and whitefronts (specklebellies). Bird callers are reed instruments made from walnut, cherry wood or plastic. Some are more exotic models made from zebra wood or mahogany. For the sound, you must blow from your diaphragm, not just from your mouth.

The fife devices bugle in bull elk and entice buck deer. These are made from bamboo, rubber or plastic. Bears may even come to some predator calls. The moose is still called with the voice, using a birchbark horn as an amplifier.

The range for predator calling is great. These reed calls, which imitate the squalling of a terrified cottontail or jackrabbit, will bring foxes, coyotes, big cats and many other animals on the run. Even cows and mother rabbits will respond!

Then there are distinct callers for crows and magpies, owls and hawks—again reed calls. Audubon Society members even use a little squeaker to bring songbirds within close range.

But why do these creations of wood, metal, rubber and plastic work? Several principles seem to be involved.

Some work because the animals involved have strong flocking instincts. Scattered wild turkeys, bobwhite quail, ducks or geese want to find more of their kind and will respond to imitations of their voices. They're lonesome.

Many kinds of game can be called during the mating season. Some species thus deluded are the moose, wild turkey, dove and horned owl.

Still others seem to answer to challenge when they think another male is invading their rightful territory. Bull moose, bull elk and deer all get fighting mad when someone is able to imitate the throaty cough, bugling or low grunting of these big game animals. In parts of the West, buck deer are brought to the hunter by rattling two antlers together. The wild tom turkey may come to a gobble on a box caller with fire in his eyes, when it's springtime in the mountains.

Predators which come to a rabbit squeal or mouse squeak are looking for food. But they are just as likely to be fooled by the imitation squeal of their own young. This response is obviously a protective instinct.

Then there's curiosity. Deer will answer a predator call, as will many other kinds of wild game which certainly have no intention of eating a rabbit! Domestic cattle and horses behave the same, often come on a dead run. Maybe they want to be where the action is.

And finally, there's the reverse-action effect! Hunters in the know often use a hawk caller to hunt pheasants. Pheasants notoriously run before a bird dog and may never stop to permit a point and a shot. However, a blast on a hawk caller and the pheasant will usually "freeze" in its tracks and stay put. He's scared to death to move for fear the hawk he hears will swoop down upon him. So, the dog points, the hunter moves in and there's a bird in the bag.

Learning to call game successfully is more than a matter of becoming adept on the mechanical device itself, although this is mighty important. It takes hours of practice to be able to get just the right note or tonal quality. The smart hunter practices while listening to the animal itself or to a good instructional record. You can get these records for a reasonable price. Better still is a tape recorder. With a small cassette type, you can record game in the off-season, practice, and be ready for opening day.

But knowing something about the habits of wild game is just as important. The hunter has to know where to find his quarry and where to place

WATERFOWL CALLERS. Wide assortment of reed types that are used for varieties of geese and duck.

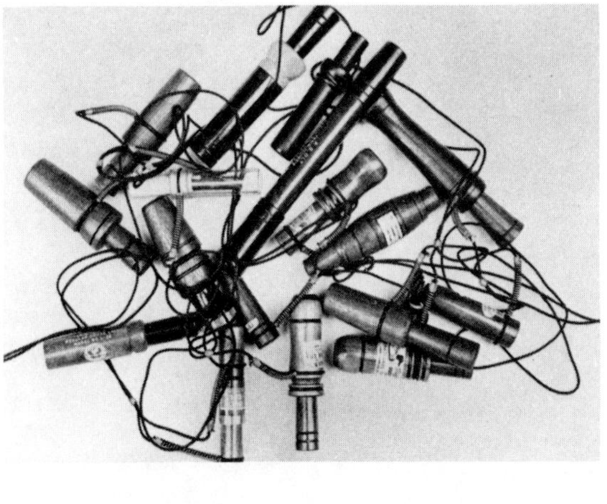

TURKEY CALLERS include slate callers (left), box callers (center), diaphragm callers and yelper.

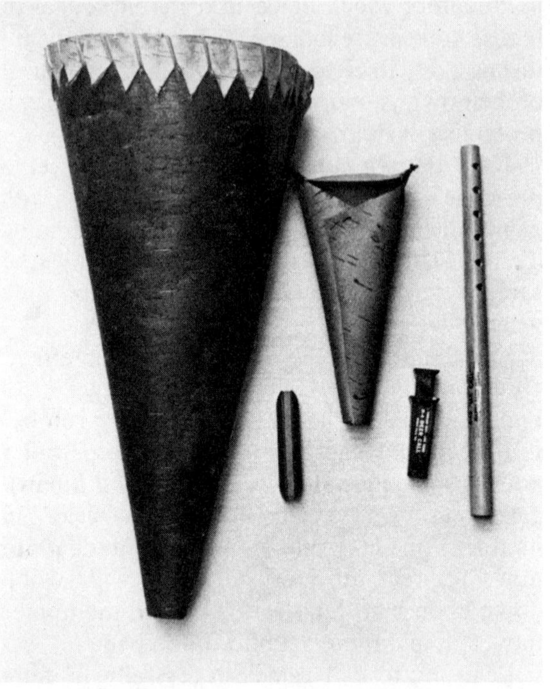

BIG GAME CALLERS. Birchbark horn to amplify moose calls; rubber-band deer callers; bamboo flute for elk.

himself for best results. For some animals which aren't color blind, like the wild turkey, you may find it neccessary to wear camouflage clothing. Turkeys, ducks, geese, coyotes and elk don't miss much and all operate under the theory that "every stump is a man."

The nimrod is warned against the reckless use of callers, too. Well hidden hunters yelping like a turkey have been filled with fine shot. Brush shooters have been known to take a "blind" shot at another hunter rattling antlers or bugling for elk. The best rule for the hunter is to leave his back open to view and to screen himself in front only where he can see anyone approaching.

But actually, calling game is safe enough and it's most certainly one of the most rewarding ways to take game or to get good pictures.

There's a double delight in success. First, the hunter must have mastered the calling technique, and his art gives him as much satisfaction as that of an accomplished musician. Then, too, there is a far greater anticipation as the game approaches, often answering as it comes. Anyone who has listened to an old turkey gobbler talking as he gets closer, or heard the angry grunting of a bull-moose crashing through the alders, or thrilled to the roar of an answering jaguar, knows full well how the adrenalin flows.

One thing sure, there's no dearth of callers on the market. The price may vary from a little for a rubber diaphragm turkey caller to a lot for a deluxe, imported wood, goose or duck caller.

One basic thing you should remember is that not all callers are good. Some are better at frightening game away than attracting it. If possible, try them out before you buy. And try them outside; using them inside a shop doesn't give you the true sound. Standard models by nationally known manufacturers are likely to be fair to good, but there are definitely outstanding makes in every category. You find out which these are only by trial and error, or by asking a local expert to try the call and give you his opinion.

PREDATOR CALLERS. Crow call (upper left), owl call (center), other four for rabbit, fox, coyote, bobcat.

SQUEAK AND SQUEAL CALLS. Squirrel caller (lower left), songbird squeaker, dove caller (upper right).

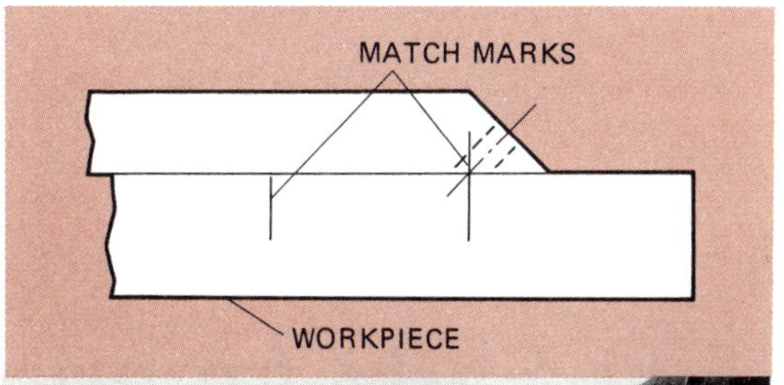

DRILLING ANGLED HOLES is easy if you make use of a doweling-jig aid. Recently I had to drill a row of angled holes in a length of stock. Here's how I simplified the task. First I cut a hole of the appropriate angle in a short block which I would later use as a template. Then I clamped the block in the doweling jig. Match marks were drawn on the workpiece and the template to align the setup at hole locations. At this point I drilled the first hole in the workpiece, using the template block as a guide. By moving the template block and jig as a unit I completed the drilling of each hole.—*S. C. Peterson, St. John's, Newfoundland.*

WOOD SCREENS can be recycled when you replace them with aluminum combinations. I made this king-size, towable leaf cart from the old screens, placing lawnmower wheels at the cart's end so it can be tilted. The axle is ¾-in. pipe. I reinforced the bottom screen with ½-in. hardware mesh. One side of the cart unhooks for fast unloading.—*R. K. Pedersen, Plainfield, NJ.*

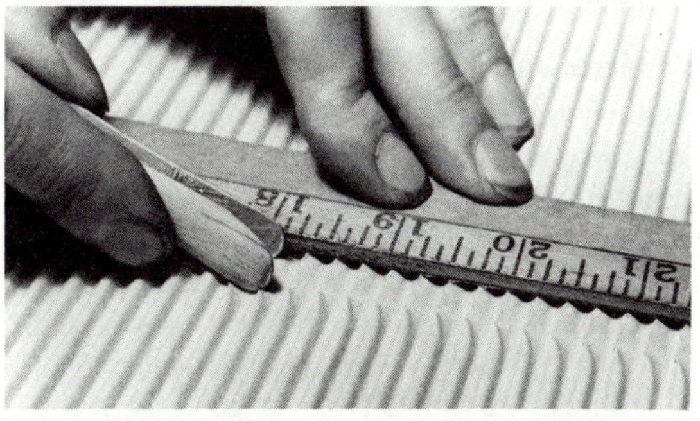

WHEN CORRUGATED CARDBOARD is used for wrapping, it must be scored to bend neatly. A knife is of no use for this purpose as it cuts the paper facing on cardboard, weakening it. I've found that an ordinary clothespin, drawn over the corrugated side, scores a neat double line that makes creasing easy.—*William Swallow, Brooklyn.*

A LARGE RUBBER BAND (or a section cut from an old inner tube) will give good protection against chipping when storing a grinding wheel. Mark wheel data—grit type, size and wheel catalog number—on the band with a waterproof felt-tip pen for speedy identification of various wheels.—*Walter E. Burton, Akron, OH.*

Early American hutch table

When not in use as a dining table, this beautiful piece serves as a handsome wall table or chair, and quickly converts to give extra tabletop space when you need it. The storage area beneath is a bonus

By HARRY WICKS

■ WHEN A CHAIR-TABLE like that on the facing page has storage area below the top, it is usually called a hutch-table. Technically, according to the antique experts, it should be called a trestle table.

This hutch-table design has been extremely popular and it is fairly easy to build. With a little time, any average home craftsman can create a beautiful piece of furniture for his living room or dining room.

Besides its charm, a hutch-table is particularly practical. When it's not needed as a table, you can position it against a wall to serve as a decorator piece fitted with a lamp or seat cushion.

table serves many uses

Our experience has proven this table to be one of the most practical—and treasured—pieces in our home. Since it is so easy to flip down the "back" to create a table, it is frequently used for buffet parties or whenever the kids have a gang in on a rainy afternoon. Because it is constructed in the primitive Early American style—distressed and antiqued—the table looks as good as, if not better than, it did new. Aging has just added to the patina of the wood, and nicks and scratches have simply been filled with a quality stain-concealer. Even if it has had some wear, it can be refinished and look good again.

Selecting materials. For best results, use either Idaho, eastern or sugar pine to make the table. However, if you have the desire, and confidence in your cabinetry skills, there's no reason not to make it of cherry, walnut or any other fine hardwood. For economy, you may prefer to use lower-cost knotty pine. (In my opinion this is a mistake over the long pull because the material is more frustrating to work with, and stands a better-than-average chance of checking and splitting over a period of time in a heated home.) But, if you do select such material, lay out the various parts carefully. Do not have knots fall along a line where cutting and shaping will occur. When you're rounding those corners, there's a strong possibility the knots will fall out entirely.

Edge-gluing. Because of the width of the bench sides, top and shelves (E), these parts are cut from glued-up stock. Use stock no wider than 4 in. to avoid any chance of warpage or cupping —if that were to happen to the cabinet, it could stop the drawers from sliding. Professionals alternate the annular rings of the boards being edge-glued as shown.

edges must be square

Edges to be joined must be perfectly square. If desired, you can have the boards pushed through a planer at your lumberyard for a slight charge. Use glue and dowels to make up the boards to desired width; then clamp the

SEE ALSO

Adhesives . . . Butler's tables . . . Chairs . . . Clamps . . . Dining tables . . . Drawers . . . Dry sinks . . . Gossip benches . . . Lowboys . . . Wood finishes

CHARM AND FUNCTION are the distinctive features of this hutch-table. When the table is not in use (left), the hutch is provided with a cushion for an extra seat. The other photos show the practical unit in service for functional table needs.

EE: FRONT RAIL 3/4 x 3/4 x 17-3/4"
26-3/8"
3/4"
4-9/16"
3/4"
4-9/16"
3/4"
3-9/16"
6"
24-1/2"
1-3/8"
1-3/4"
SHELVES E LET INTO 3/8 x 3/4" RABBETT
FRONT

14-3/8"
18-1/2"
E: SHELF
E: SHELF
D: SIDE
F: 1 x 2-1/2 x 18-1/2" (2 REQD.)
G: FOOT
PART D NOTCHED FOR PART F

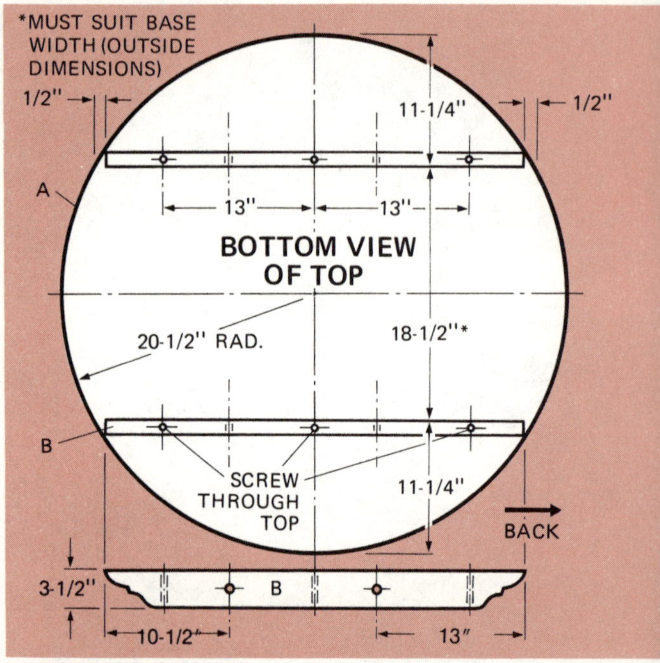
*MUST SUIT BASE WIDTH (OUTSIDE DIMENSIONS)
1/2"
1/2"
11-1/4"
A
13"
13"
BOTTOM VIEW OF TOP
20-1/2" RAD.
18-1/2"*
B
SCREW THROUGH TOP
11-1/4"
BACK
3-1/2"
B
10-1/2"
13"

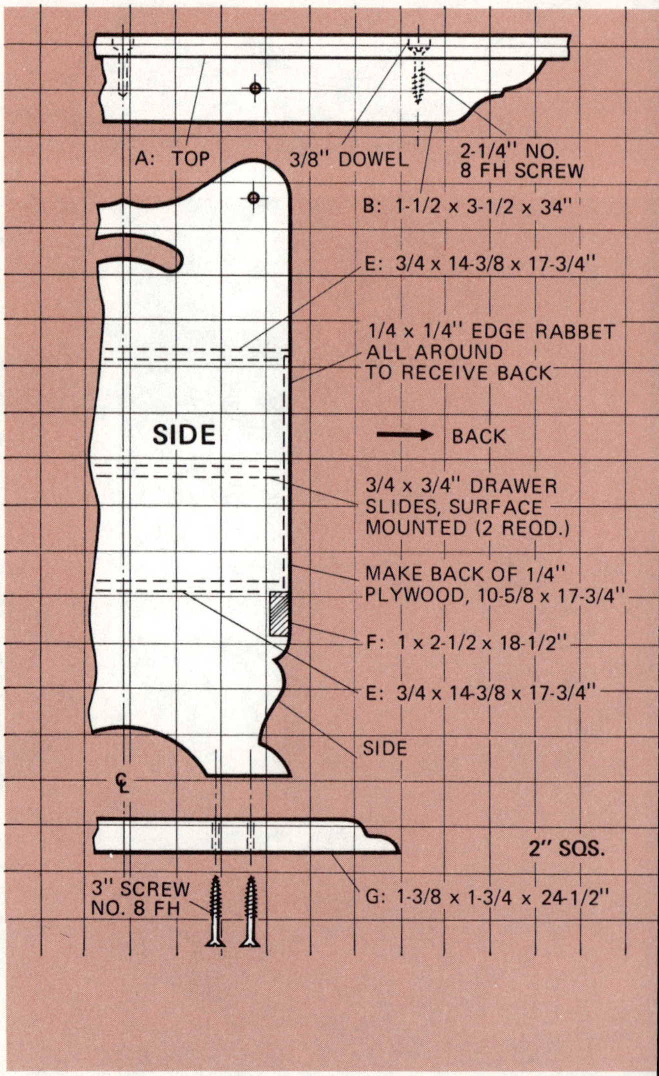
A: TOP
3/8" DOWEL
2-1/4" NO. 8 FH SCREW
B: 1-1/2 x 3-1/2 x 34"
E: 3/4 x 14-3/8 x 17-3/4"
1/4 x 1/4" EDGE RABBET ALL AROUND TO RECEIVE BACK
SIDE
BACK
3/4 x 3/4" DRAWER SLIDES, SURFACE MOUNTED (2 REQD.)
MAKE BACK OF 1/4" PLYWOOD, 10-5/8 x 17-3/4"
F: 1 x 2-1/2 x 18-1/2"
E: 3/4 x 14-3/8 x 17-3/4"
SIDE
℄
2" SQS.
3" SCREW NO. 8 FH
G: 1-3/8 x 1-3/4 x 24-1/2"

boards, but don't overtighten them. Simply run the clamps to close all joints neatly. Sight along the edge to make certain you haven't "clamped in" a warp. When satisfied with the setup, wipe off all excess glue and set the section aside to dry for at least 24 hours. Follow the same procedure for all edge-glued members.

While these parts are drying, use the patterns shown on 2-in. squares to lay out the curved members: feet and top braces. These are best cut by a band-saw and next-best cut by a sabre saw with a long blade. You can of course, do the shaping with a coping saw (as the old craftsmen did); it will just take longer. After cutting, sand the shaped portions until smooth and rounded.

cut both sides together

The next day, you can lay out the sides and top and cut to shape. Important: Temporarily tack the sides together and cut both at the same time. Then, lay out the locations for the dadoes for the top and bottom shelves (E) and push the pieces through the dado-head cutters. To prevent any chance of the piece drifting as you cut the dadoes, use your miter-gauge clamping device. There's no need to dado the sides for the drawer slides. These are simply surface-mounted ¾-in. square strips of hardwood.

With all parts cut and sanded, temporarily assemble the piece and mark the back (side and shelves) for rabbeting for the plywood back panel. Disassemble the piece and, using your router and a ¼-in. rabbet cutter, make the edge rabbet. Then chuck a ¼-in. rounding over (¼ round) bit in the router and round all edges including top and bottom edges of the top. You will not be able to use the router to round over the shaped edges of the ends of the feet. Here, I found the Surform file and round file did the job best. Finally, sand all pieces, working up to a fine-grit paper.

Locating the top. Lay the top good-side down on your workbench. Turn the bench upside down and center it on the top. *Note: For strength, braces should be perpendicular to direction of boards in the top.* When you're satisfied with the fit, position the braces along the outside of the cabinet, leaving some tolerance (about ¹⁄₁₆ in. on each side). Next, mark the brace locations and remove the bench. Making certain that the braces stay aligned with your pencil marks, tack the braces in place using 4d finishing nails through the ends of the braces. Flop the top and use a long straight-edge to draw a line directly over the center of the braces. Drill and counterbore three holes for each brace as indicated in the drawing. Turn in the screws and, after applying glue, push in short lengths of dowel plugs. (Good doweling technique calls for leaving dowel plugs slightly above the surrounding surface. When glue has dried, the protruding dowels can be sanded flush with the top.)

Hinge pins are simple affairs. All four are made alike, each from two parts, a 3-in. block of pine and a 4¼-in. length of ½-in. dowel. It's easier to make these production style, cutting all blocks at the same time. Ditto the dowel cutting, chamfering, drilling and sanding steps. Dowels are simply glued in the blocks.

To locate the holes in bench sides and braces (part B), set the bench right-side up on your workbench. Position the tabletop on the bench. Note there is a difference in spacing of holes—you need greater distance at the back where the top will pivot. When the top is lined up, use two C-clamps on the ends of one brace to lock the top securely to the bench side. You'll need a ¹⁄₁₆-in. shim to maintain that clearance mentioned earlier. If you're right on, a scrap of Formica is just the thing for a perfect shim.

Carefully bore holes in sides

With a ½-in. spade bit, bore the holes through the first brace using a backup board on the side to prevent splintering when the bit breaks through. Then, leaving the clamps in place, swing around to the other side and bore the pair of holes required there. Remove the clamps and test-fit the hinge pins. They should fit snugly and not slide freely. If they are too tight, enlarge the holes slightly with a round file. Later, when the table is completed, you can always spray on silicone so that the pins will slip in and out of place without fracturing.

Drawers are of standard construction. The fronts are of ¾-in. stock; sides and back of ½-in. stock and the bottom of ¼-in. plywood. The front and sides are dadoed (½ in. up from the bottom edge) to receive the drawer bottom. And the sides are let into an edge-rabbet on the drawer front. Notice that the drawer back is cut narrower than the sides. This method simplifies construction; the back simply fits into edge-rabbets on the sides, and the bottom is attached by driving brads up through the bottom into the back. Lay out for the drawer knobs and drill these holes to suit the knob screws.

Finishing the piece. When satisfied that the piece is sanded smooth, give it a thorough dusting. Next, apply a honey-tone pine stain and after

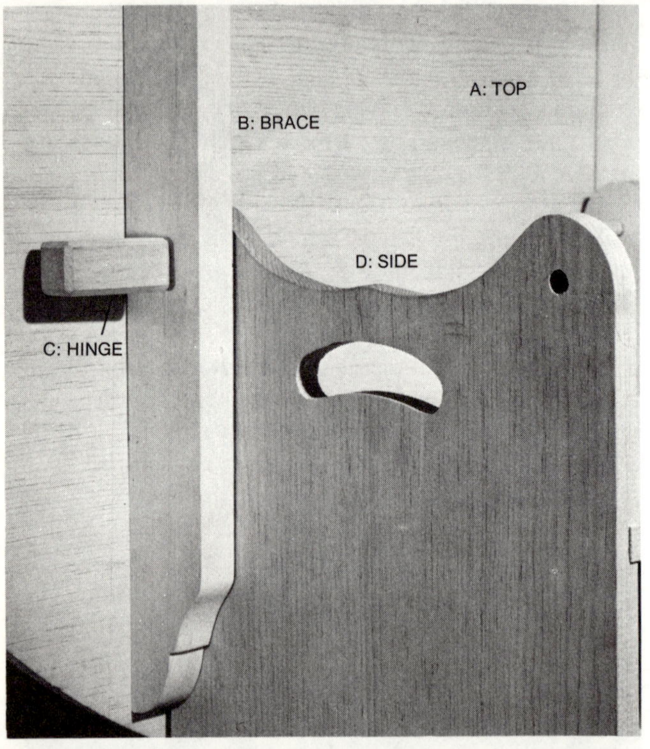

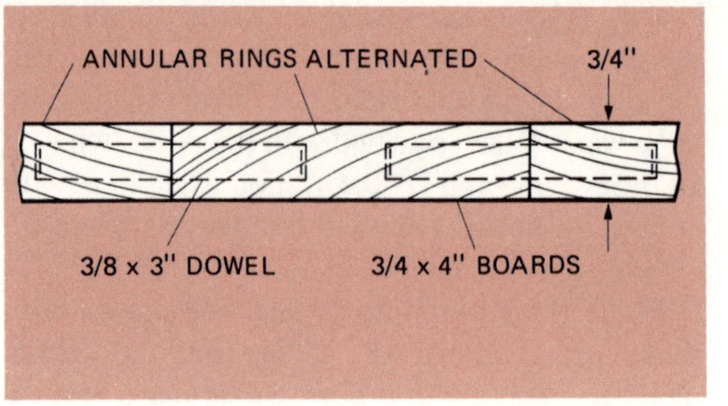

10 to 15 minutes, depending upon desired shade-depth, wipe off the excess stain and allow the piece to dry overnight. Apply a wash-coat of shellac to seal the wood and allow to dry.

My preferred finish is McCloskey's egg-shell, or satin, Heirloom finish. It's a varnish but it sets rather quickly, thus diminishing the amount of dust that settles on the surface. Apply at least two coats at least 24 hours apart and buff lightly with 00-grade steel wool between coats. Let the piece cure for four to six weeks; after that, if desired, it can be rubbed with paste wax.

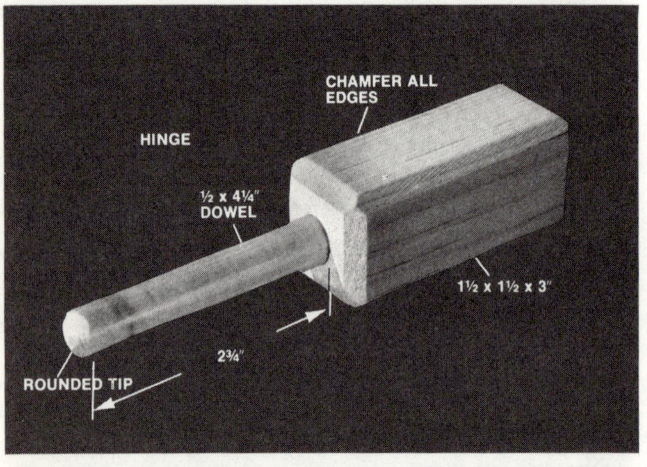

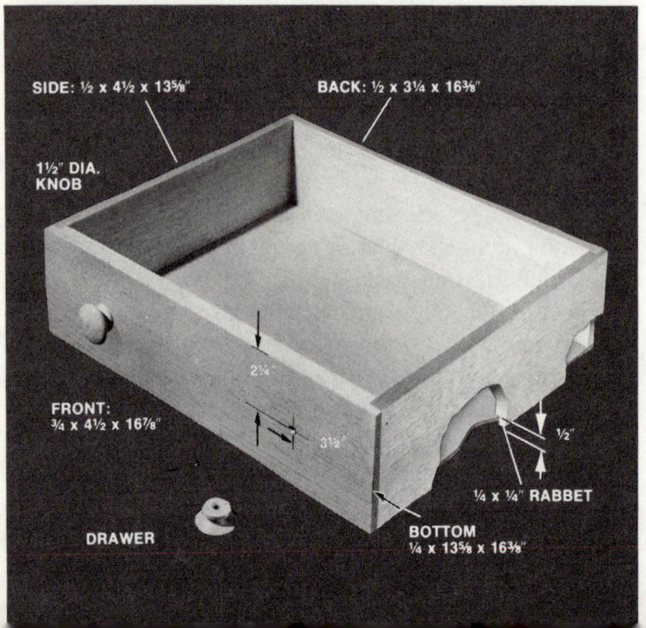

TABLETOP PIVOTS on pair of "hinges" (upper left). When top is down, second pair is used at front to securely lock the top in place. The required four hinge-pins are constructed alike (middle). All pins (dowels) should fit snugly in holes in braces and sides. Drawer construction is basic (lower left); bottom is let-into sides and front. To affix back, use 4d finishing nails up through bottom. In the diagram above, narrow boards are edge-glued and doweled to make up pieces for sides, shelves (E) and top. To lessen chance of warpage, annular rings should be alternated.

Two gadgets for ice-fishermen

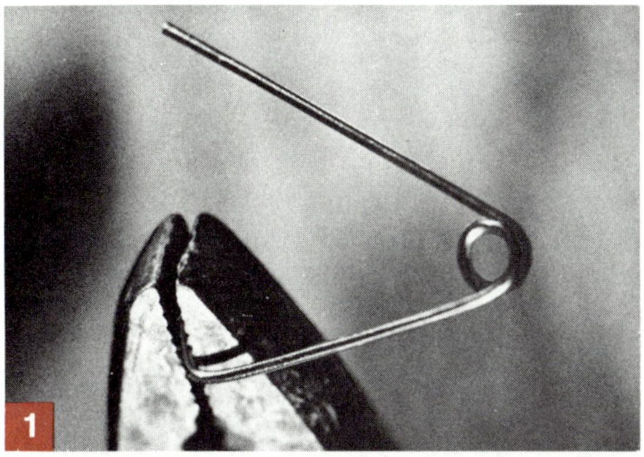

TRIM THE ENDS off a safety pin and then bend the tips.

SHAPE A DOWEL and then bend the pin over

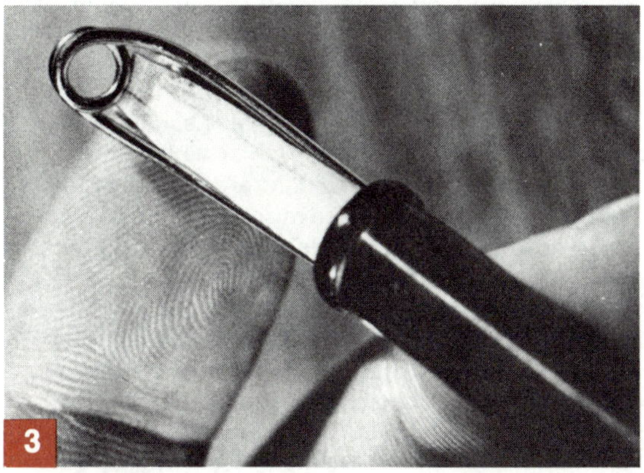

SHAPE UNTIL dowel and pin fit into the ferrule.

REEVE THE LINE through the safety-pin. Catch fish!

■ A BICYCLE HORN lets the fisherman know there's action when he uses this rig. He no longer needs the red tip-up flag.

To make it, all you need is the tip of an old steel rod, an inexpensive reel, a broomstick and a battery-operated bicycle horn with button. Attach the horn button at the end of the broomstick. Run insulated wire back to the horn. Position the rod and reel so the slightest wiggle of the rod activates the button. Attach folding tripod legs.

■ A HANDY ICE-FISHING rod can be made from the butt end of any spinning rod. All you need is a dowel, safety pin, knife and pliers. After clipping the ends off the pin, bend the two open ends (Step 1) so they'll clamp over a dowel. Bend the pin loop at a right angle, then shape the dowel so it fits firmly in the ferrule opening. Now clamp the pin onto the dowel (Step 2). Keep whittling the dowel so the pin and wood slip almost all the way into the ferrule (Step 3). Only a small part of the dowel extends from the ferrule when the fit is a correct one.

SEE ALSO

Casting, fly . . . Fishing tackle . . . Fly fishing . . . Lures, fishing

How to keep your ice skates sharp

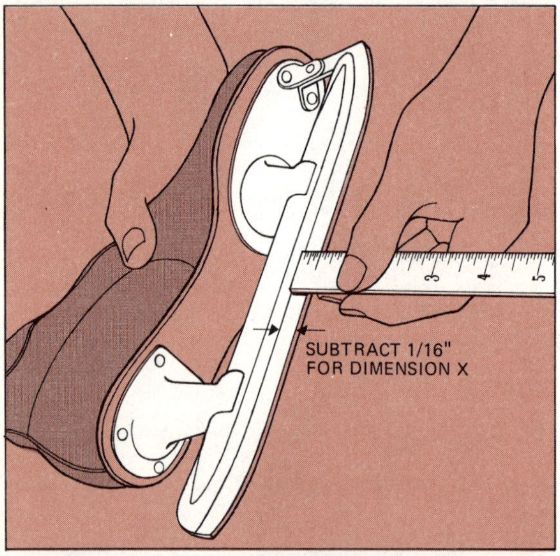

MAKE A SHARPENING JIG

Midwinter is the time of year when the kids—and maybe even you—are getting in a lot of ice-skating. And nothing's more frustrating than trying a graceful figure eight with dull blades. By making the simple jig (lower right) and clamping it to your bench saw, you'll be able to touch up blades with perfect hollow-ground edges as often as needed.

To make a jig, use two scrap pieces of ¾-in.-thick lumber, long enough to span width of your saw table. After measuring depth of skate blade and subtracting 1/16 in. to get dimension X (right), cut mating rabbeted edges on pieces A and B (lower right) with a dado head or make two cuts at 90° with an ordinary saw blade. Temporarily secure A and B together with two small scrap wooden strips tacked across top of jig. With saw blade or dado head lowered, center jig over cutting area across width of table, clamp work securely, and raise spinning saw blade or dado head to make 7/16-in.-deep, ⅝-in.-wide crescent groove on *underside* of jig.

Replace saw blade or dado head with a ½ x 5-in., 80-grit abrasive wheel on the saw arbor. With saw off, check jig with grinding wheel to make certain there is clearance. Determine the exact center of the wheel and mark clearly across top edge of the wheel. Place piece A across width of table, with crescent groove fitting over abrasive wheel and vertical face of the rabbet offset from marked center-line on wheel by a distance equal to half the thickness of the skate blade. Make sure piece A is exactly at right angle to grinding wheel by using the saw's miter gauge before clamping A in place. Position skate in the rabbet, slide piece B in place, and clamp to form a slot for the skate blade to ride over the abrasive wheel (right).

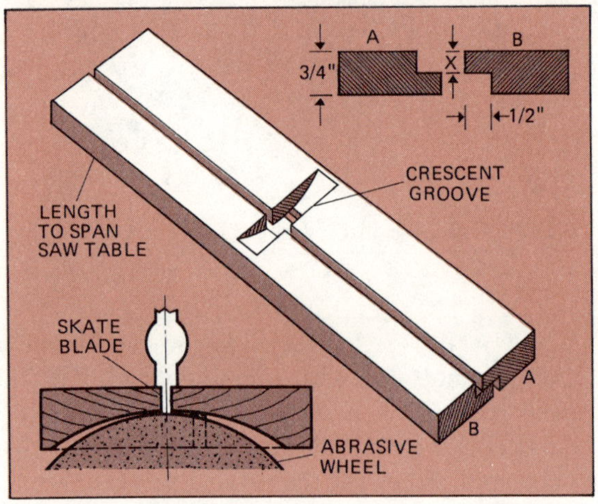

USING THE JIG

With jig clamped in place, raise grinding wheel until it just touches skate blade. Turn saw on and slide skate back and forth over wheel. If needed, wax or silicone spray can be applied to slot to facilitate movement of the skate to and fro. After every few passes, check edge of skate with your thumb as you would when sharpening a knife. Grinding marks should show along full edge of blade. Skates are sharp when, held like a pair of scissors, they cut strips of newspaper easily.

If the blade has a rough edge to it before you begin sharpening, you may have to raise the wheel a bit and grind off slightly more than usual. Don't forget to give the curved tip of the blade a good sharp edge. To do it, lift the back of the skate as shown in the drawing at left.

How to make an ID photo

Need a photo for a passport or some other identification? Here are simple hints to improve your shots

By CHARLES SMITH

IDENTIFICATION PHOTOS for use on applications, passports, permits and licenses are sometimes hard to have taken for you (they're not profitable for most portrait studios)—but they're easy to take yourself.

The average snapshot won't do, but just follow a few rules to lift your ID photos out of the snapshot class:

■ Backgrounds should be plain and white—light, unmarked plaster walls will do indoors or large sheets of white cardboard anywhere. (White bedsheets aren't suitable—they wrinkle too easily, and the wrinkles show up in the background unless you take a lot of extra trouble with your lighting.)

■ Distance should be at least 4½ feet between camera and subject to avoid distortion. Ten feet is still more flattering, but unless you use a short telephoto lens, you may have to order a large print to get a big enough head size at that distance.

■ Lighting should be soft and simple—bounce light indoors, open shade or overcast skylight outdoors.

■ The print should be made on matte or semi-matte-surface paper, especially if it will have to bear a signature. But if you can't have a matte print made, get a glossy one and spray it with dulling spray from a photo, art or drafting shop.

■ The pose need not be dead straight on or the expression as grim as on the mugshots on the post-office wall; a slight turn of the head and relaxed smile are permissible and pleasant.

A SIMPLE BACKGROUND, such as the white cardboard taped to the wall in the photo at the upper left, accounts for some of the difference between a mere snapshot (above, left) and a good ID photo (right). Soft, even lighting (here, a wall in open shade), the right distance from your subject and a relaxed expression also improve the quality of the shot.

SEE ALSO

Candid photography . . . Close-up photos . . . Copy photography . . . Developing, photo . . . Filters, photo . . . Mountings, photo . . . Photography . . . Prints, photo

How your car's electrical system works

STORED IN your car's battery is the energy for all the electrical systems. As you turn the ignition key, it goes to the starter to crank the engine and to the ignition system for boosting so it can fire the spark plugs. It feeds lights and the host of other accessories. To ensure you of ample energy, a generator or alternator replaces that used from the battery's supply.

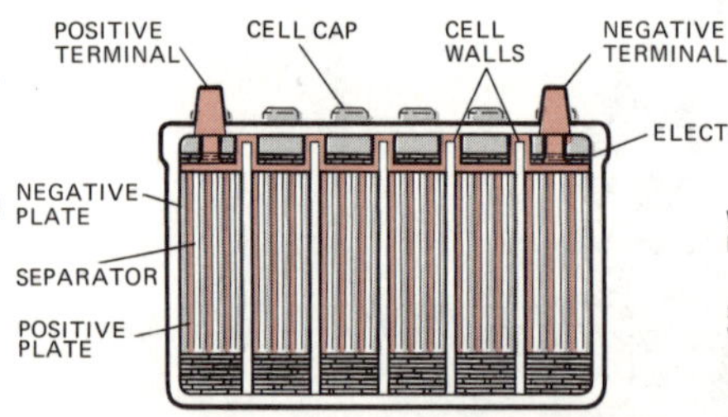

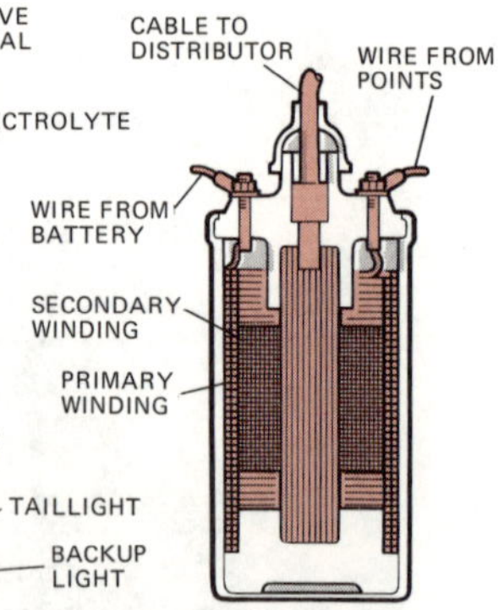

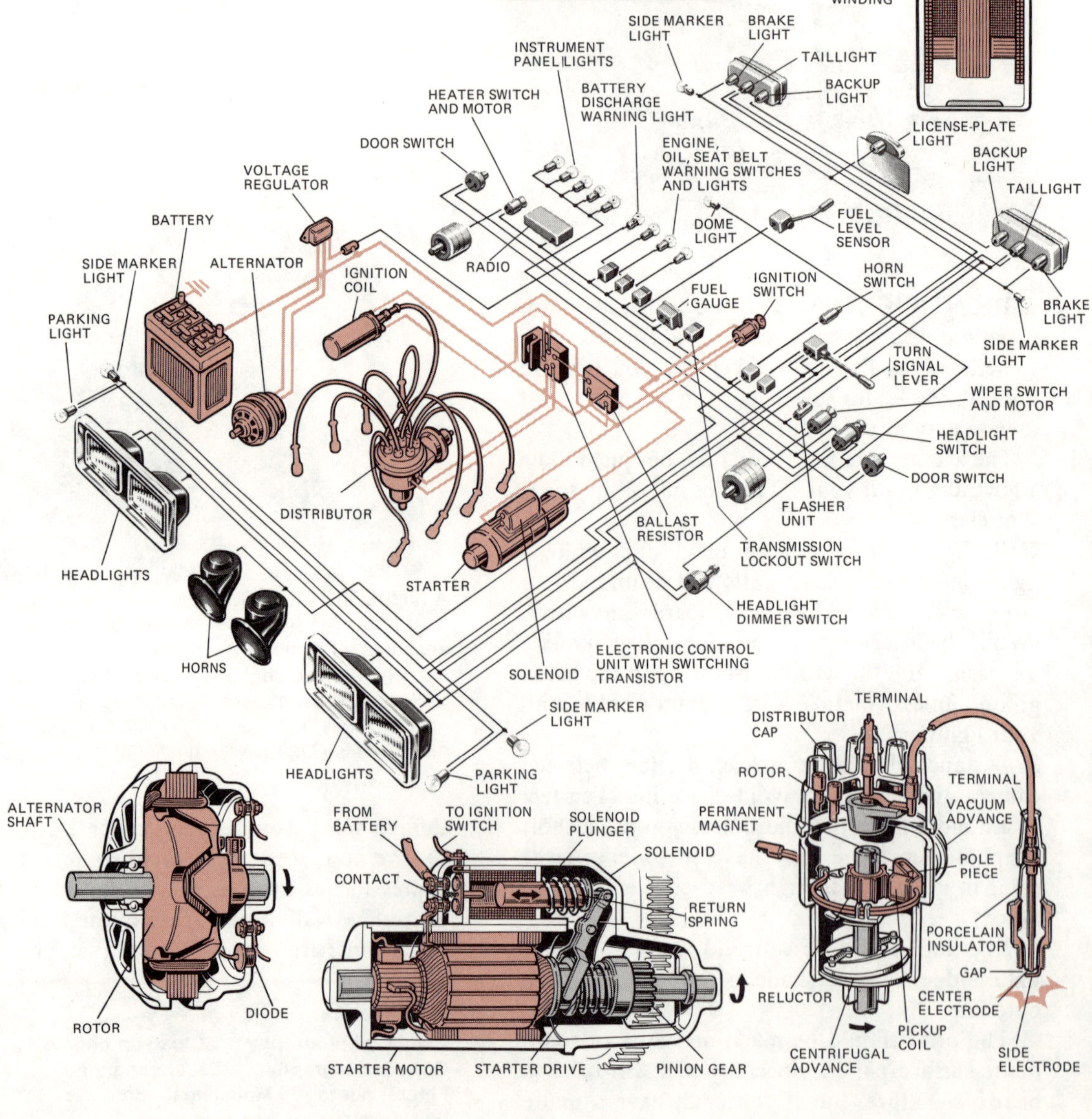

Service the ignition system yourself

By MORT SCHULTZ

■ IGNITION SYSTEM tune-up includes replacing sparkplugs, reconditioning the distributor, and setting the dwell and timing. This program is essential to avoid such problems as missing, hard starting and excessive fuel consumption.

You do the job yourself for the cost of parts alone—saving half or more of a professional's bill. You can save $40 or more with an hour's work. Shopping around for parts saves even more.

you must have the tools

The first time you service your ignition will probably be the most costly, since you may have to buy instruments you don't now have. You will need a timing light and dwellmeter/tachometer. For the sparkplugs, get a plug gapping tool and gauge and a sparkplug wrench; for the distributor, a feeler gauge, distributor wrench, and distributor-tower brush.

We're concerned here with conventional ignition systems, not the electronic breed. Since electronic ignitions dispense with condensers and distributor points, servicing that version takes neither the feeler gauge nor the point file. And a simple tach replaces the dwellmeter/tachometer.

Here's the essential procedure:

Replace badly worn or damaged plugs; otherwise clean and regap good ones. Wipe off and examine the coil; if its case is cracked, replace it.

If primary wires' insulation is cracked, replace them. Be sure they're tight at the terminals.

Remove the heavier secondary cable from the coil tower by twisting and pulling the boot (not the cable). A badly eroded terminal or cracked insulation calls for a new cable. Brush out the coil tower and reseat the cable firmly if it's in good shape.

Now disconnect that cable at the distributor. Hold it with a clip-type wooden clothespin to avoid a shock and put the end ¼ inch from a clean ground. As someone cranks the engine, a strong blue spark should jump the gap. A weak yellow spark means the distributor needs service. If that doesn't help, replace the coil.

A molded rubber boot may be impossible to pull back. Then poke an insulated-handle screwdriver into the boot to contact the terminal and move the shaft close to a ground for the test.

check the cap carefully

Unhook the distributor cap. Wipe it clean inside and out, and check for cracks, chips, carbon tracks and broken or eroded terminals. If it's damaged, replace it. If terminals are just blackened, clean them with fine sandpaper.

Remove one secondary cable at a time and check towers for damage. If they're OK, clean them with the tower brush. Be sure cables are good and each goes back to its own tower since

SEE ALSO
Auto batteries . . . Battery testers . . . Carburetors, auto . . . Dieseling, auto . . . Distributors, auto . . . Emissions controls . . . Sparkplugs . . . Stalling, auto . . . Tune-up, auto

CHECK PRIMARY ignition wires carefully. They must be tightly attached at the coil terminals and must have sound insulation. Otherwise replace them.

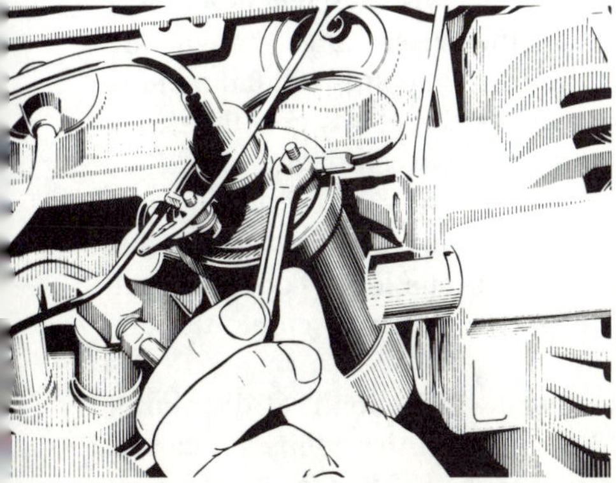

CLEANLINESS IS important at the coil and distributor towers. A distributor tower brush will clean both, but you can also improvise a tool.

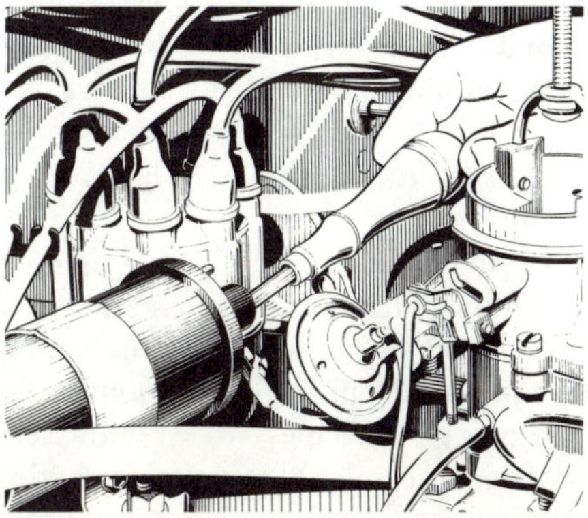

DON'T OVERLOOK the inside of the distributor cap. Even hairline cracks disqualify it for any further service. Wipe it clean before restoring it.

THE ROTOR carries high voltage from the coil to plug wires. Inspect it with care and always carry a spare.

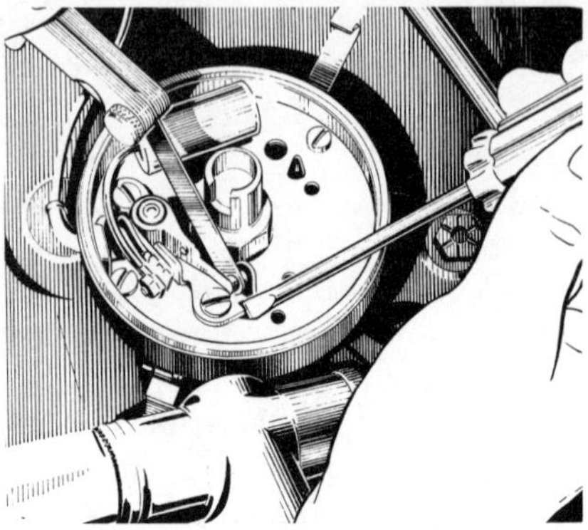

DISTRIBUTOR points are sometimes adjusted by twisting a screwdriver in a slot near the mounting screw.

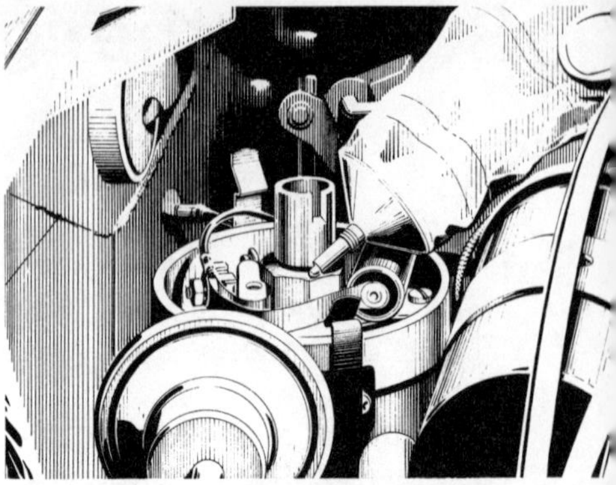

CAM LOBE lubrication takes a steady hand. One matchhead-sized drop goes on one cam lobe only. Don't over-do.

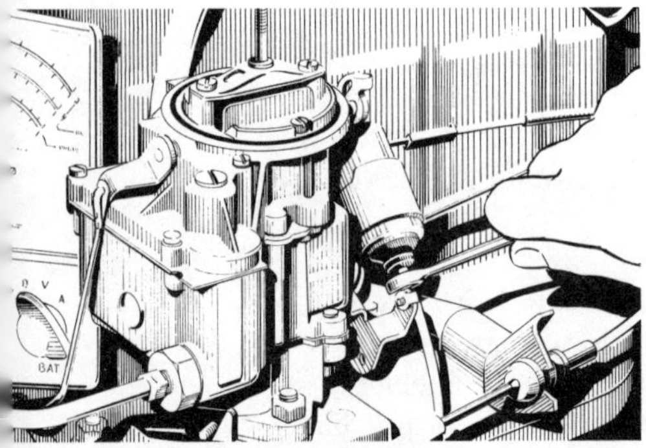

SET SLOW-IDLE speed at the carb before setting the dwell angle at the distributor. The idle-stop solenoid, as here, is often the means to use.

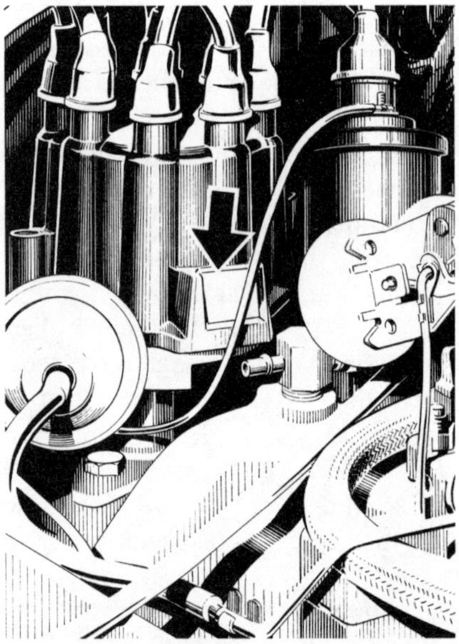

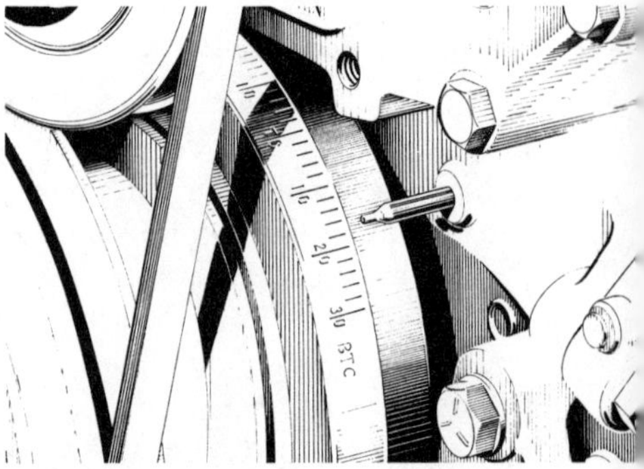

THE TIMING mark and pointer may be hard to see. White paint smeared on the pointer and degree marks will make your subsequent jobs far easier.

DWELL ANGLE can sometimes be set by sticking an Allen wrench into an access door in distributor's side. But don't forget to close the door.

confusing the firing sequence could damage the engine.

Remove the rotor from the distributor shaft; it, too, must be replaced if damaged. A radio-frequency or dust shield over the distributor can be set aside.

Find the distributor's direction of rotation by having someone crank the engine briefly. Then turn the shaft in that direction and release it. If it doesn't snap back, the distributor should get new springs and counterweights.

It may be hard to inspect breaker points within the distributor. To remove them, unscrew clips holding the distributor primary and condenser pigtail wires. Check their condition. Then unscrew the point assembly and lift it out.

Grayish or slightly rough points need only a pass or two (no more) with the point file. Wipe them clean with a cloth moistened with mineral spirits or alcohol, then reinstall them.

Get the point gap from a service manual, your owner's manual or the service decal in the engine compartment. Move the cam lobe under the movable point's rubbing block by having the engine cranked in brief spurts as you watch.

Some points are gapped with an Allen wrench in an adjusting screw. On others, you loosen the mounting screw, then twist a screwdriver in a nearby slot. Hold the feeler gauge straight. Be sure it's clean since dirtied points will fail rapidly. The gap is right when the points grip the gauge lightly as you move it between them.

If the distributor has a wick lubricating pad resting on the cam, replace it. Otherwise put just a drop of cam lube on one lobe. Too much will cause points to burn. Then reassemble the distributor.

Now set the dwell—the amount of distributor cam motion during which the points are closed. A smaller gap means the points are closed longer

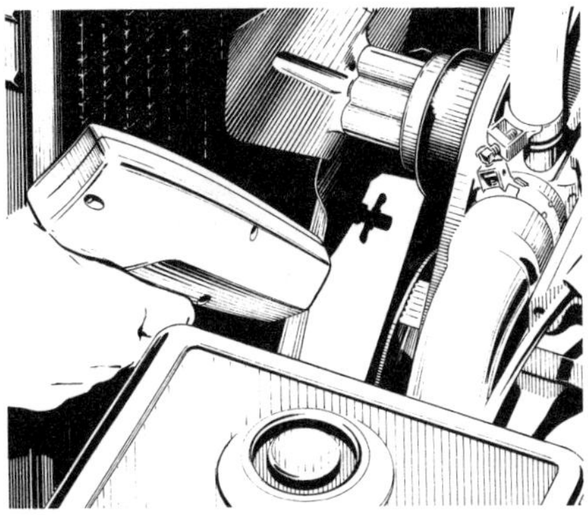

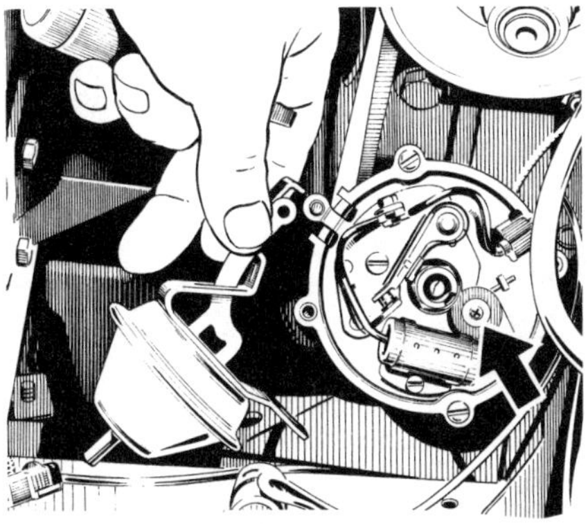

HOOK THE timing light into the No. 1 sparkplug circuit and to the car's battery. When you shine it on the timing mark (far left), be sure to aim the light straight down to avoid any parallax.

THE VACUUM advance is removed by unscrewing it from the distributor's breaker plate (left). The arrow points to the lubricating wick.

and the dwell angle is larger. The dwellmeter will let you refine the setting you got with the feeler gauge. If they're closed too long, points may arc and shorten their life; if too briefly, the engine may miss at high speed.

Hook the dwell/tach's black lead to a clean ground, the red to the distributor primary terminal on the coil. With the engine running and warm and the instrument set for engine rpm, use the idle-speed screw or solenoid on the carburetor to bring idle speed to specs.

Switch the meter to **DWELL** and fine-tune the point gap. If the distributor housing has an access door, you can adjust the gap through it with an Allen wrench as the engine's running. If not, shut the engine off, remove the distributor cap, and reset the dwell. A wider gap reduces dwell angle. You may have to repeat the process several times.

Spark timing is adjusted according to the relation of an index pointer to a timing mark on the crankshaft pulley, block or flywheel. Connect the timing light. The heavily insulated lead goes to the No. 1 plug, often with an adapter between the plug and its cable. Some timing lights have inductive pickup clamps that grip the sparkplug cable. Other timing lights go to battery terminals—black to negative and red to positive.

Find the right timing mark. Those on U.S. cars are usually on the pulley or block. Some imports have them on the flywheel. Light paint or chalk can help them stand out.

Pull the hose from the vacuum advance mechanism and plug its end with a pencil. Start the engine and leave the transmission in **PARK** or **NEUTRAL.** The timing specification is based on an engine running at the specified slow-idle speed.

Aim the timing light straight down at the timing mark and reference pointer. The light's flashes should make both seem to stand still, aligned with each other. If this doesn't happen you'll have to adjust timing.

Leave the engine running and loosen the distributor's hold-down bolt with your distributor wrench. Aim the timing light at the timing mark. The vacuum-advance mechanism on the distributor makes a good handle; grab it and rotate the distributor slowly. This will have the effect of changing the relationship between the reference pointer and timing mark. You move the distributor to bring the mark into line with the pointer.

clockwise retards timing

Turning the distributor clockwise retards the timing, counterclockwise advances it. Remember that if the pointer seems to move farther from the timing mark instead of toward it, you've moving the distributor in the wrong direction. Reverse your wrist.

When the timing is right on the money, turn off the engine and tighten the distributor hold-down bolt.

Check your work now: Start the engine and recheck the timing. You may have to repeat the procedure.

Now check the functioning of the distributor's centrifugal and vacuum-advance mechanisms. Aim the timing light at the timing mark and advance the throttle until the engine is running at 1500 rpm (hook up your tach). The timing mark should advance as engine speed increases and drop back to its original setting when you allow engine speed to fall back to idle. If not, the distributor should be overhauled.

Reconnect the vacuum-advance hose. Again, aim the timing light at the timing mark and increase engine speed to 1500 rpm. The timing should advance itself farther than it did when you checked the centrifugal advance. If it doesn't, replace the vacuum advance.

Plug leads are vital links, the only way electrical energy can reach the cylinders and trigger the combustion process. But deteriorating cables may let you down

How to replace ignition cables

By MORT SCHULTZ

THINK OF THE BOOT as a handle: Pull on it (above), never on the cable itself. Numbered tape patches (left) identify the individual cables and the right location for their terminals. Sparkplug pliers (below) make removal of the cables easier and prevent any damage to them. The tool isn't expensive.

SEE ALSO

**Alternators, auto . . . Auto batteries . . .
Battery testers . . . Cables, auto . . .
Electronic ignition, auto . . . Sparkplugs**

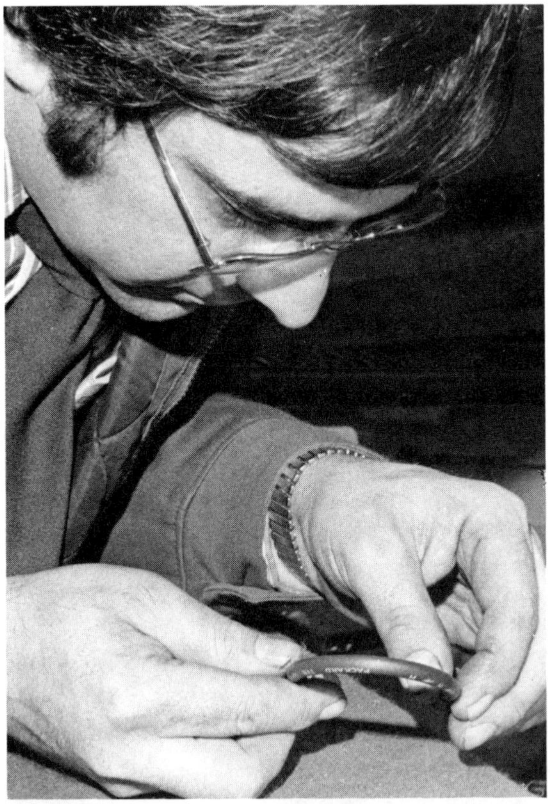

STUDY CABLES closely for cracks or frayed areas and bend them gently to check for brittleness.

■ NOTHING LASTS FOREVER—not even the heavy cables leading from each of your engine's distributor-cap towers to respective sparkplugs. These cables carry high-voltage jolts (about 20,000 volts per jolt) to the plugs. If they fall down on the job, your engine may misfire.

As for a cable, the way in which misfire occurs depends largely on the degree of damage to the cable and the amount of resistance offered by engine compression.

That is why one engine may misfire only when the engine is under load; another at all throttle speeds, and a third only when the air is damp. (Moisture is an ideal conductor; a cable beginning to fail may do so only in the presence of moisture.)

In a sound electrical system, the path of least resistance, the path over which electricity finds it easiest to flow, is across sparkplug electrodes. However, when a high-voltage cable develops a defect in its insulation, this path may be through the insulation to a ground presented by the engine near which the cable passes. If the cable "sparks," less or no current will be available at the sparkplug for *it* to spark.

When engine misfire occurs—no matter under what conditions—think cables! Repairing "something else" when it isn't the problem costs money for nothing.

Many factors you can't control affect the life of high-tension cables. Age, heat, cold, oil and grease attack insulation, making it brittle and causing it to crack. Where salt is used on roads during winter, cables can become coated with salt spray. A salt-coated, cracked cable will short out since salt is a conductor.

watch for corona, too

Corona, the magnetic field surrounding high-tension wiring, is another phenomenon affecting cables. The magnetic field created by high-current surging is so strong that it breaks down oxygen, converting it to ozone which is particularly detrimental to rubber insulation.

Disconnect and examine one high-tension cable at a time. At the distributor cap, grasp a terminal boot and disconnect it from the tower with a twisting, pulling motion. You should never pull the cable itself. Sloppy handling of cables is the main reason they fail before their time.

When the cable has been disconnected from the tower, trace the cable to its sparkplug. The process of relating the distributor-cap tower to its cable and then tracing each cable to the specific sparkplug it serves is very important.

For a simple way to identify components, use masking tape. Suppose the cable you disconnect serves the first sparkplug on the left-hand (driver's-side) bank of a V8 engine. Snip off three pieces of masking tape and write on each the designation "L1," meaning first plug left side. Stick a strip on the distributor-cap tower, another around the cable and the third near the sparkplug. Disconnect the cable at the plug—grasp and pull the boot only, not the wire.

A good tool you might consider buying is a sparkplug-cable pliers. It helps prevent cable damage and lets you grasp the terminal boot firmly. The "scissor-grip" permits a tight hold as you pull off the boot.

With the cable disconnected and all components identified, clean the cable with a kerosene-moistened cloth. Wipe it dry with a clean cloth. Now, bend the cable over its entire length. Discard it if cracks show, if it is chafed or if insulation is brittle.

Also check the cable terminals. If one is black, it tells you there has been a poor connection with either the plug terminal or the distributor cap.

FAULTY CABLES CAN CAUSE ENGINE MISFIRE

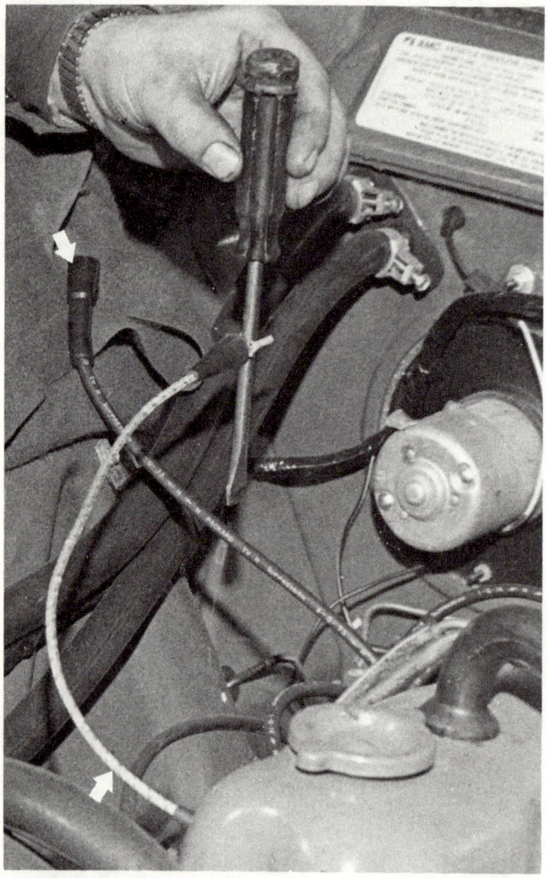

TO PROBE A cable, disconnect it from the plug and put that end where it won't ground out (upper arrow). Then hook the probing instrument to a good ground (lower arrow). With the engine running, probe along the cable's full length; any spark jumping to the screwdriver means the cable is faulty.

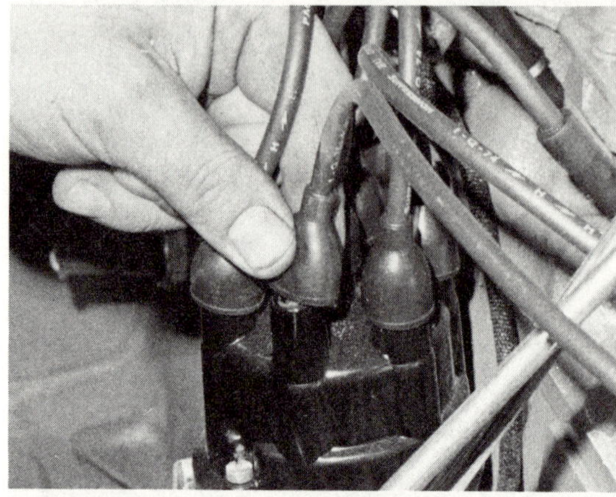

SEAT CABLES by pushing lightly down on them as you squeeze the boot to let trapped air out.

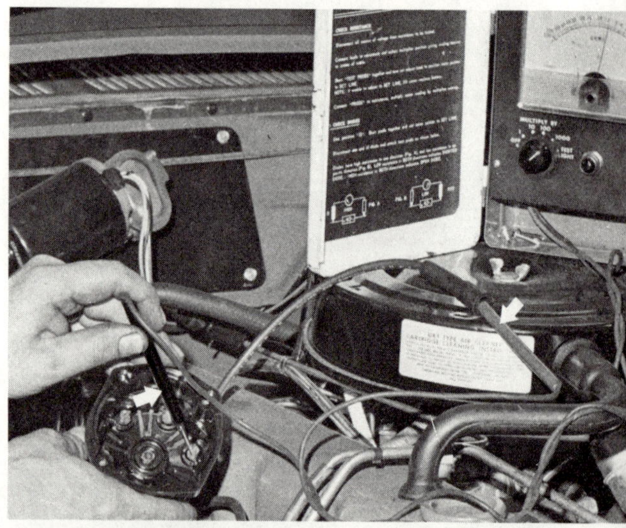

AN OHMMETER CHECKS a cable's resistance. Arrows show where the meter's probes are connected.

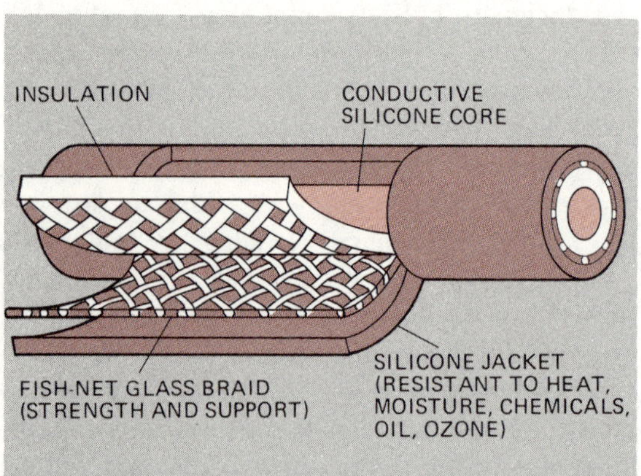

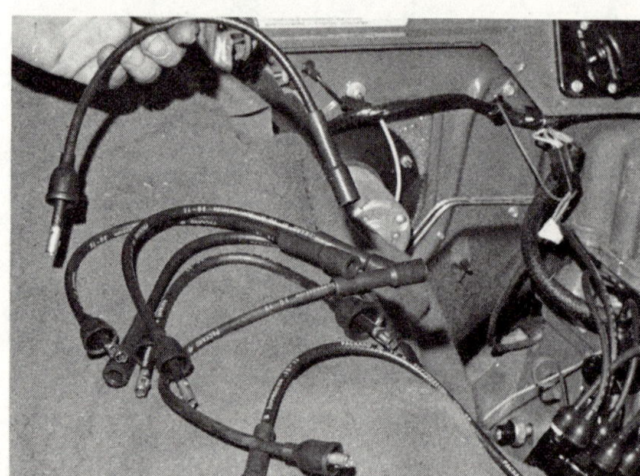

GOOD REPLACEMENT CABLES are well made (left)—and they aren't cheap. Unless severely mistreated, however, their long life can make them worth their cost. A custom-made replacement set (right) comes cut to length. They will already be assembled and ready for installation on your car.

Secondary current has been forced to arc across the gap.

If this arcing has eaten at the cable's terminal, the cable should be replaced. If there has merely been carbon deposited on the terminal, wipe it clean and be sure the contact is a good one when you restore the cable.

For your inspection, you can often slide the boot back along the cable a bit to expose the terminal, although the boot should fit snugly. It won't slide along the cable as though greased. Original-equipment cables—and some replacements—have boots molded in place at the cable ends. Don't try to break this bond.

clean the distributor cap

If a cable shows evidence of arcing at the distributor-cap end, remove the distributor cap and clean deposits from each socket with a distributor-cap cleaning tool. Clean the coil tower. Deposits increase resistance.

The visual inspection shows clearly if cables are cracked and also lets you check the condition of terminals. You can also "probe" the cables to reveal small punctures that might go unnoticed. To make the problem test, get a jumper wire with an alligator clip at each end. Clip one end to a clean ground on the engine and the other to the shank of a screwdriver.

Start the engine and let it idle. Remove one cable from the sparkplug. Be sure that the boot end of the cable is positioned so it doesn't point to a ground. Probe all around cable and its boot. If a puncture is present, a spark will jump from the defective area to the probe. Discard the cable.

To test the high-tension cable between the center tower of the distributor and the coil tower, keep the cable connected, but be sure to disconnect one sparkplug cable.

If cables pass your tests, reconnect them. To install cables into distributor towers enter each terminal into its tower. Push lightly as you pinch the large diameter part of the boot to release air trapped between the boot and tower. Continue pushing until the cable is firmly seated.

Before seating cables on sparkplugs, wipe off sparkplug insulators. All connections must be secure to avoid arcing.

one more possibility

Even though cables pass all tests up to this point, they may still be the cause of misfire. A cable that looks perfectly sound can be damaged internally. Internal damage is caused primarily by manhandling. When a cable is pulled, the inner core can break. This increases resistance, reducing current to the sparkplug.

If you have an ohmmeter, you can find out if cables are damaged internally by testing resistance. Do one cable at a time, as follows (this test assumes that your car is equipped with electronic suppression cable, identified by marks on it):

1. Disconnect the cable from the sparkplug and attach a sparkplug adapter between the cable and sparkplug if your ohmmeter lead has an alligator clip.
2. Remove the distributor cap, but keep cables connected.

hook up the ohmmeter

3. Connect ohmmeter between sparkplug adapter and the correct electrode inside distributor cap for the cable you are testing. If ohmmeter leads are probe types, you can disconnect the cable from the plug and insert the probe so it touches the terminal. Check that probes make good contact.
4. If resistance is more than 30,000 ohms for cables up to 25 inches long and 50,000 ohms for cables longer than 25 inches, remove the cable from the tower and check its resistance by probing the terminal. Replace cables that fail to meet the 30,000- or 50,000-ohm specifications.
5. If a cable meets specification when disconnected but flunks when hooked to the distributor, a problem exists in the distributor cap. Clean out deposits from inside the cap and test again.
6. To test the cable between the coil and distributor cap, connect the ohmmeter between the center contact in the cap and either primary terminal at the coil. Combined resistance should not exceed 25,000 ohms. If it does, remove the cable at the coil and test resistance. If it is more than 15,000 ohms, replace the cable. If less, check for a loose connection at the tower and for a faulty coil.

The best replacement high-tension cables are expensive, but worth it. The latest design uses tough silicone rubber for the core, jacket and even boots. It is by far the sturdiest and longest lasting cable yet made. You should get an easy 50,000 miles of service unless you start playing tug-of-war.

Most cable makers offer sets as "custom" or "universal." A "custom" set is designed for a specific engine; a "universal" set for several engines.

Quick care for your electronic ignition system

By MORT SCHULTZ

■ ELECTRONIC IGNITION has arrived. By the beginning of the 1980s, every U.S. and foreign auto maker had made it standard on most models. Solid-state systems aren't all identical, but they have many characteristics in common. And they deserve care.

All electronic systems eliminate old distributor breaker points, the distributor cam and condenser. A toothed armature (Chrysler calls it *reluctor;* GM, *timer core;* Ford, an armature) on the distributor shaft teams with a stator or magnetic pickup—a small magnet and coil. They replace the old cam and points.

how solid-state works

That armature has a tooth for each engine cylinder. As one passes near the pickup, magnetism builds up and cuts off inducing a voltage pulse.

This slight pulse tickles the transistor switch in a "black box" so a pulse of primary voltage goes to the ignition coil. When it cuts off (as if old breaker points had opened), the collapsing field induces high voltage in the secondary windings. Fed back to the distributor cap, this goes through the rotor to individual sparkplug leads. The "black box" containing the transistor switch is known by various names, including control module, electronic control unit, and igniter. We'll stick to "black box."

what are the advantages?

Here are some of the advantages of electronic ignition:

SEE ALSO
Auto batteries . . . Cables, auto . . .
Dieseling, auto . . . Distributors, auto . . .
Electronic ignition, auto . . . Sparkplugs . . .
Tune-up, auto

- No point problems such as erosion or fouling.
- Dwell angle is no longer a factor. Dwell angle is the distance in degrees that the cam of a conventional distributor rotates when points are closed. It goes out of adjustment, because the cam and point block rub against one another and wear down. But no parts of an electronic ignition distributor rub against one another.
- The whole concept of ignition tune-up is changed radically. Tune-ups are simpler and timing checks are needed only as often as you clean or change sparkplugs.

Manufacturers claim that because of electronic ignition and unleaded gasoline, sparkplugs give suitable performance for 20,000-plus miles.

it isn't service-free

But don't fall into the common error of thinking service is unnecessary. That isn't so. It's called for every 20,000 or 30,000 miles. Make these checks:

- When you replace sparkplugs, remove the distributor cap and inspect the rotor for cracks and burned areas on the metal terminal. Replace the rotor if it's damaged.
- Inspect the distributor cap. Wipe it clean with a dry rag and look for cracks, corroded terminals and carbon tracks. Replace a damaged cap.
- Replace high-tension cables if insulation is brittle or frayed. Test them for excessive resistance with an ohmmeter for the resistance values in the service manual. If you don't have a service manual, replace those cables that exceed the resistance values in this table:

Length of cable	Maximum resistance
up to 15 inches	10,000 ohms
15-25 inches	15,000 ohms
25-35 inches	20,000 ohms
over 35 inches	25,000 ohms

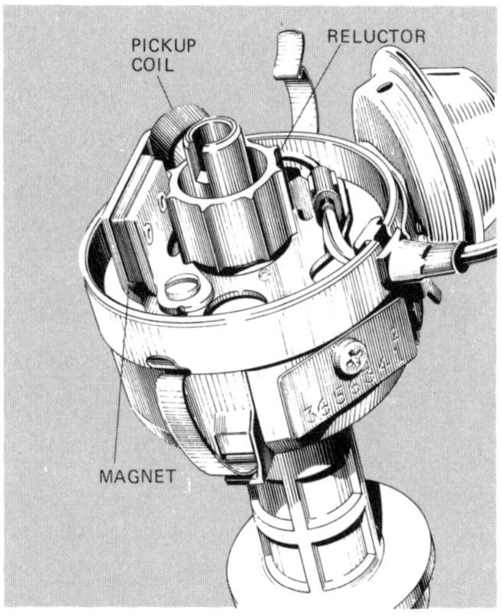

TYPICAL electronic ignition systems distributor differs from a conventional unit on the inside. Instead of breaker points and cam, most of the devices have a toothed armature and stator or magnetic pickup consisting of a small coil and permanent magnet.

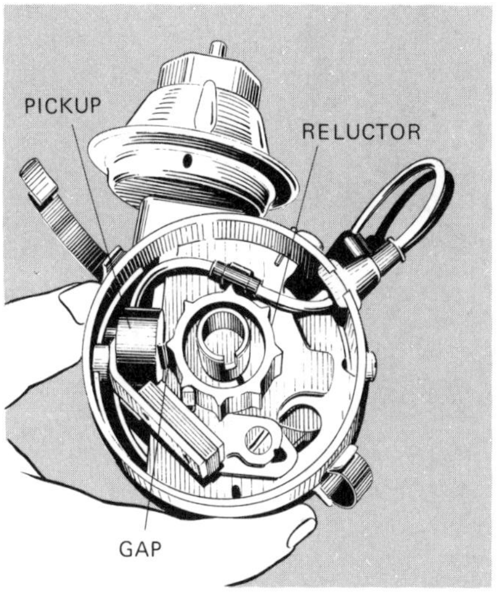

THE SMALL gap between the magnetic pickup and the toothed armature in an electronic distributor corresponds to conventional breaker points, but the gap never closes completely.

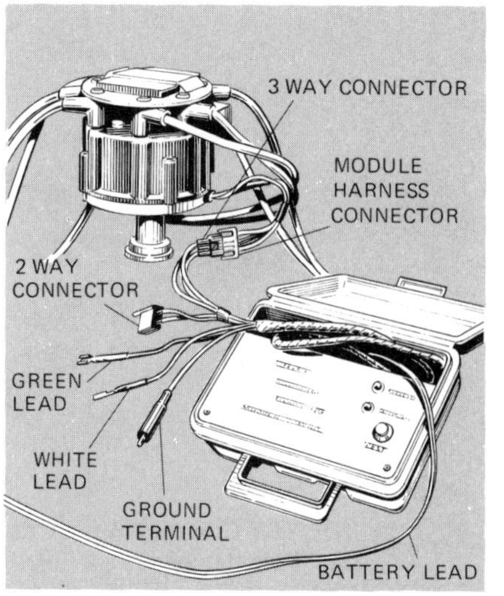

SPECIAL TEST instruments make tests simpler, giving go/no-go readings on a display panel. This one is testing a General Motors electronic ignition.

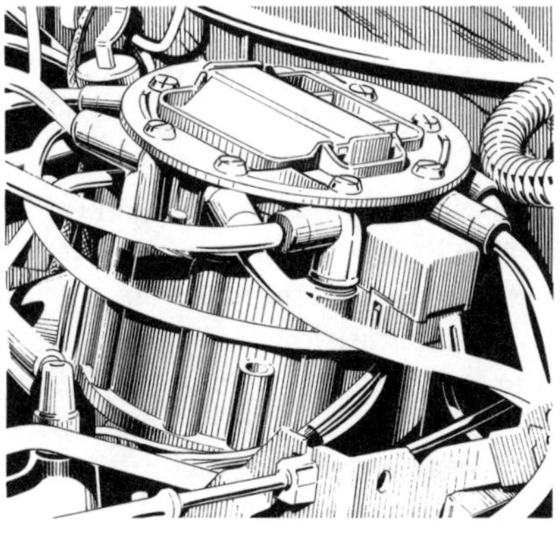

ELECTRONIC IGNITION distributors from GM are larger than those from other builders because they also contain the ignition coil and control module.

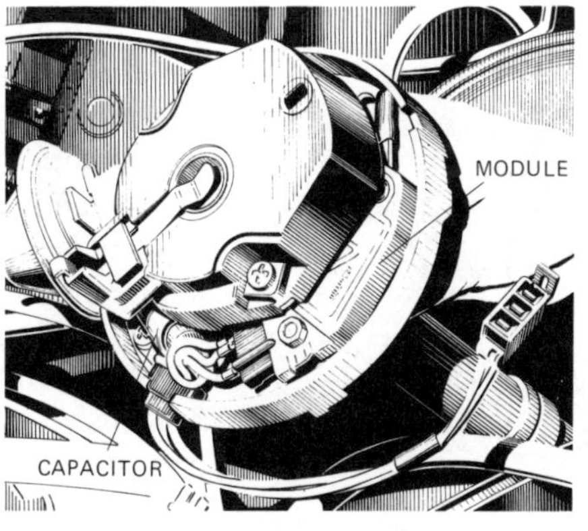

THE BIG rotor takes lots of space in GM's oversized electronic-ignition distributor. The capacitor is a radio noise suppressor, but the electronic control module is part of the modern ignition system.

THE IGNITION coil in GM's electronic ignition is a rectangular device inside the cap. A separate item, it can be removed and replaced individually if that becomes necessary.

Replace only cables that fail. Don't replace the entire set. Cables for electronic ignition systems are expensive.

• Finally, check ignition timing. The conventional old method still works with solid-state.

testing instruments available

Special instruments that make electronic ignition troubleshooting particularly easy are available. They present go/no-go displays on a panel. Although considered professional testing units, they are available if you decide you want one.

A unit designed for testing GM's HEI (High Energy Ignition), which is different from other electronic ignitions, is available from Kent-Moore Tool Div., 29784 Little Mack, Roseville, MI 48066. It has part No. J-24642-E. HEI has all components, including the ignition coil, inside the distributor.

A universal tester is available from Miller Special Tools, 32615 Park Lane, Garden City, MI 48135. It consists of a basic tester (part No. C-4503). You also need one of nine adapters (C-4503 "dash"/through 9)—whichever one makes the basic tester compatible with the one out of nine different electronic systems currently in existence that's in your vehicle.

In place of a special tester, you may use a sen-

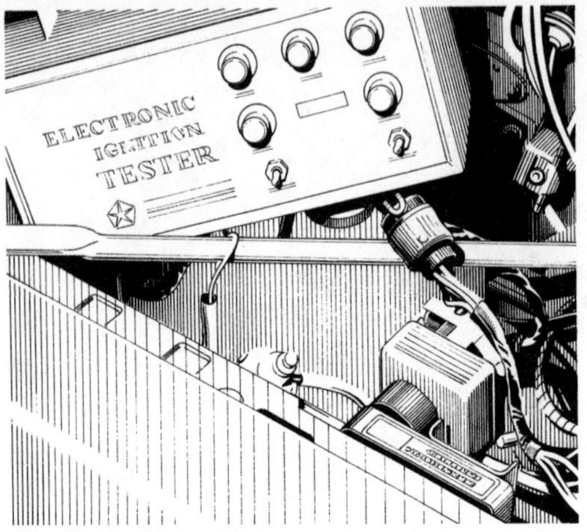

TO TEST CHRYSLER'S electronic ignition, plug the tester right into the electronic control unit. Once hooked up, it gives readings on the whole system.

SWITCHING transistor in Chrysler's system is on the control unit. It's "hot" when the ignition is on, so take care not to touch it.

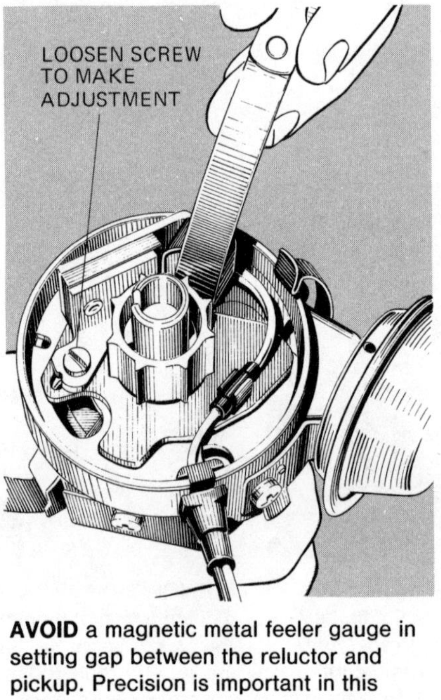

AVOID a magnetic metal feeler gauge in setting gap between the reluctor and pickup. Precision is important in this setting; follow the specs for your car.

sitive dc voltmeter/ohmmeter, but only if you know how or have specific instructions. There are many potential pitfalls and a wrong connection can burn out the system—a costly slip.

In servicing the various systems, I found there are several points that may not be mentioned in instructions. Here are a few:

• You can get an overall indication of electronic-ignition functioning by disconnecting the high-tension cable from the center tower of the distributor. Insert a paper clip into the boot so it touches the terminal and hold it about ¼ inch from a ground. Use insulated pliers to hold the cable; bare hands ask for a stiff jolt. Crank the engine. A fat blue spark between the paper clip and ground indicates a solid system.

Caution: With a conventional ignition system you can use a sparkplug cable for this kind of test. But don't do it with electronic ignition. Holding the wrong cable to ground of some systems could result in damage from arcing in the distributor.

• Be careful around switching transistors that are exposed. They're "hot" and can set you on your tail if you touch one when the ignition is on.

• In GM's big, solid-state distributor, you'll find what looks like the conventional primary-circuit condenser. Don't be confused. It isn't actually part of the ignition system, but a capacitor that serves as a radio noise suppressor.

• If replacement of the pickup in a Chrysler unit is followed by hard starting, suspect the armature teeth-pickup coil air gap is maladjusted. A nonmagnetic feeler gauge is essential for measuring this gap. A plastic gauge is preferred.

• Be careful around the pickup coil. Its wires are very delicate and split easily.

• A hairline crack in the pickup coil won't usually show up when you test the electronic ignition system. Hairline breaks widen under heat and can stop the engine. It will start when heat dissipates. If this is happening to you, suspect the pickup coil.

• Use sparkplugs recommended by your automaker only. Sparkplug gap is much wider than with breaker point ignition, and plugs have been designed with a longer side electrode. Trying to gap any other plug to specification will cause you to bend the side electrode to an extraordinarily wide angle, and lead to operational problems.

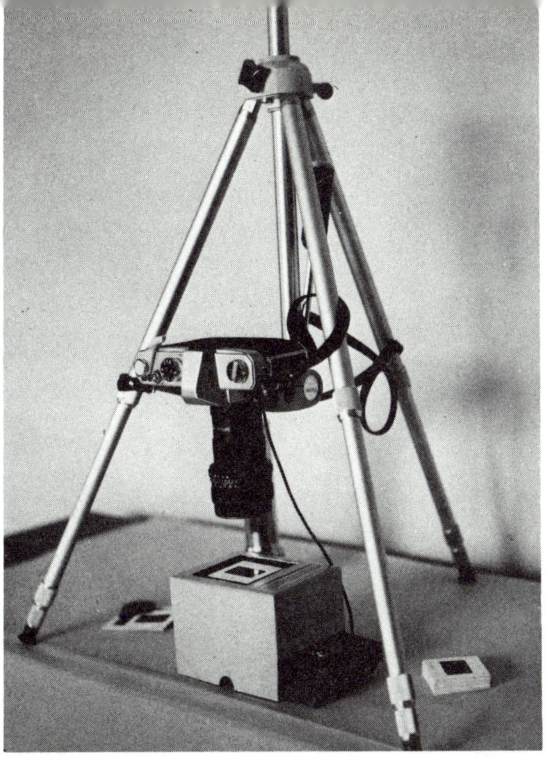

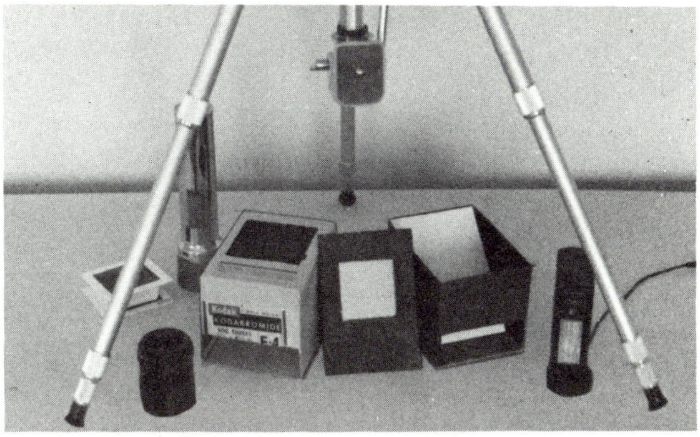

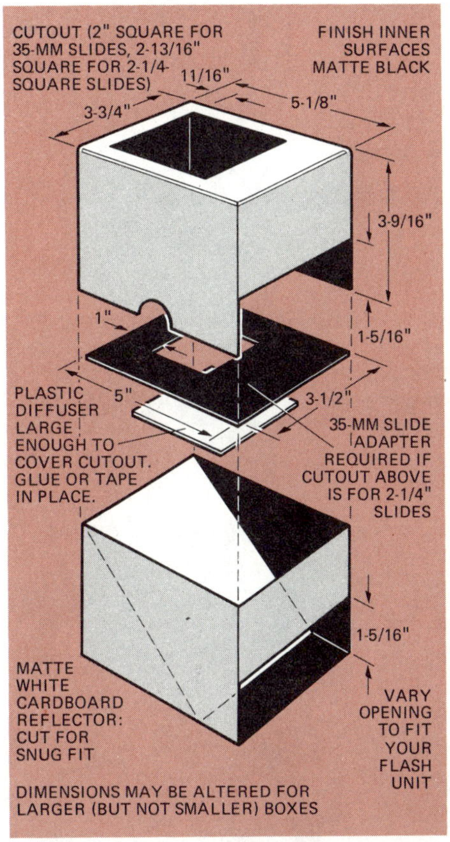

ALL YOU NEED to copy slides is a camera having close-up gear, an electronic flash and this box—which you build for about $1. The disassembled view (below) shows the simplicity of construction: just a photo paper box, a white cardboard reflector, a cardboard mask and a piece of plastic diffuser. The flashlight is used to illuminate the slide for focusing. The dimensions shown at left aren't critical, but a smaller box might not fit your flash.

Slide-copy illuminator for less than $1

By JAMES L. ABBOTT

■ I CALL THIS BOX a "slide converter" because it lets me shoot with slide film all the time. Then I can convert the results into any other type of film; black-and-white, color negative or duplicate slides. I can also make 35-mm copies of 126 (Instamatic) or 2¼x2¼ (120) slides, and sandwich negatives or positives for unusual effects. But the best of all is the box's cost: less than a dollar.

The box originally held 3½x5-inch photographic printing paper. The 3½x5-inch card that goes just below the lid and the 45° matte-white reflector both can be cut from scraps of poster card stock. A piece of diffusion plastic is available from plastic dealers, among others, for a few cents. You may be able to do without the plastic entirely; but if you try it, make test shots to be sure the opening is evenly illuminated without dark corners.

To use the box, slip your flashgun into the slot, mount your camera above the box with extension tubes or bellows to let you get close enough, and drop the slide you want to copy into one of the holes on top of the box. The 2x2-inch lower opening will block off part of a 2¼-square slide—but not as much as you think: just 1/16 inch from each edge of the visible image area. If you use only 2¼-squares, you can do without the inner adapter plate. (If you don't make 2¼-square slides, then you simply can cut a 2x2-inch hole in the box top, and do without the inner adapter.)

One last tip: Since the flashgun illuminates only the slide as you shoot, keep a flashlight handy to light up the slide as you focus and frame your camera.

SEE ALSO

Close-up photos . . . Darkrooms . . .
Dryers, photo . . . Lightboxes . . . Photography . . .
Projector stands . . . Slides, photo . . .
Theaters, home

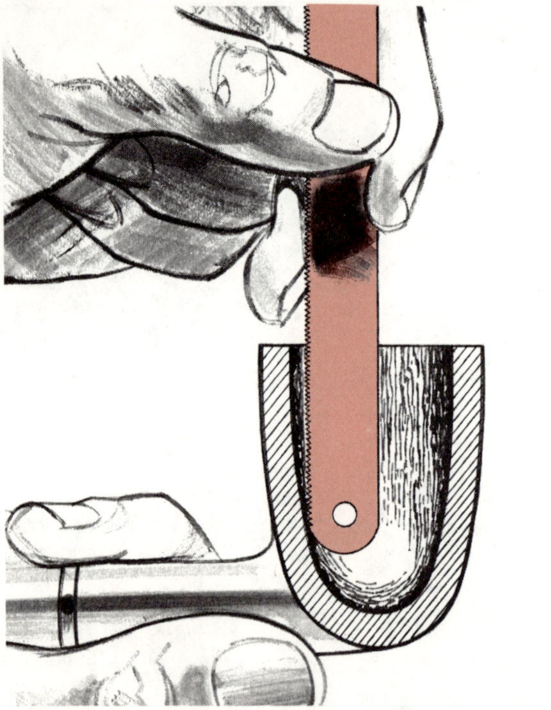

WHEN THE ASH COATING needs scraping from the bowl of your pipe, a piece of hacksaw blade makes a fine reamer. The teeth are perfect for scraping and the rounded end of the blade won't harm the bowl.—*S. H. Rynk*

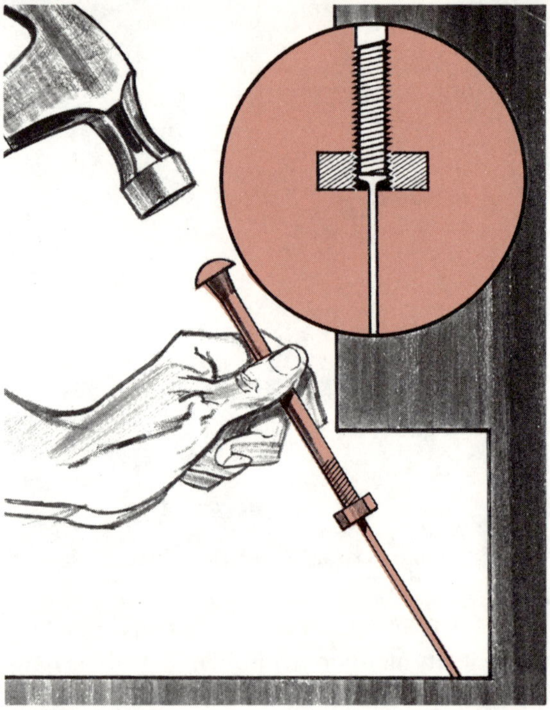

DRIVING A NAIL in an inaccessible spot is no problem if you use a carriage bolt. Turn nut partway on the end so bolt won't slip off the nail and use the bolt like a regular nailset.—*Victor H. Lamoy*

TO MAKE SURE an extension ladder won't slip when standing on wet grass, anchor it with a spading fork. Simply press it in the ground and secure the handle to the bottom rungs with wire. —*Victor H. Lamoy*

WHEN YOU BUY a new aluminum ladder with tubular rungs, it's a good idea to insert wood dowels in the rungs as soon as you get it. Snug-fitting dowels will keep the rungs from bending.—*John Krill*

By WALTER E. BURTON

Cloth tape inlays

AT FIRST GLANCE, the colorful design on the lid of this trinket box looks like expensive enameled inlay work. Actually it's nothing more than patterned fabric tape cemented in shallow channels and coated with a clear plastic finish, but the simulation is nearly perfect.

Any fancy cloth tape, 1/4 to 1-in. wide, can be used this way; a metallic braid will produce a handsome inlay of delicately wrought gold bands.

The picture sequence shows how you first create 1/32-in.-deep channels for the tape with a router and chisel. Then you miter the tape like the corners of a picture frame with a 45° template and a wood chisel, after which you apply white glue sparingly to the channels and press the tape in place flush with the surface.

Finally, you finish both box lid and cloth tape with two coats of a transparent urethane to enhance the wood grain and bring out the beauty of the tape pattern.

SEE ALSO
Gifts, Christmas . . . Jewelry boxes . . . Marquetry . . . Routers . . . Veneering . . . Wood finishes

SHALLOW CHANNELS are first routed to equal thickness of the tape, then corners are squared.

ENDS OF TAPE are mitered by holding sharp wood chisel against 45° template and cutting over hardboard.

WHITE GLUE is spread evenly in channels, then tape is pressed in place. Wipe excess glue with damp cloth.

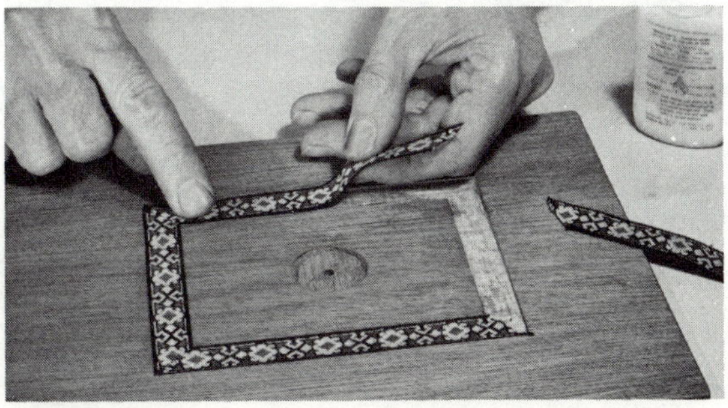

WHEN GLUE is dry, tape is given two coats of clear urethane finish. Then the wood is coated.

Say good-bye to patio bugs

By M. J. DISTEFANO

■ SITTING ON AN OPEN patio during a cool summer evening sounds great, but how many times have you been chased inside by mosquitoes and other nighttime insects? I was chased for the last time when I rigged up the hanging bug trap you see here—it solved the patio bug problem for good.

Knowing that black light attracts most insects, I placed a 100-w. black-light bulb in a plastic flowerpot after cutting a hole in the bottom. Using the pot as a funnel, I fastened it over a same-size hole in a piece of plywood, then bolted a small electric suction fan (4½ in. sq.) to the back to suck the insects from the bulb into a bag made from pantyhose. Once drawn in the trap, the bugs can't escape back through the fan—it works like a charm.

SEE ALSO
Barbecues . . . Cookout bars . . .
Garden shelters . . . Gazebos . . . Patios . . .
Picnic tables . . . Screened summer rooms

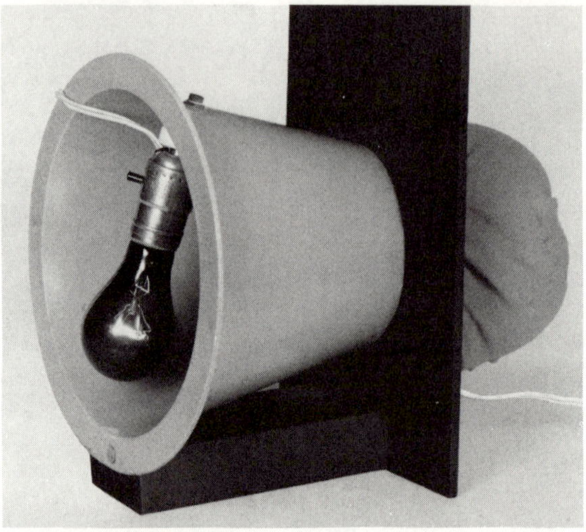

WHEN MOSQUITOES flock to the light bulb, the fan immediately sucks them into the trap for later disposal.

I bought the fan in a surplus store for $3 and attached it to the back of the plywood with four small stovebolts. The drain hole in the bottom of the plastic pot can be enlarged to 2 in. or so with a round file, leaving a flange around the inside for attaching the pot to the plywood with two small bolts. A short ⅛-in. pipe nipple and nut holds the socket to the pot.

I made the trap from discarded pantyhose by cutting off the legs as shown below and tying the ends in a square knot. The elastic top of the hose grips the fan snugly.

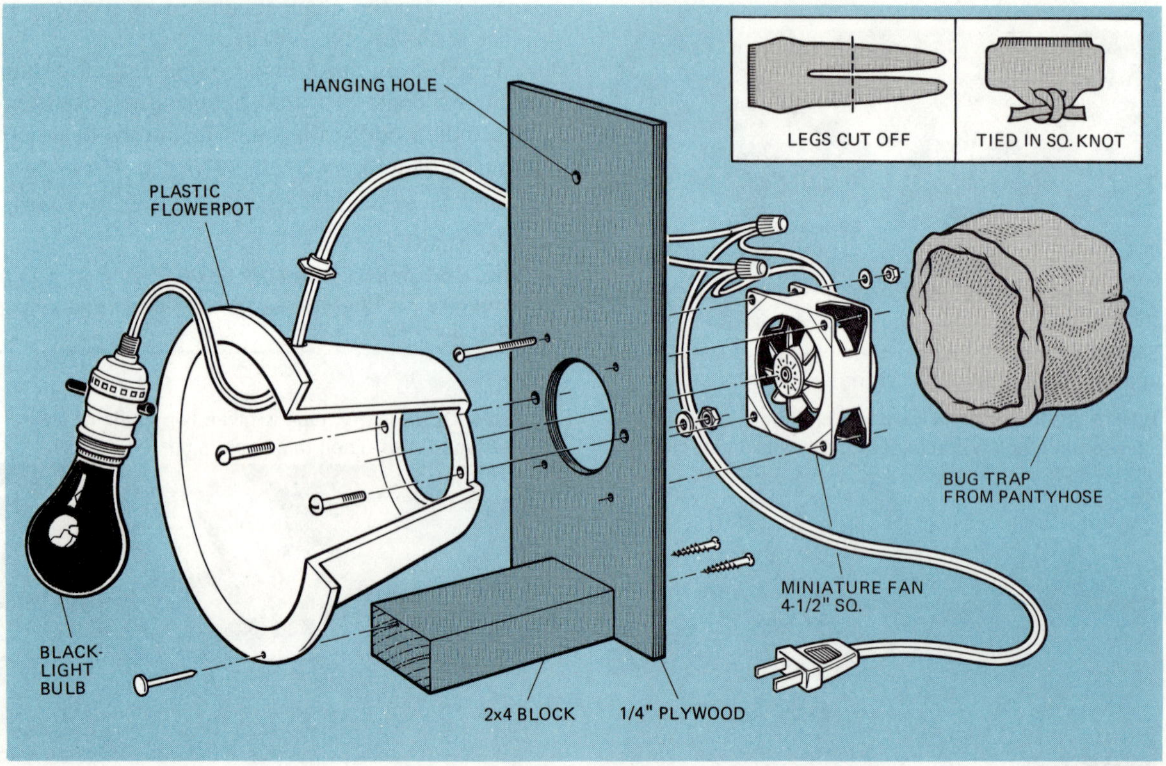

INSULATION DESIGNED for use between furring strips on masonry walls is called Pre-Panel by Johns-Mansville.

continued

How to install insulation

THERE ARE FOUR good reasons why you should insist on adequate insulation when buying a new home or remodeling an existing one. *First:* The cost of heating and cooling in any given locale is proportional to the heat-loss/gain factor of the dwelling. You pay for heat and cooling that escapes through those walls. *Second:* Comfort. Insulation, installed properly, eliminates drafts and increases comfort appreciably and measurably (by the thermostat). *Third:* Acoustical privacy, particularly important if you own a multiple dwelling. Insulation in wall and floor cavities helps to reduce airborne noises, such as loud voices, and impact sounds, such as heavy footsteps. And *fourth:* A reason seldom considered when insulation is being discussed—its effectiveness as a fire barrier. Mineral-wool insulation is noncombustible; when it fills a wall cavity, it acts as a deterrent to the vertical spread of fire. In fact, if the walls in new construction are filled with insulation, then fire-blocking (fire stops) can be eliminated. What you will thus save on labor and materials can be deducted from your insulation cost.

SEE ALSO

Basement waterproofing . . .
Heating systems, home . . . Home winterizing . . .
Remodeling . . . Sheathing

how to install insulation, continued

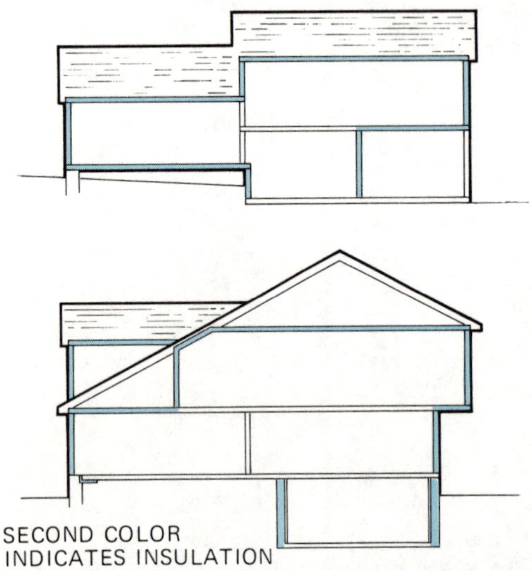

EFFECTIVE LOCATIONS for insulations are indicated by colored lines in the drawing above. To assure that your home is free of moisture problems, remember that you must install adequate vapor barriers. If you use one of the types of insulation that comes without a vapor barrier, install polyethylene, as described at right. The vapor barrier is always installed between the insulation and interior of the home.

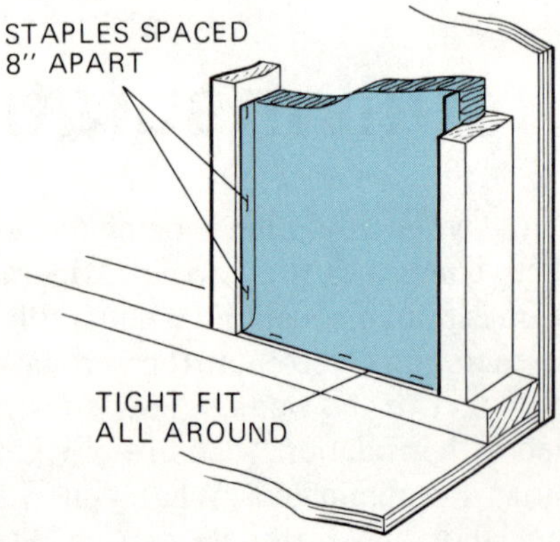

BLANKETS should be pushed into stud spaces so they touch siding or sheathing. Working from the top down, space the staples about 8 in. apart, pulling flanges to fit snugly over studs. Cut the blanket end slightly overlength and staple through the vapor barrier to the plates by compressing the insulation.

WHEN YOU USE pressure-fit blankets without a vapor barrier, wedge them into place and then cover the wall with 2-mil-thick polyethylene vapor barrier stapled to the top and bottom plates. Unroll the sheet to cover the entire wall area, including window and door openings, then cut to length. Staple to end studs, cut out openings and staple around openings.

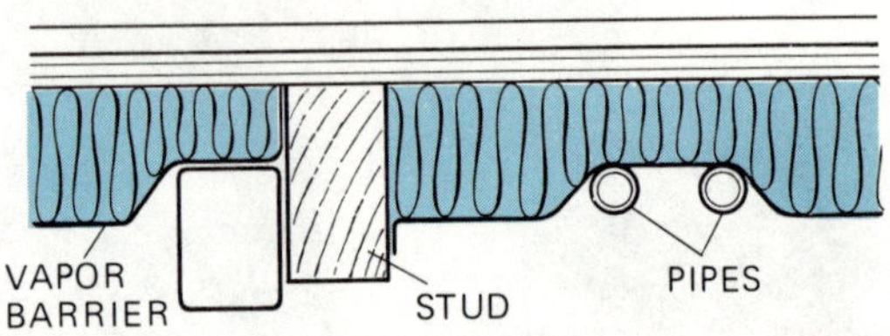

IF OBSTRUCTIONS—ducts, pipes and the like—are located in your wall cavities, push insulation behind (to the cold side in winter) those pipes before stapling. Or you can pack the space with loose insulation or cut a piece of blanket insulation to fit the space. If you do pack the space with loose insulation, make certain you cover it with 2-mil polyethylene.

USE SCRAPS of insulation to stuff into small spaces between rough framing and door and window heads, jambs and sills. You can fill even the narrowest cracks by using a putty knife to force the pieces of insulation in until the crack is filled. Staple scraps of the insulation vapor barrier, or polyethylene, in place to cover those small stuffed spaces.

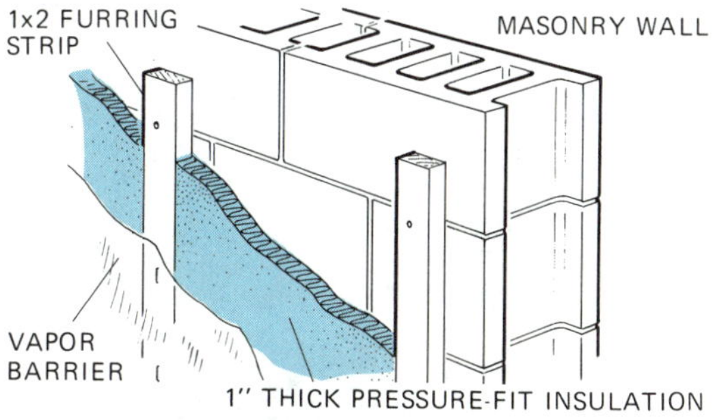

EASIEST WAY TO INSULATE MASONRY WALLS is to space nominal 1x2 furring strips 16 in. on center with nominal 1-in. pressure-fit masonry-wall insulation between strips. Cover with polyethylene vapor barrier. If you prefer 2x2 furring, and use R-7 insulation (with vapor barrier), strips can be spaced 24 in. o.c. This insulation backs up wall panels.

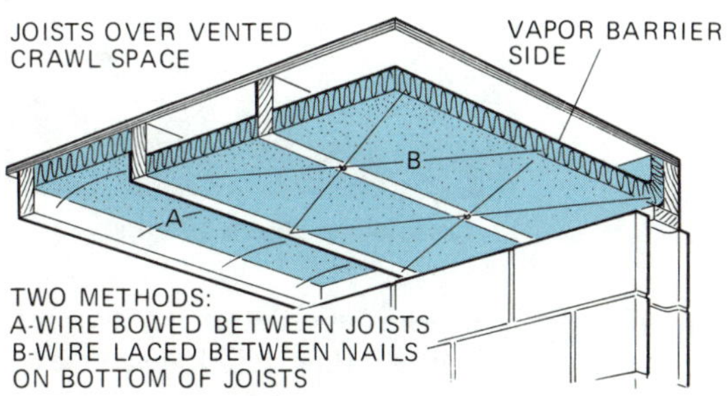

FLOOR OVER VENTED CRAWL SPACE can be insulated if insulating material is held between joists, using either of these methods: (A) By using heavy-gauge wires pointed at both ends, made especially for this purpose. Just bow wires and wedge them underneath insulation between joists. (B) By lacing wires between nails placed in bottom of joists.

HEADER JOIST should be covered with insulation, too. You can do it by wedging oversize pieces of blanket insulation between joists behind the band of header joists and stapling edges to the joists. Or, when you are using insulation at the bottom of joists, you can insulate the header joist by "folding" the end of the blanket 90°, pushing it back against the header and then driving in a few staples.

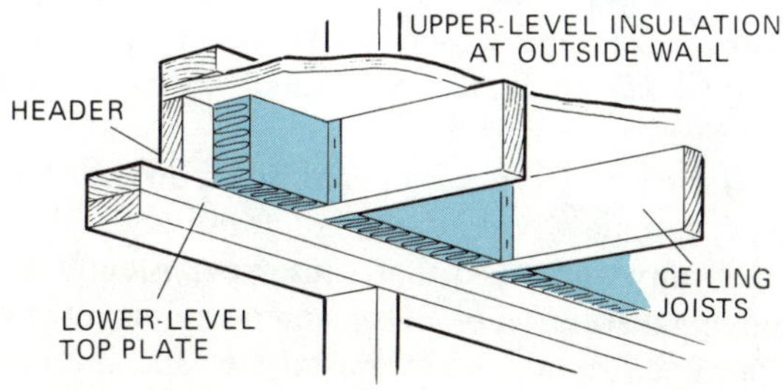

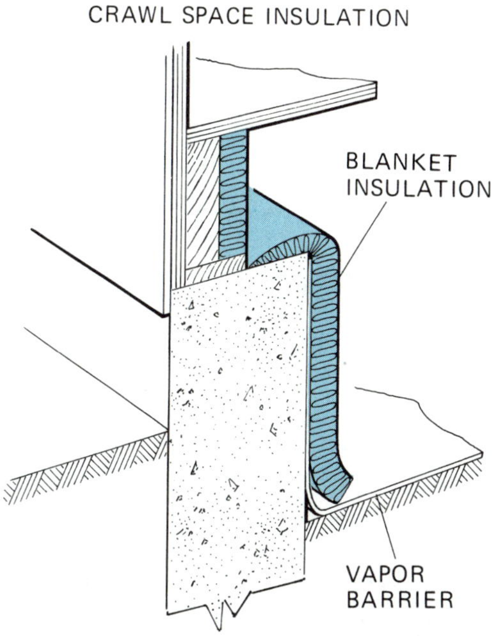

FLOOR OVER UNVENTED CRAWL SPACE usually can be insulated more economically as shown above than by methods given at left for floor over vented crawl space. Spread the vapor barrier over ground in crawl space, let it turn up onto the walls and hold it there with tape. Then place one edge of the blanket insulation on top of the foundation wall and let it drape over and against the inside of the wall. The vapor barrier must face inward.

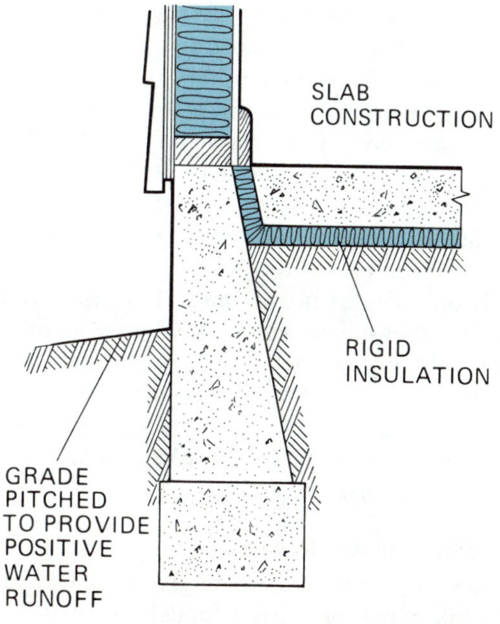

SLAB-FOUNDATION HOMES should always be insulated. The correct way is to lay a 6-mil polyethylene vapor barrier over tamped gravel and use rigid insulation between barrier and slab. The same material should also be used for perimeter insulation, installed as shown. For any insulating job, don't scrimp on quality or thickness. The material is relatively inexpensive and you will recoup its cost in the form of heating and cooling savings.

How to beat TV interference

By JORMA HYYPIA

1 Weak signal—grainy, degraded

5 Ghosts—multiple imaging

A FEW YEARS AGO, there was considerable hoopla about the alleged disruption of television by citizens band radio. Today, there are rumblings and grumblings that hobby computers are the real TV-interference culprits. Tomorrow, latter-day Don Quixotes bent on protecting the purity of TV transmissions may have reasons to joust with *real* windmills, as well as with CB radio and computers.

1. Weak TV signals

These can be mistaken for television-interference (TVI) problems. If all channels have the same grainy, degraded appearance, look for corroded or broken connections all along the lead-in cable, from the antenna to the TV set. This type of maintenance is indicated if you formerly had good reception. If you have never had satisfactory picture quality, you may need a better antenna, or the existing antenna should be placed higher up and perhaps be fitted with a signal amplifier for improved reception.

If only one or two channels have the overall grainy appearance, your cable connections are probably in good shape. Perhaps you are simply located in a fringe area with respect to the particular channels affected. Better antenna orientation (direction and height) and use of a signal amplifier should solve the problem.

2. Electrical interference

If very pronounced, this might be mistaken for a weak signal condition, although the two effects are actually quite easy to differentiate. A weak signal causes uniform degradation of the entire picture area. On the other hand, even severe electrical TVI tends to form changing bands of flickering, short, horizontal lines, or else more randomly spaced, bright pinpoints of white light. The latter effect is very common when an electrical storm is in the viewing area.

If you observe pinpoints of light dancing around on the screen when there is a breeze blowing outside but no storm, check the lead-in wire connections to the antenna. Odds are you will find at least one connection either badly corroded or broken off.

To track down other intermittent electrical TVI, go around the house and turn off operating appliances one by one.

If a portable radio is affected by the same interference, carry it around your home area and see where it sounds noisiest. It's just possible that you will get loudest radio interference when you move closer and closer to a neighbor's property; maybe *his* appliance or engine is creating the problem.

If the interference is caused by a power drill or saw, you may live with the minor nuisance. However, any appliance that causes persistently annoying disruption of TV or stereo equipment performance should be corrected (see illustration).

SEE ALSO
Amplifiers . . . Antennas, TV . . .
Cassette recorders . . . Cassette tapes . . .
Citizens band radio . . . Masts . . . Speakers . . .
Television antennas

2 Electrical—bands of snow

3 FM radio—hash-like stripes

4 Computer—similar to radio

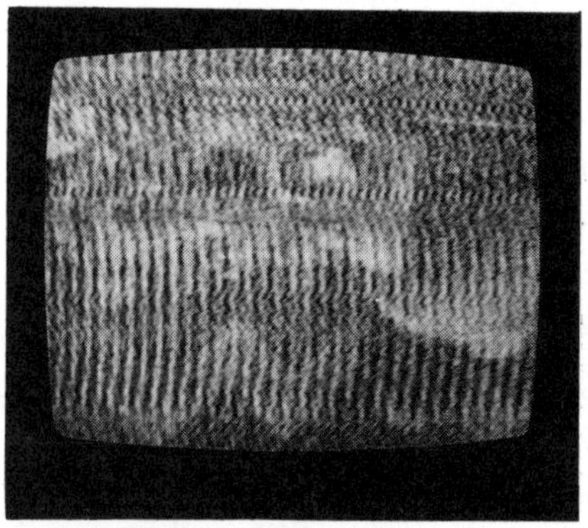

6 CB radio—pulsing lines

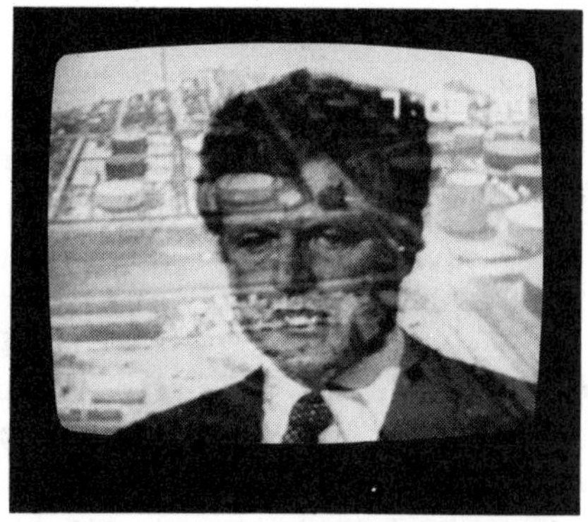

7 Co-channel—different images

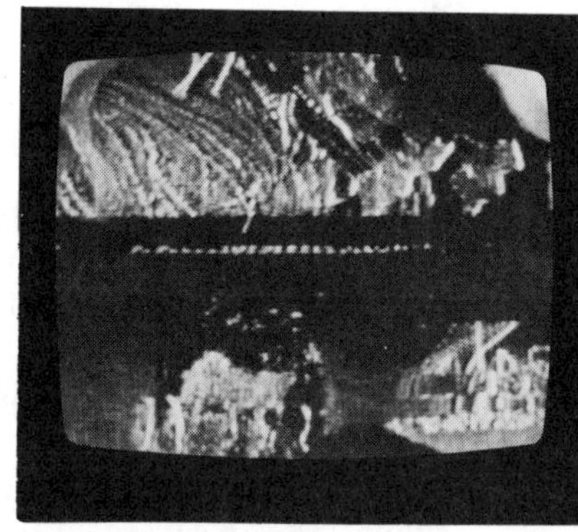

8 Airplanes—picture tears

3. FM radio interference

This can be caused by a nearby FM broadcast station and may create a herringbone pattern that is easy to confuse with a similar pattern caused by misadjustment of the TV set's fine-tuning control. If the tuning control is at fault, the interference pattern fluctuates with sound changes in the TV program; if FM interference is present, the pattern fluctuates with variations in the sound of the FM broadcast, *not* with the sound of the TV program.

FM TVI is usually most bothersome on Channel 6, although other channels in the 2 to 13 series may also be affected. Before attempting a cure, make certain that the FM interference is not caused by a nearby FM *receiver.*

To become familiar with FM interference, hold a portable FM receiver near a TV set tuned to Channel 13. Dial the radio down to the 96- to 97-megahertz range and observe the variety of interference patterns on the screen.

If your own FM receiver is the problem, just move it a little farther away from the TV set. If the FM TVI is caused by a broadcast station, start by installing an inexpensive FM-band rejection filter at the rear of the TV set. Connect the filter to the antenna leads as instructed in the literature that comes with it. Use a connector cable of the same type as the existing antenna lead. This may be a simple twin-lead wire or a coaxial cable; just don't mix the two types.

If you have an antenna amplifier, install one filter before the amplifier and a second one ahead of the TV receiver input terminals. You may also be instructed to add a ground wire which should be kept as short as possible. If the filters don't solve the problem, call a serviceman for in-set modifications.

4. Computer-generated TVI

This is generally not a problem unless the computer is quite close to the TV set. During our tests, Channels 2, 4 and 13 were found to be most sensitive to computer radiation. However, the radiation put out by some other computer might affect a TV set differently, perhaps on other channels, and produce other types of interference patterns.

If a neighbor buys a hobby computer, don't be in a rush to blame him for all your TV interference problems. It's simple enough to check it out by turning the computer on and off while watching the TV set. Not all computers create TVI, even when operated next to the television receiver.

5. Ghosting

This is a formation of double images and occurs when the TV signal travels along two paths of different lengths from the broadcast tower to a receiving antenna. However, ghosting can also be caused by a poor TV antenna and/or lead-in wire, or merely improper aiming of a directional-type antenna. Check these possibilities first.

If the problem obviously relates to multipath reception of a reflected signal, try moving the antenna to a different location. If that doesn't cure the problem, replace the antenna with a more directional type, and be sure to use shielded-type lead-in wire.

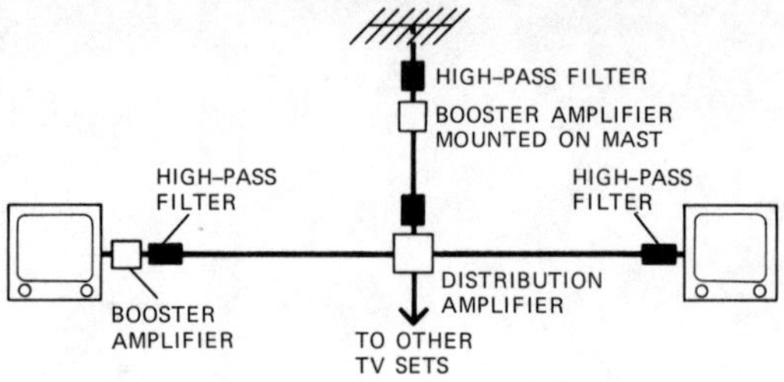

6. CB radio interference

This can be caused by citizens band and amateur "ham" radio transmissions, but also by transmissions by police and other public service radios.

Such TVI characteristically occurs in the form of dark parallel lines tilted slightly off the horizontal. These patterns are easy to confuse with similar effects caused by horizontal-hold problems in the TV set. But these aren't the only interference patterns produced by radio transmitters.

The actual effects vary greatly depending on many factors, including the strength of the radio signal and whether the radio operator is actually talking or merely sending out an unmodulated carrier wave.

If the TVI is, in fact, due to radio interference, the pattern will pulsate as the radio operator talks, and may even bounce back and forth between the parallel-line pattern and more random patterns.

You will not observe such pulsations if the parallel lines are caused by horizontal-hold problems; instead you may hear a high-pitched tone. To cure a hold malfunction, readjust the horizontal-hold control. If that doesn't work, have a serviceman replace a bad component.

Eliminating radio transmitter TVI can be a problem. You should begin by installing an inexpensive high-pass filter at the antenna terminals of the TV set. Be sure to use the same type of connecting cable as is used for the antenna lead-in (either twin-lead wire or a coaxial cable). Put one filter ahead of an antenna signal amplifier you may be using and a second filter at the TV set.

If the filters don't fully cure the problem, consult your serviceman about possible modifications of the TV set's internal circuitry.

7. Co-channel images

This resembles ghosting, but is easily recognized because the second image is usually of a *different* program, which means it is coming from a second TV broadcast station. Remember, true ghosting involves a duplication of the same TV program material.

Co-channel interference is most commonly caused by atmospheric conditions that permit signals from a very distant station to bounce back down from the upper atmosphere and thereby "skip" to receiving areas they normally wouldn't reach. There's nothing to do about a temporary problem except wait until the atmospheric condition clears, usually within an hour or two.

However, if you experience *persistent* co-channel interference, it means that you are located where it is possible to pick up signals regularly from two broadcast stations on the same channel. You may be able to cure or minimize the problem by installing a highly directional antenna. If some interference persists, try reducing the signal strength with a tunable signal attenuator that actually weakens the signal getting into the TV set.

8. Airplanes and windmills

Here are but two examples of miscellaneous outside sources of TVI. The whirring blades of a helicopter (eggbeater) or the wings of a banking 747 can cause TV interference. The display may tear badly, and there may be a temporary loss of color. The problem is really troublesome only near busy airports.

Some channels may be more sensitive than others to such disturbances, perhaps partly because of weak TV signals. The installation of a better antenna, use of a shielded coaxial lead-in cable, and addition of an antenna signal amplifier can greatly reduce the effects of aircraft.

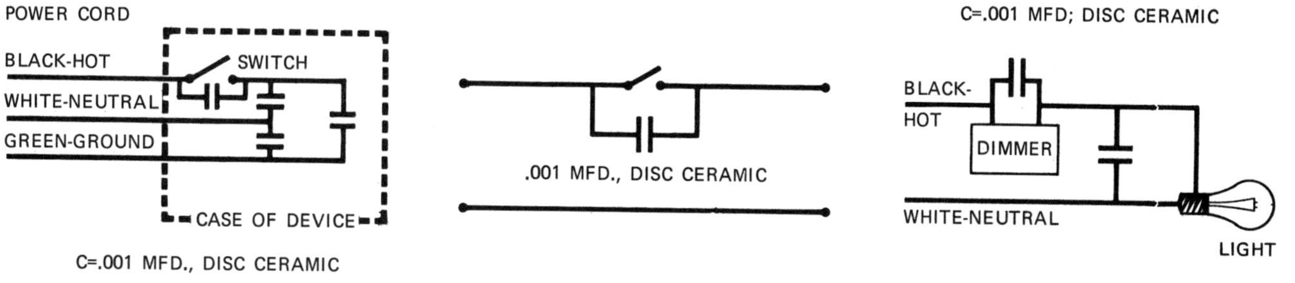

HIGH-PASS FILTERS can be useful if installed as shown at the left. Don't forget to put one on each side of a booster amp. Try the three cures shown above to solve the interference from appliances or dimmer-switches—but be careful of a.c. wiring if you make modifications. See text for further instructions.

A similar problem can be caused by windmills! People living in rural areas may already be familiar with this source of TVI, and the problem may become more widespread if windpower develops into a significant energy source in the years ahead.

Of course, there's also TVI that originates from malfunctioning equipment at the TVI broadcast station, and the broadcaster usually—but not always—announces that fact. If you observe bad color or other picture distortions during the presentation of field-recorded news broadcasts, for example, it may be due simply to a malfunction or inexpert use of the broadcaster's portable camera equipment.

additional tips

If a specific ham or CB transmitter in your area obviously relates to your TVI problem, work with the operator to check his equipment for proper performance. See if the rig is properly grounded, test for harmonics and/or spurious emissions, and add a good earth ground if the transmitter cabinet radiates energy. Install a *low-pass* filter on the transmitter antenna circuit to see if the TVI pattern is affected by changes in harmonics and/or spurious emissions.

check antenna connections

If these measures fail, go back to the TV receiver and recheck all antenna connections. If there's an antenna signal amplifier, remove it temporarily. If this eliminates TVI, reconnect the amplifier, but protect it against radio frequency (RF) pickup as follows: 1. Add grounding; 2. enclose the amplifier in a metallic RF-proof housing and ground the housing; 3. install a high-pass filter at the input to the amplifier; 4. install a second such filter in series if the first one is not adequate.

Add a purchased a.c. power-line RF filter to determine if the RF from the transmitter is entering the TV set by way of the power cord. If the TVI persists, even when the antenna is disconnected, look for the problem inside the TV set, especially at the tuner. Disconnect the antenna input lead inside the set at the tuner. If the TVI is eliminated, install a high-pass filter at the tuner. If this doesn't cure the problem, each stage of the TV must be tested—a job for a repairman.

Electrical TVI caused by sparking home appliances and tools can often be eliminated by adding capacitor bypasses. *However, the modifications must be done with extreme care, especially when bypassing appliances having capacitors.* Dangerous voltages may exist, the a.c. power line might accidentally be shorted and an inexperienced do-it-yourselfer can invite electrocution!

interference from tools

Arcing between the brushes and commutators of infrequently used power tools are best left alone. If the tools are in constant use, TVI can be reduced by bypassing each side of the line to the other side and to ground with capacitors. The on/off switch also should be bypassed.

Also, .001-mfd. capacitors may be used to bypass arcing contacts in such thermostatically controlled appliances as electric blankets and fish-tank heaters. Defective TVI-producing doorbell transformers should be replaced. Dimmer switches that utilize SCRs or triacs can cause much hard-to-eliminate TVI. However, bypassing with capacitors may help somewhat.

Internal carving: a little-known art

By AL WESTERFIELD
and HARRY WICKS

Development of clear plastics cleared the way for this craft—you carve from the back instead of the front, using a power tool employing various burrs and cutters

DESIGN to be carved in clear plastic is drawn on the front of the sheet with a felt-tipped pen or grease pencil. Then an entry hole is made in the back and the carving begins. Use burrs and cutters. Check depth of cut by peering through sides.

SEE ALSO
**Bottle craft . . . Carving, wood . . .
Gifts, Christmas . . . Jewelry . . . Lapidary . . .
Stained glass . . . Wood sculpture**

■ ACCORDING TO EXPERTS in the acrylic plastic field, internal carving was the first popular plastics craft. The fine optical characteristics of clear plastic not only make this art possible, but enable you to create effects that are impossible with any other carving technique.

The biggest delight for most internal carvers, after they have acquired the necessary skills, is to produce objects which are edge-lit. The Lincoln head, for example, when mounted on a wood base containing a 7-w. bulb, produces a striking three-dimensional look when the bulb is lighted. The reason: the light passes through the uncarved area and is not visible to the eye. But, the carved-out portion will reflect every mark that you've made with your cutters.

A fine tool for small carving projects is the Dremel Model No. 260 Moto-Tool. It was used to carve all the projects you see on these pages. With a foot rheostat, the tool performed well on light chores. Though it did require some cooling-off periods when large areas were being ground out, the tool did all that the maker claims it will when restricted to the hobbyist-type chores for which it is intended.

If you're a beginner, you should start with simple designs which will keep you pretty much confined to using round or barrel-type cutters. Don't be disappointed if your first few tries don't even resemble the design you've drawn on the face. It takes practice and more practice to learn the nuances and tricks that the art demands. But once you've mastered the tools of the trade, you'll be more than pleased with what you can turn out.

To carve, hold the piece of plastic between thumb and forefinger of your left hand, and the carving tool in your right hand with the drill bit facing up to the bottom of the plastic. As you carve, you will look down into the work. With a round burr, form a cavity in the underside. Don't hurry the job and do let the drill do the work. A good project to start with is a simple shape such as your house number or initials. After a while you'll automatically manipulate the drill expertly enough to take on such sophisticated projects as flowers, birds and fish. For more information on internal carving and the Moto-Tool, write Dremel Manufacturing Co., Box 518, Racine, WI 53201.

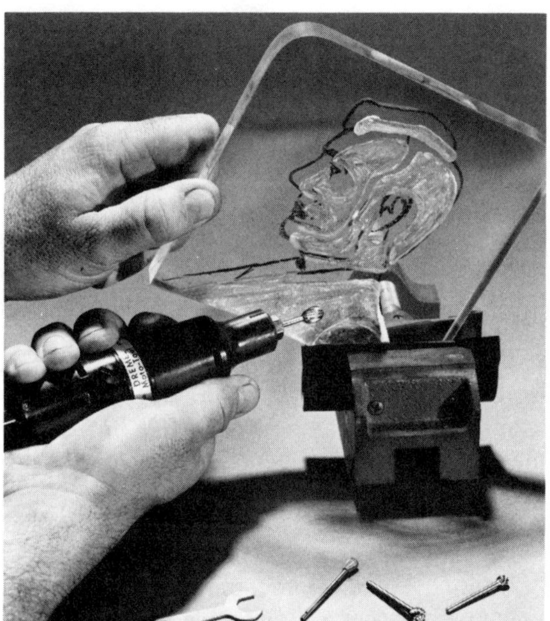

BACK VIEW of carving shows varying depths of cut. When the carving is finished, a colored sheet plastic (right) is affixed to it by means of double-faced tape. If desired, the carving can be painted.

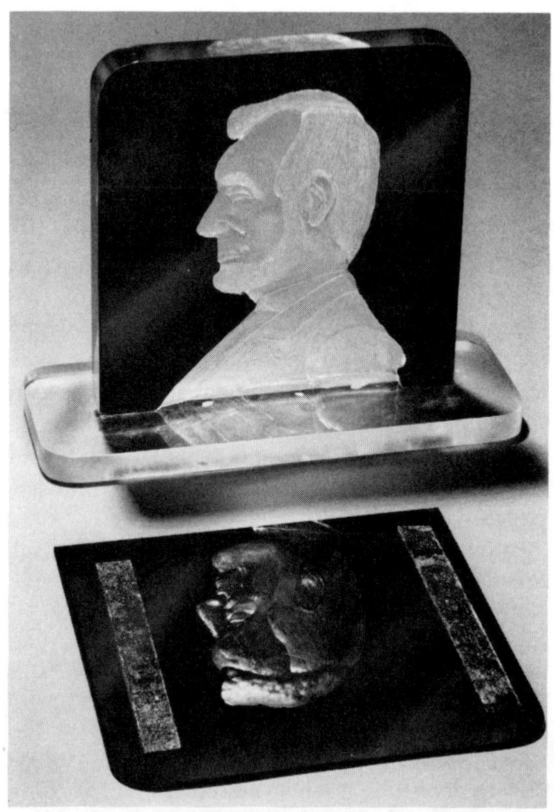

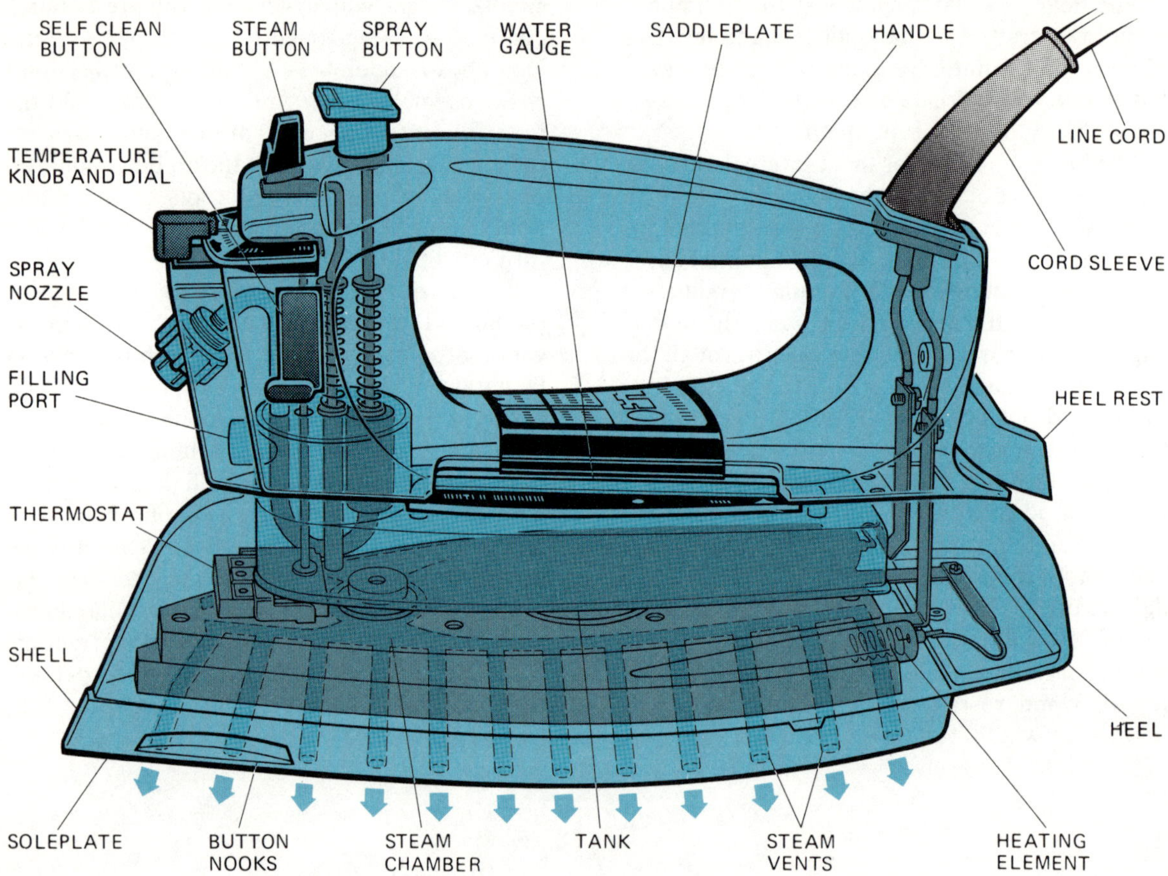

How to repair an electric iron

■ ELECTRICALLY, AN IRON is simple; its electrical circuit consists of cord, thermostat and heating element. Iron thermostats are of two types: bimetal and base-expansion (see drawings on page 1551). In the first, a bimetal strip makes and breaks contacts as temperature changes. In the second, a thin metal strip welded to the base of the thermostat falls and rises to make and break contacts as the base contracts and expands with temperature changes.

In either type of iron thermostat, the spring tension on thermostat elements is varied to give different temperature, settings, and the iron, once hot, will cycle on and off within a few degrees of the desired temperature. Thermostat contact points may become pitted or corroded in time, and if an iron is dropped, insulators and bimetals may break.

It is usually better to replace a thermostat than to repair it. Thermostat calibration requires an iron tester; one may be worthwhile only if you plan to check a number of irons. One tester maker is Waage Manufacturing Co., 632 North Albany Ave., Chicago, IL 60612. Write for your local dealer's name.

Heating elements are chrome-nickel resistance wire, either a replaceable ribbon element wound on a sheet of mica, or a round wire element in a ceramic form cast into the iron's soleplate. The cast-in type is expensive to replace when found defective; you're better off buying a new iron than trying to replace such an element. Heating-element failures are opens (breaks),

SEE ALSO
**Appliance repair . . . Appliances . . .
Clothes dryers . . . Washing machines**

Iron does not heat

POSSIBLE CAUSES	WHAT TO TRY
1. Blown fuse or tripped circuit breaker.	Replace line fuse or reset circuit breaker. If blowing or tripping is repeated, check iron for shorts.
2. Defective cord or plug.	Inspect cord and plug for fraying or breaks. Disconnect cord from outlet and iron and test each wire for continuity. If either gives no reading, replace with cord of correct size.
3. Loose connections at iron terminals.	Tighten both connections at eyelet terminals on iron.
4. Loose thermostat-control knob.	Replace knob and tighten on shaft.
5. Defective thermostat.	Disassemble iron for access to thermostat. Replace thermostat if parts are broken.
6. Defective heating element.	Test element for continuity. If there is no reading, replace removable element; discard iron with cast-in element.

DRY IRON

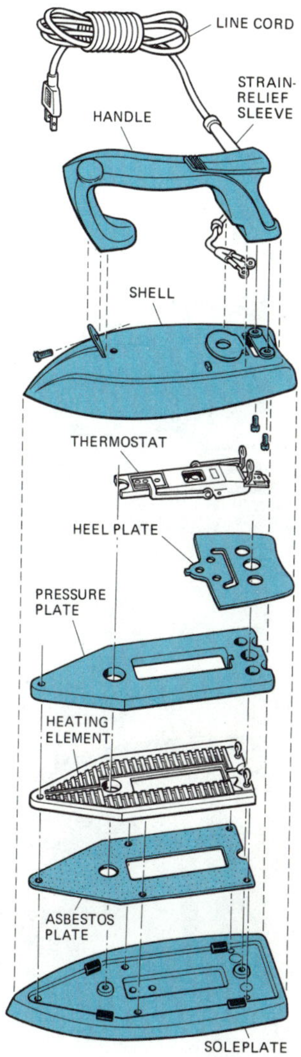

Iron produces too little heat

POSSIBLE CAUSES	WHAT TO TRY
1. Low voltage.	Test voltage at wall outlet with voltmeter. If not within 10 percent of normal, call local power company.
2. Thermostat out of calibration	Recalibrate iron only with an iron test stand. Set text for information on source.
3. Defective thermostat.	See preceding chart.
4. Loose connections at terminals.	See preceding chart.

Iron produces too much heat

POSSIBLE CAUSES	WHAT TO TRY
1. Thermostat out of calibration.	See preceding chart.
2. Defective thermostat.	See chart, "Iron does not heat" (top above).

CAUTION: Be sure power is turned *off* before you handle components. Make all continuity tests with power *off*. Use your manufacturer's manual to locate components, and use only replacement parts that meet his specifications.

grounds and shorts. A shorted element will usually blow itself apart when it is turned on, in turn blowing the line fuse; afterward it will test as open.

Steam irons operate two ways: with a tank that also serves as a boiler or, in the flash type, with valving that drips water into a steam chamber—a recess in the hot soleplate—where it vaporizes. A spray feature adds a pump to the hardware. Hard water is the enemy of steam irons, as it leaves mineral deposits that build up and clog valves and ports. Distilled water is recommended in its place.

When a steam-iron problem involves inaccessible parts, disassembly should be done with caution because of the complexity of valves and linkages. Get the manufacturer's service instructions, and take the iron apart only as far as necessary to gain access to the faulty component.

BOILER-TYPE STEAM IRON

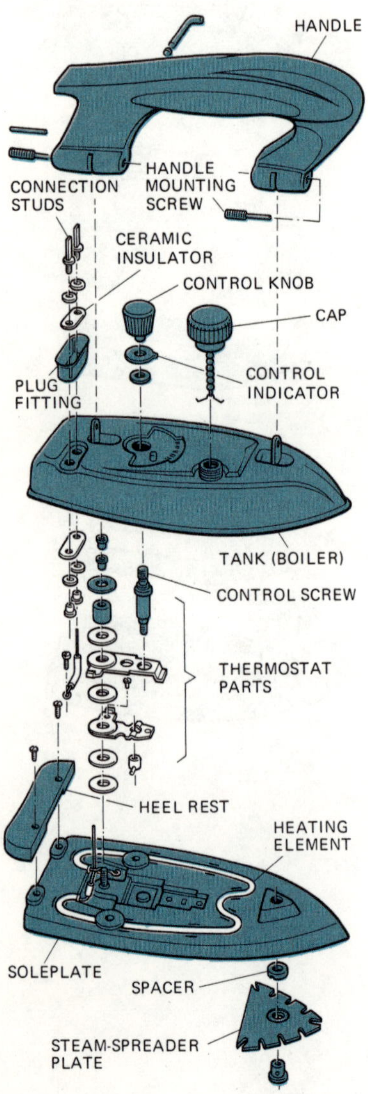

Water leaks from iron

POSSIBLE CAUSES	WHAT TO TRY
1. Tank overfilled.	Do not fill tank completely. Water expands when heated.
2. Defective seam or tank weld.	Disassemble iron for access to tank, replace tank, reassemble iron.
3. Damaged tank gasket.	Disassemble iron for access to gasket, replace gasket, reassemble iron.

Iron does not steam

POSSIBLE CAUSES	WHAT TO TRY
1. Tank nearly empty.	Refill tank.
2. Thermostat set low or out of calibration	Set thermostat higher or recalibrate if necessary. See chart, "Iron produces too little heat."
3. Valve OFF.	Turn valve to ON position.
4. Clogged valves or steam ports.	Clean iron by filling its tank with vinegar and turning it on.

Iron spits

POSSIBLE CAUSES	WHAT TO TRY
1. Wrong setting of thermostat.	Set thermostat higher. Spitting usually is caused by low thermostat setting.
2. Internal mineral deposits.	Clean iron with vinegar as described in preceding chart.
3. Tank overfilled.	Do not fill tank completely.

Spray does not work

POSSIBLE CAUSE	WHAT TO TRY
1. Defective plunger or assembly.	Disassemble iron for access to plunger and the plunger assembly. Replace any worn or broken parts.

Iron stains clothes

POSSIBLE CAUSES	WHAT TO TRY
1. Starch on soleplate.	Clean soleplate with damp cloth, buff with steel wool and polish with dry cloth.
2. Minerals in water.	Use distilled water in iron.
3. Sediment in tank.	Clean with vinegar. See chart, "Iron does not steam."

Iron tears or snags clothes

POSSIBLE CAUSE	WHAT TO TRY
1. Rough, spot, nick or burr on soleplate.	Buff soleplate with fine emery, polish with dry cloth.

Iron gives shocks

POSSIBLE CAUSES	WHAT TO TRY
1. Defective cord.	Check cord for frays, cracks, exposed bare wires. Replace with cord of correct size for iron.
2. Thermostat insulation break.	Disassemble iron to get at thermostat; look for broken porcelain or asbestos. Replace assembly.
3. Heating element grounded.	Test for ground with one lead of continuity tester on element, other on iron chassis. A reading indicates a ground. Replace removable element; discard iron with cast-in element.

Iron sticks to clothes

POSSIBLE CAUSES	WHAT TO TRY
1. Dirty soleplate.	Clean soleplate. See chart, "Iron stains clothes."
2. Excess starch in clothing.	Reduce amount of starch used and lower temperature setting.
3. Temperature roo high for fabric.	Lower temperature setting. Consult manufacturer's instructions on fabric type involved.

BIMETAL THERMOSTAT

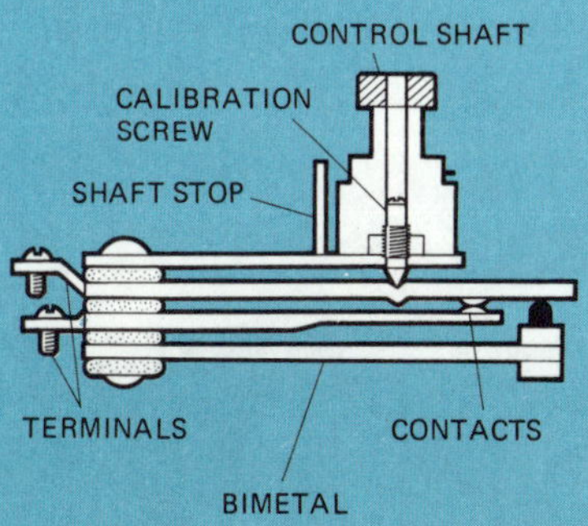

BASE-EXPANSION THERMOSTAT

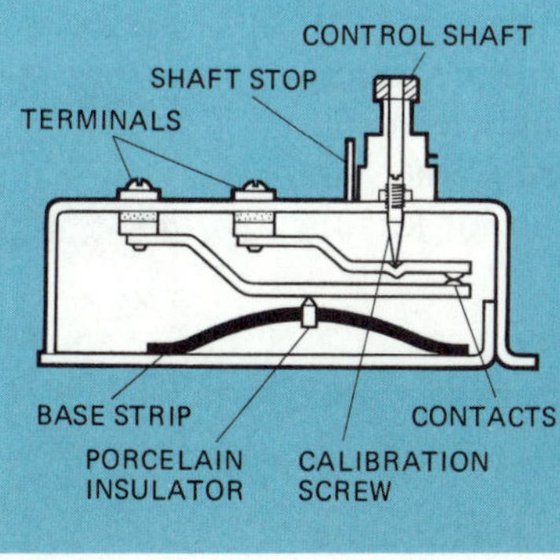

FLASH-TYPE STEAM IRON

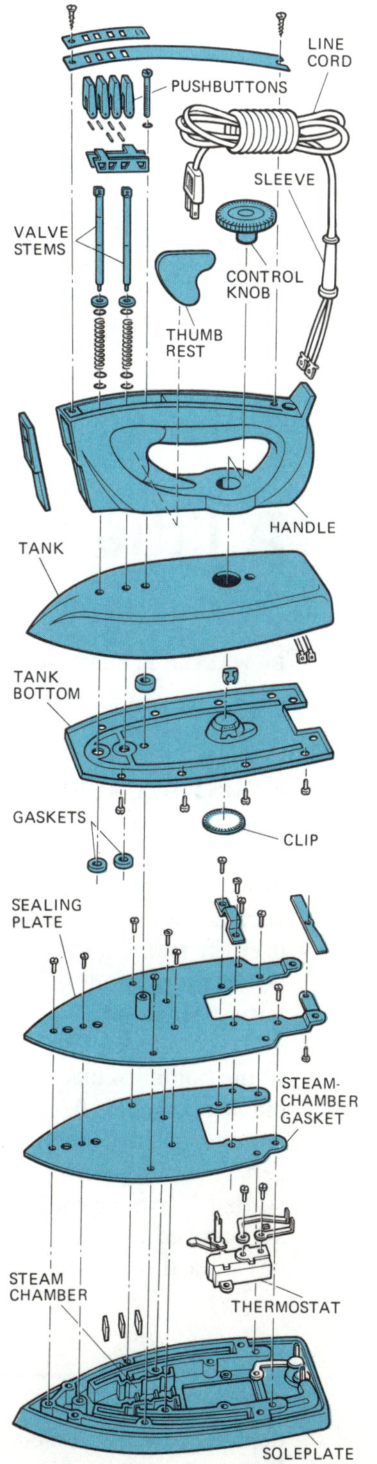

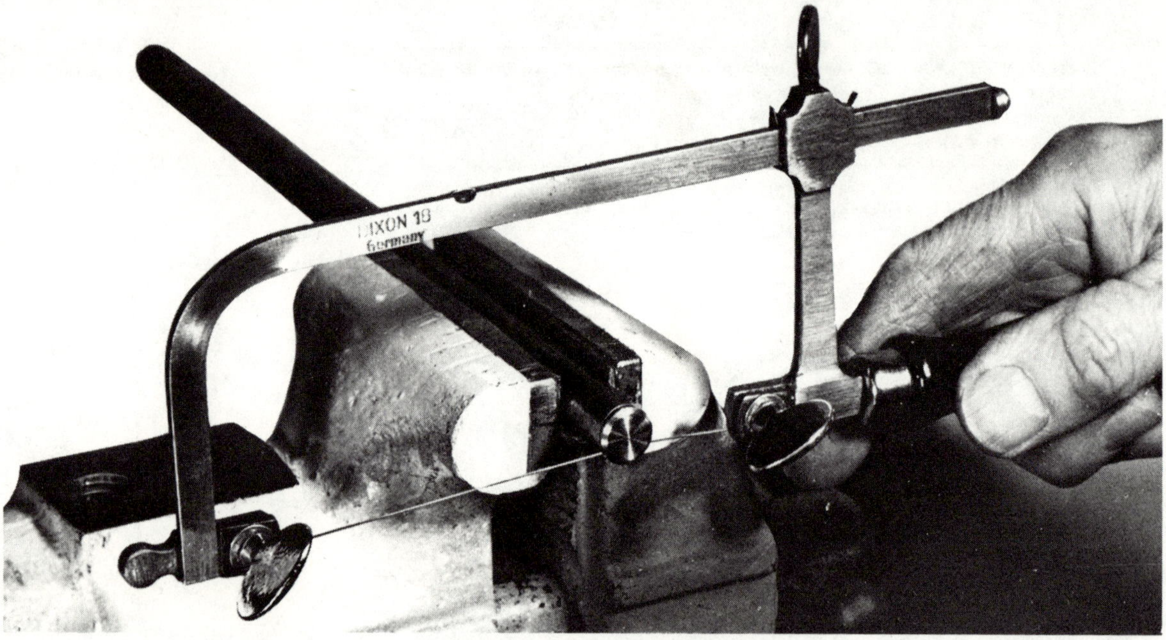

A little tool with a big bite

By WALTER E. BURTON

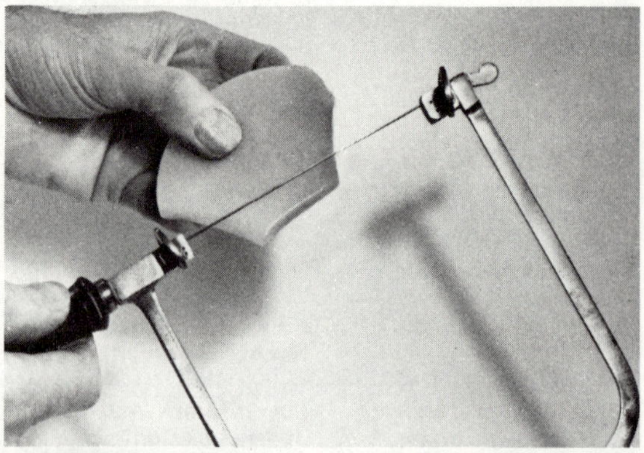

LUBRICANT APPLIED to blade helps with the cutting. Use beeswax or paraffin, or even a cutting oil.

SAW TEETH should be cleaned periodically whether or not wax is used. Suede-shoe brush will work fine.

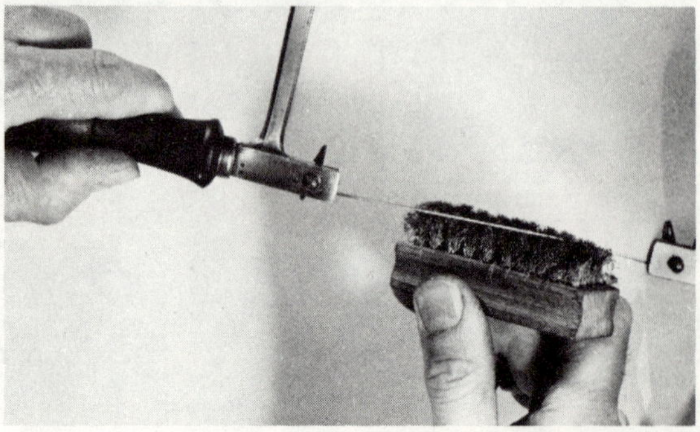

■ JUST BECAUSE they're labeled "jeweler's piercing saws" is no reason for not adapting these handy tools, with their ultra-thin blades, to other jobs about the home and shop. The fact is, such a saw and a variety of blades to fit it can be used in many ways by the homeowner, do-it-yourselfer, modeler or almost any garden-variety tinkerer.

Essentially, a jeweler's saw is a C-shaped frame holding a blade capable of cutting various materials ranging from wood and plastic to brass and unhardened steel. The blade normally is inserted with its teeth pointing toward the handle so that it cuts on the pull stroke and cleans the kerf on the push stroke. A shallow frame, one having a throat dimension of 2¼ in. or less, is

SEE ALSO
**Bolts . . . Jewelry . . . Modelmaking . . .
Power, hacksaws . . . Tools, hand . . . Workbenches**

TYPICAL BLADES in pairs (from top): Nos. 8/10, 3, 14. Blades and frames are by William Dixon, Inc.

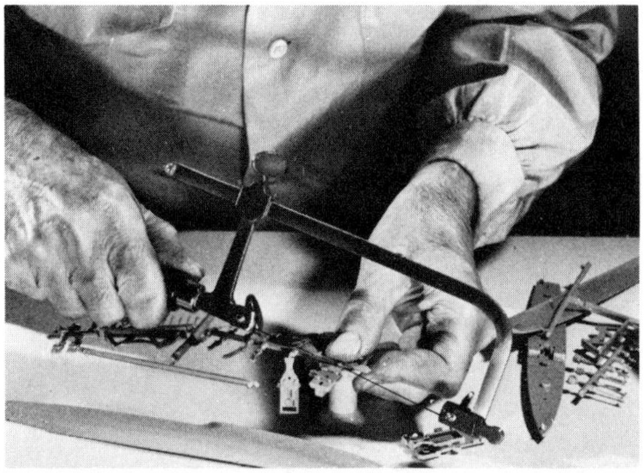

ON MODEL WORK, jeweler's blade produces very fine cut and seldom requires further finishing.

most often used for jewelry work, modelmaking and similar light-duty chores. For work where the blade has to cut to the center of a large circle, a deeper frame is necessary. In the average workshop, one saw with a 2¼-in. throat and another 6 to 8 in. deep will be adequate to handle most challenges.

Blades, commonly 5 in. long, come in thicknesses and widths ranging typically from No. 8/0 (.006 in. thick and .013 in. wide) to No. 14 (.024 in. thick, .068 in. wide). Most hardware stores sell the blades by the dozen or the gross. They are not expensive.

Thumbscrew clamps on the frame hold the blade tips. Distance between clamps should be adjusted so that when you press the frame ends slightly toward each other and clamp a blade in position, the frame will spring back enough to pull the blade taut.

It should be noted that the degree of blade tension is often a matter of personal choice. Some craftsmen prefer more or less tension than

COARSER BLADES can be used for cutting wood, but because of set, they often do not clear themselves.

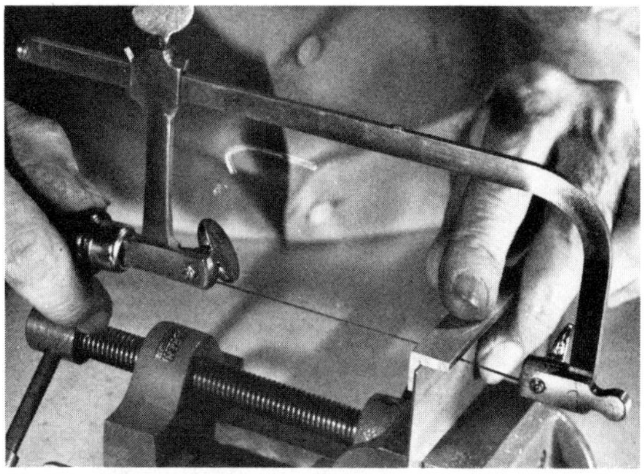

TO PREVENT BLADE WANDER, cut groove on under side, hold piece so groove is at cut starting point.

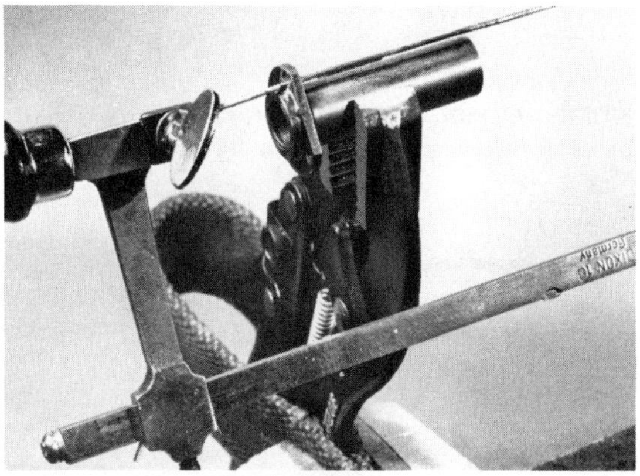

COPPER WIRE installed in frame can be used as lap for smoothing, increases clearance in small grooves.

RIVET often can be removed—with less damage—by slicing off projecting part with a jeweler's saw.

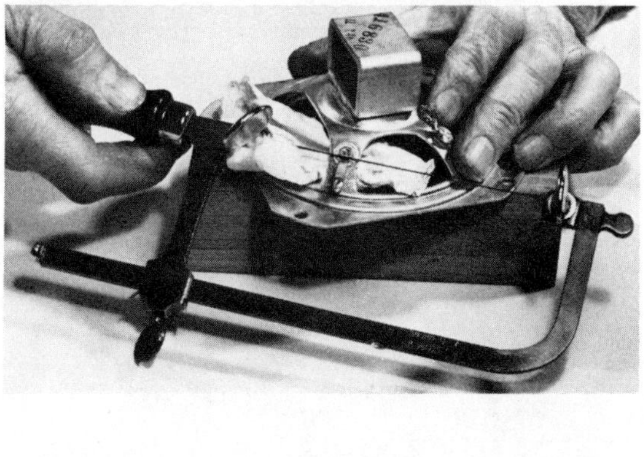

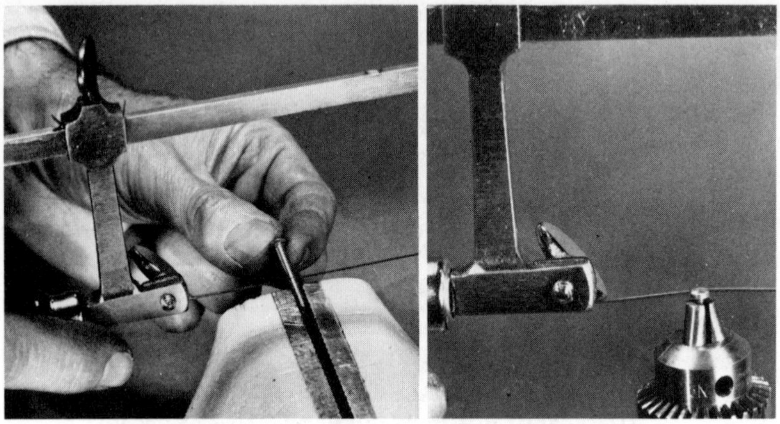

CHUNK OF BOLT can be whacked off (left) without leaving any burrs. Screw slot (right) clogged by paint or rust is quickly cleaned.

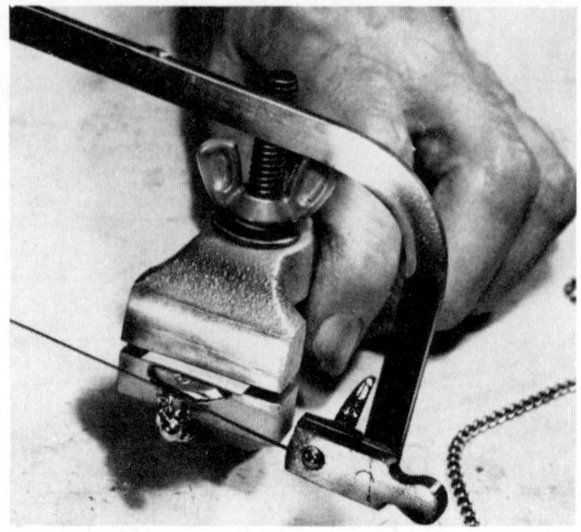

PENDANT is easily cut from an earring. Work should be held in a small vise.

WORK TO BE SAWED is normally rested on wooden bench with saw operated to cut on the down stroke.

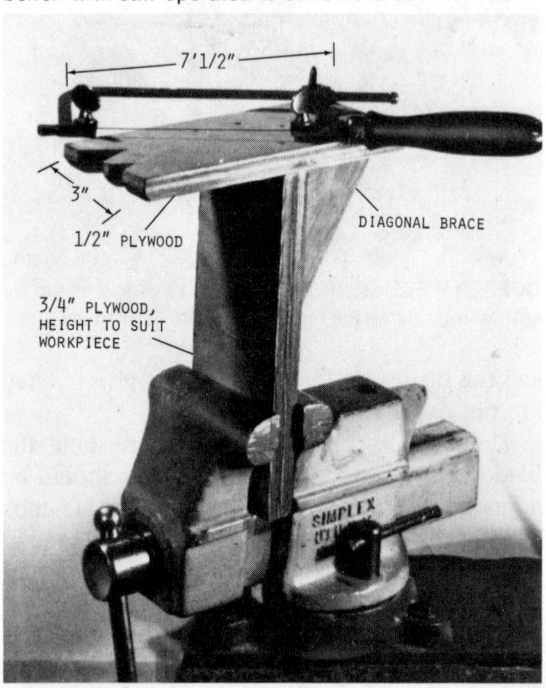

a fellow sawyer would. A good rule of thumb is to tension the blade so that when plucked like a guitar string, it will emit a moderately high "ping."

The term "piercing" originated from the use of the tool in making delicately pierced work in metal. To do this, the blade is threaded through a predrilled hole and then used to cut an opening of the desired (usually irregular) shape.

A number of uses for a jeweler's saw are illustrated on these pages. As the pictures show, they can be used on such jobs as jewelry work, light wood and metal-cutting jobs, centerhole cutting and shortening bolts.

As with conventional hacksaw work, more effective cutting action can be maintained if the blade is kept lubricated. You may find that wax tends to trap chips between teeth, thus slowing cutting action a bit, but it does reduce friction and thus increases blade life. One source for frames and blades is William Dixon, Inc. 32-42 Kinney St., Box 89, Newark, NJ 07101.

OPENING can be cut in the center of a large piece of work by first drilling pilot holes at four corners.

TO CUT STRAIGHT LINE in sheet metal, clamp parallel strips such as lathe-bit blanks shown.

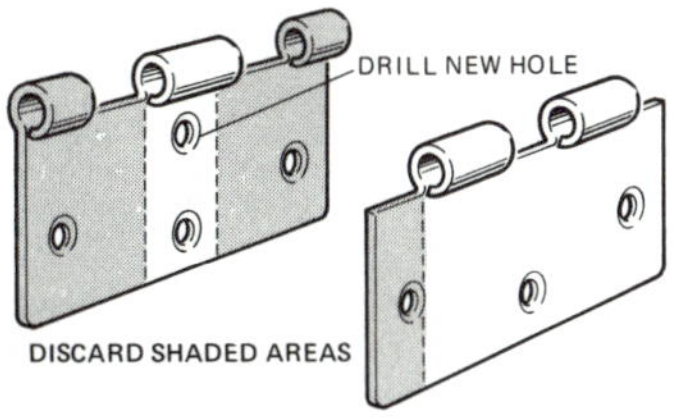

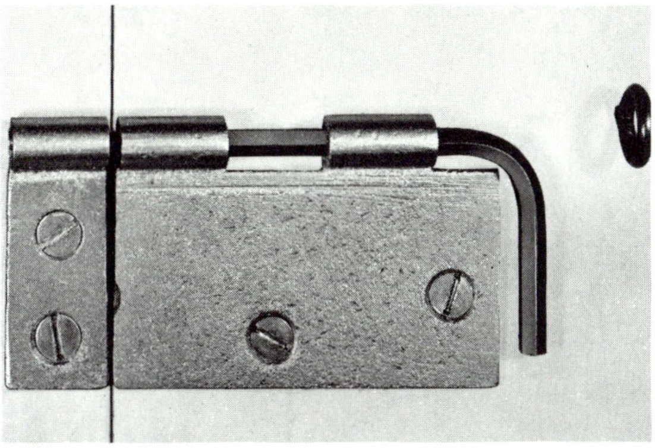

A DOOR OR CABINET can be secured with a bolt latch made from a removable-pin butt hinge, an L-shaped Allen wrench and a screw eye. The screw eye acts as a stop to keep the wrench from being pulled out too far, yet can be turned to release the wrench when it is needed for its original purpose.—*Walter E. Burton, Akron, OH.*

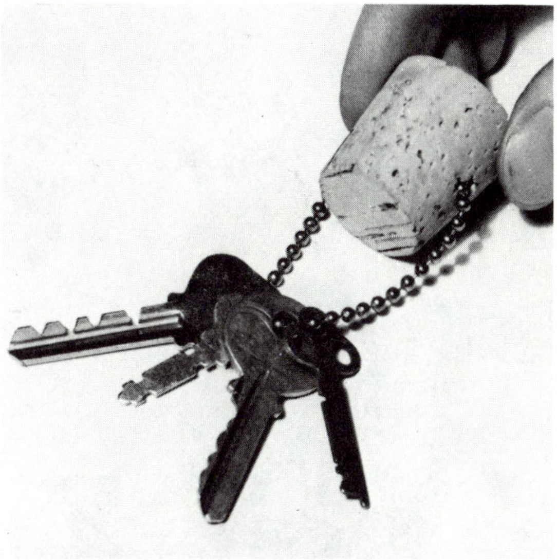

WHEN BOATING, fishing or working around water, it's a good idea to take this simple precaution against losing your keys. String a large cork on the chain to keep your keys afloat. Or you can keep chain and cork in your boat and attach them to your regular key ring before going out on the water.—*William Swallow, Brooklyn, NY.*

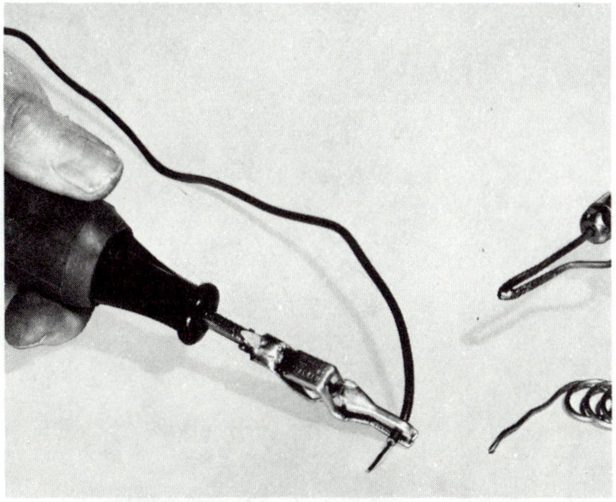

AN ALLIGATOR CLIP soldered to the end of an old, small screwdriver is an extremely versatile tool. I use it to hold wires for soldering, especially in hard-to-reach places. It is also useful for lighting candles in deep vases.—*George Hagstrom, Stevens Point, WI.*

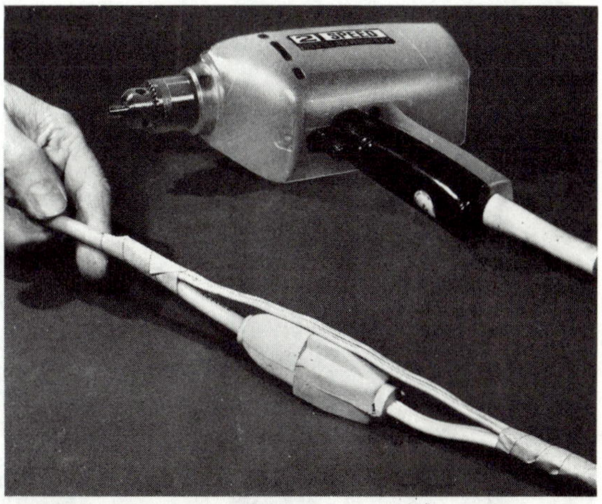

IF YOU CAN'T FIND a regular "cord connector" for reinforcing extension-cord connections, you can make one from a length of lamp cord or small rope and masking tape. When no longer needed, the reinforcement is quickly removed by peeling off the tape.—*W. B. May, Oak Park, IL.*

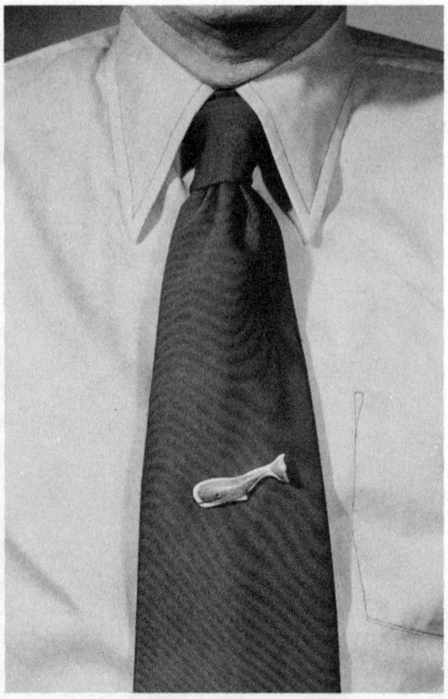

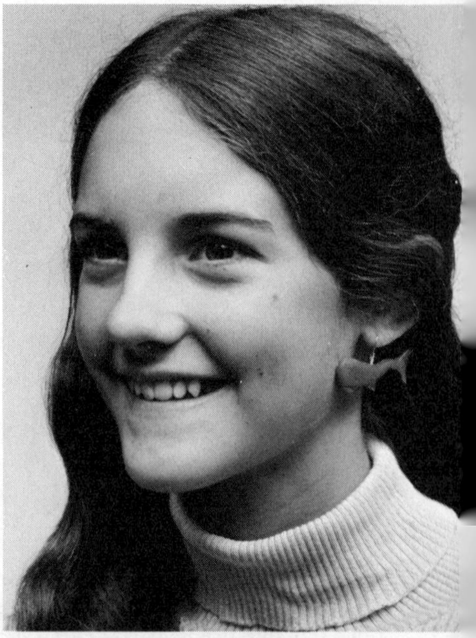

THE CARVINGS SHOWN in the top photograph are of wood, plexiglass, veneers or combinations of these. You can duplicate some of these shapes using the grid drawin on page 1676. The peace dove pendant on the left is of white plexiglass on tinted plas suspended from a rawhide thong. The whale tie-tack, above left, was created using two woods. The rounded-off edges reveal the lighter backup piece. The same carving c the whale is red plexiglass, above right, was used for earrings.

Jewelry you can carve

These mini carvings actually take shape right in your hands. You can create the jewelry you see here from a few scraps of material and the tools described. Here's a step-by-step explanation of how it's done

By JOHN GAYNOR and HARRY WICKS

THESE MINIATURES can be carved, from start to finish, on a kitchen table, so you won't need a king-sized workshop for the project. And the nature of the job requires just a small amount of material—even scraps which you probably have on hand can be used. Further, the tools that make it all possible are available at reasonable cost.

Mini carving is a wise choice for beginners. Unlike sculpture, you needn't be either an artist or an advanced craftsman to try your hand at it. As can be seen in the step-by-step photos showing the creation of an elephant in the round, a minimum number of steps is required. Because of their small size, any errors or imperfections will be virtually invisible. Ideas are easy to come by; encyclopedias, magazines and books are excellent sources for inspiration.

Carving in the flat. Actually, some of these pieces are not carvings at all. Letters, the peace dove and the like are simply drawn on a piece of wood from 1/8 to 3/16 in. thick and then cut

SEE ALSO
Gifts, Christmas . . . Internal carving . . . Jewelry boxes . . . Jigsaws . . . Lapidary . . . Marquetry . . . Mobiles . . . Plexiglass projects . . . Wood sculpture

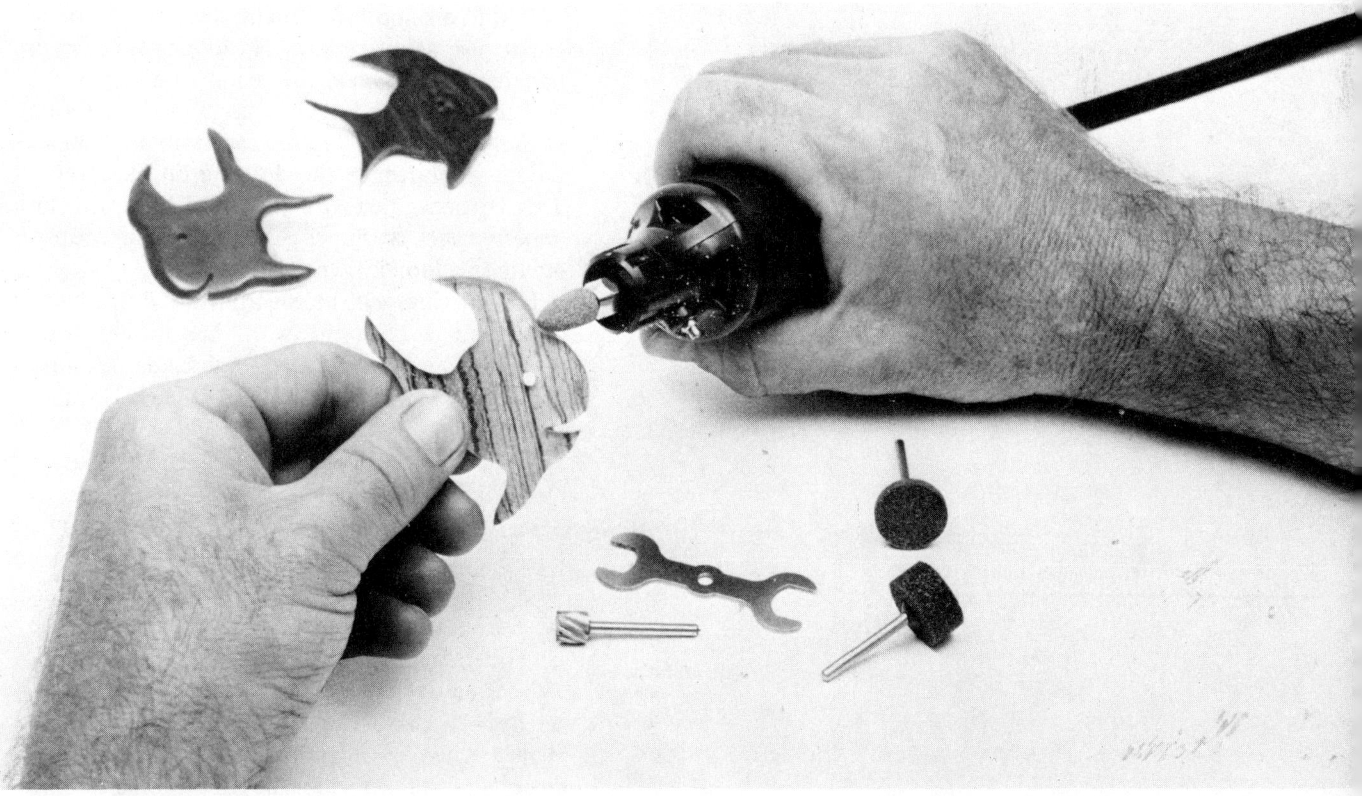

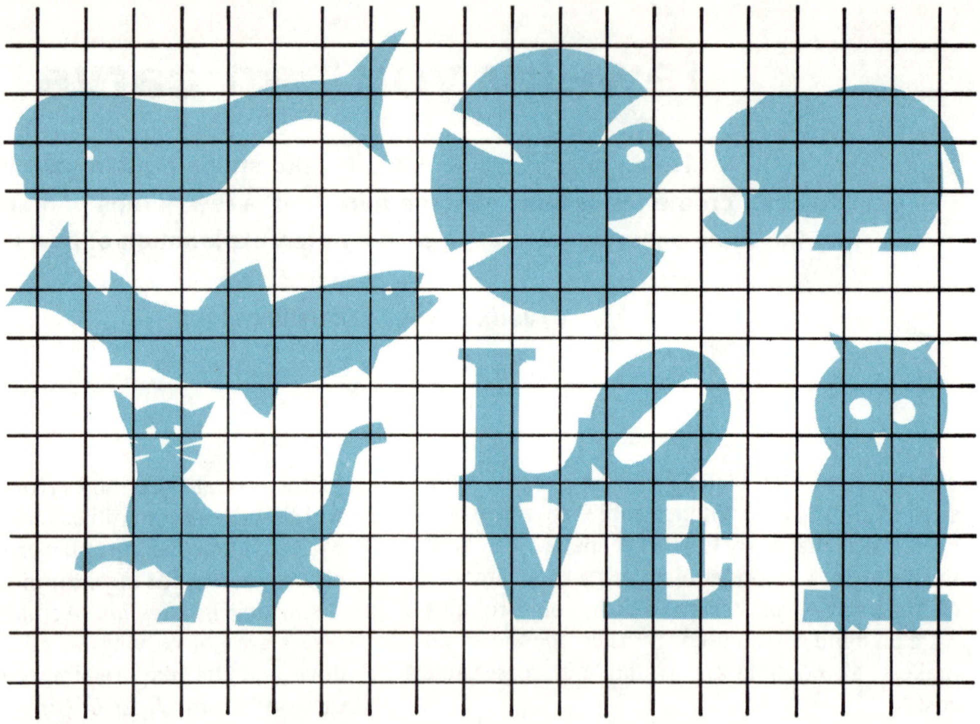

SOME OF THE articles shown on page **1556** were made using the patterns shown above. Using the square grid, you can adjust the size to fit your needs.

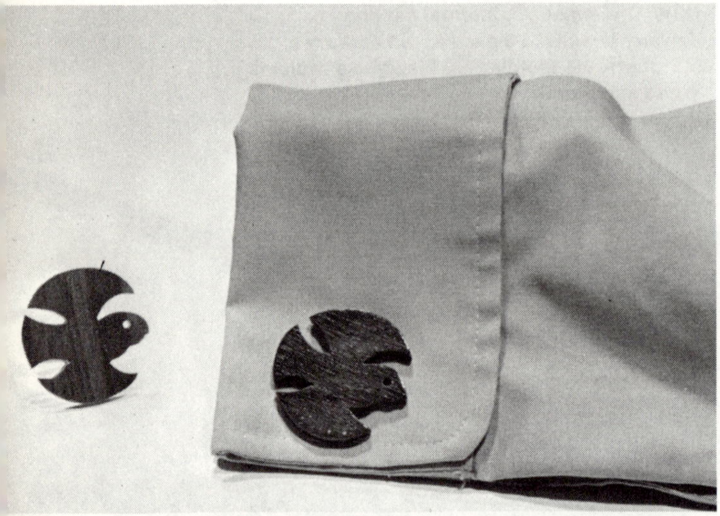

MASCULINE cuff links were "carved" on a jigsaw, sanded smooth, then glued to jewelry hardware.

continued from previous page

out on a jigsaw. The edges are then sanded and buffed to a smooth finish and the carving can be put to use as a pendant, pin or tie tack. For a hanging piece, such as the pendant on page 1556, you simply drill a hole and use a rawhide thong as the "necklace." Or, you can fashion a hanger mount as shown in the drawing on page 1560. This is then glued in a predrilled hole with an adhesive such as Super Strength. The appropriate finding loop is then attached.

Flat carvings can be cut from wood or plastic or a combination of the two. When cutting plexiglass with a jigsaw, use a 14-tooth blade. (A finer blade causes heat which welds the plastic behind the saw cut.)

To glue veneer to plastic or plastic to plastic, we found that Daybond Thickened Cement worked best. Apply cement liberally to the surfaces to be joined and clamp the piece overnight between two pieces of wood. Make certain the wood is separated from the workpiece with wax paper because glue oozes out as the clamp pressure is increased.

Next day, remove the hardened excess glue using a sharp knife. The flat is now ready to saw to shape. After sawing, sand and buff the edges smooth. Drill the hole for the hanger if the carving

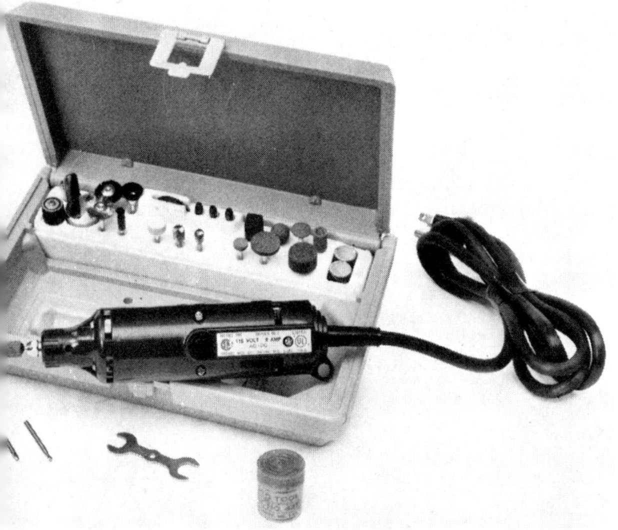

BASIC TOOL used for the carvings is the Dremel Moto-Tool which comes in a 34-piece kit including wrench. Tungsten carbide bits are extras.

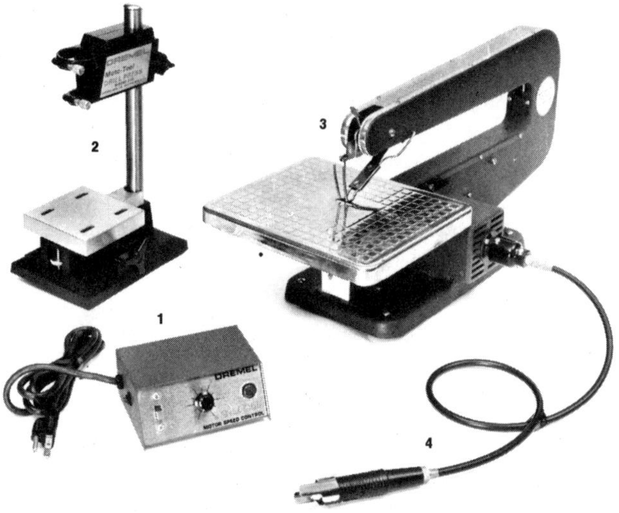

OTHER TOOLS that will speed work: 1. variable-speed control; 2. drill-press accessory; 3. Moto Shop jigsaw; and, 4. flexible shaft (used with jigsaw).

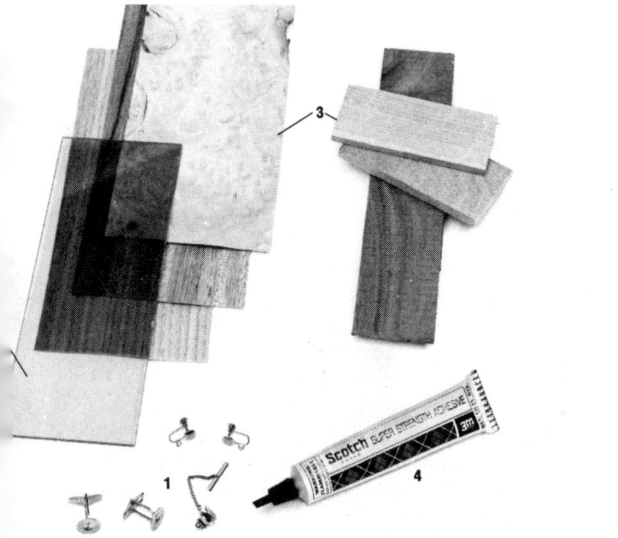

MATERIALS used: 1. jewelry findings (cuff links, earrings, tie-tack shown); 2. plexiglass; 3. veneers, solid wood; and, 4. glue to affix carvings to hardware.

CARVINGS shown above are examples of plastic glued to plastic (top), wood to plastic, and plastic glued over veneer. Use Daybond Thickened Cement.

is to be a necklace or simply glue the carving to the appropriate jewelry finding with Super Strength Adhesive. For a hand-rubbed look, we found that a clear plastic coating, the type which comes in an aerosol container, works best. Three light coats are better than one thick one. It is also best to spray flat pieces with them lying down rather than suspended—when the first side is dry, flop the piece and spray the second side.

Carving in the round. Though three-dimensional carving is slightly more difficult than flat carving, it is also more satisfying. For these carvings, use thicker stock—5/16 to 3/8 in. Steps for carving in the round are shown in the photos. After cutting out the shape, use the powered carver and various cutters to begin rough shaping to give the piece form in the third dimension. Although cutter No. 194 is not included in the kit,

TRANSFER the design from grid paper to a wood block using carbon paper beneath the drawing. Tape the carbon and drawing so they can't shift.

CUT THE figure out with the jigsaw. The stock for the elephant is cherry, 5/16 in. thick. Using the blade guard helps you reduce chatter.

MOUNT THE carving tool in the drill press accessory and drill the eyehole first. Unlike large presses, this one's head remains stationary. The work table is raised to the drill with the knob.

CARVING starts with knurled cutter (No. 194 shown). The shop-built jig facilitates handling the small piece. Jig (below) is gripped in a vise.

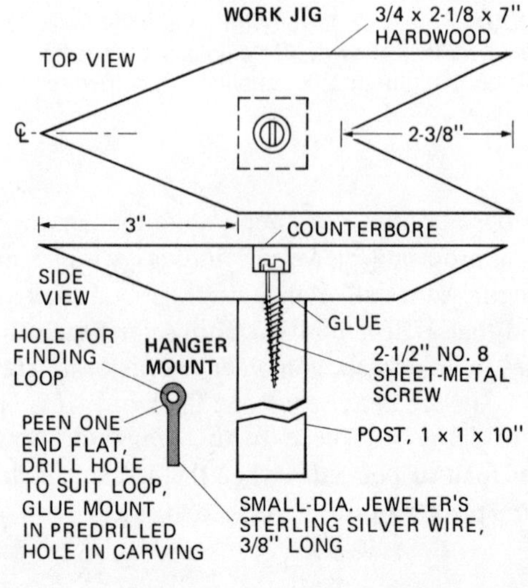

AFTER ROUGH shaping, grind the carving smooth with an emery-point dressing wheel. Since the form is hand-held, power carving calls for extra care.

THE FINISHED gift from the workbench is ready for gift-wrapping. For looks, line the box with black velvet around a card or tissue as shown.

TO FINISH, the carving is polished with buffing rouge and a cloth pad chucked in the tool. The pad is recharged by dipping it in the rouge.

Manufacturers of Materials

Tools: Moto-Tool kit No. 281 (about $55), Moto Shop No. 571 (about $60), and accessories. Dremel Mfg. Co., Dept. PM, Box 518, Racine, WI 53401.

Jewelry findings: American Handicrafts Co., Dept. PM, 1011 Foch St., Fort Worth, TX 76107.

Wood and veneers (by mail order): Albert Constantine and Sons, 2050 Eastchester Rd., Bronx, N. Y. 10461. Also, Craftsman's Wood Service, 2727 South Mary St., Chicago, IL 60608.

Plexiglas and Daybond Cement: Rohm and Haas Co., Dept. PM, Philadelphia, PA 19105.

Super Strength Adhesive: Adhesives Div., 3M Center, St. Paul, MN 55101.

Clear plastic coating: No. 1301, Krylon Div. of Borden, 50 West Broad St., Columbus, OH 43216.

NOTE: All items listed above, except for woods and veneers, are available at hobby, hardware and department stores. If you have difficulty obtaining a product, locate nearest source by writing direct to the manufacturer at address given above.

we found it best for this stage of carving.

Keep in mind that the Moto-Tool's cutter rotates at 30,000 rpm. And since the carving is small, thus fingertip held, care should be taken to keep fingers clear of the cutter's path. Never start a cut from the end and work toward the middle; always start a cut in a "meat" portion of the wood and progress shaping toward an end. If you start a cut at the end grain, the tool may jump in the opposite direction. Also, don't try to cut away too much wood in one pass. A series of light passes is easier to control and permits more graceful shaping.

final finishing

With the piece roughed out, start smoothing using a grinder such as No. 992 or 997. For this step, using the variable-speed control, adjust the tool speed to lower rpm. High rpm will leave burn marks on wood and plexiglass. To sand hard-to-get-at spots, trim an emery board to a point. When satisfied with the smoothness, spray the piece with a clear plastic coating. When completely dry, polish the piece with the buffing wheel and polishing rouge as shown in Step 6.

These mini carvings make excellent gifts for Christmas or birthday giving. The ideas shown here are just some of many possibilities. Use your imagination. Try making a peace pendant or dove for a teenager, a lapel pin for your wife, or a fish tie-tack for any anglers you know. To give the carvings that expensive jewelry look for gift giving, wrap them in boxes lined with black velvet.

Jewelry box fit for a queen

Made of rare woods and featuring a Swiss musical movement, this craftsman's work of art is sure to be an appreciated gift. And it may very possibly become a treasured family heirloom

By TOM H. JONES

■ THERE COMES A TIME in any serious woodworker's career when he has a desire to build pieces that his family will treasure. An anniversary gift for his wife, perhaps, or a graduation present for his daughter. Maybe the daughter will cherish and eventually pass it on to *her* daughter. This jewelry box is just such a project.

Surprisingly, it is a lot easier to build than a first look may imply. It features a case veneered on all sides and a single-tune musical movement which plays when the lid is opened. Though veneering requires care and accurate cutting, none of the steps is particularly difficult if you take your time.

• *Panels.* Cut all veneer blanks slightly oversize. And, since it is brittle, the face of thuya, or any fragile crotch or burl veneer, should be taped (masking or kraft) near all edges and across any cracks before you cut it with a knife or veneer saw. Apply white glue liberally to the veneer (remember, keep the taped side outside) and affix the veneer to hardboard. Clamp this between waxed paper and cauls and, applying pressure slowly, work from the center out.

Trim the oversize veneer blanks to remove loose veneer and excess glue from edges, peel off tape and rough-sand the veneer to remove all glue that has seeped through. Finish the blanks by trimming to dimensions shown in the drawing.

Cut oversize backing panels from plywood and glue them to the back of each veneered panel. Trim the plywood panels flush with veneered panels on all sides, except the ends of the back panel which are trimmed 1/16 in. oversize to fit the grooves in the rear corner posts.

• *Drawers.* Cut three blanks for drawer fronts from ¼-in. hardboard and veneer them with thuya. After rough-sanding the veneered blanks, trim two of them for drawers and the third for the false drawer. Glue rosewood veneer to all four edges of the two drawer fronts and sand these to size. Now remove ¼ in. of thuya from all four sides of the three draw fronts with a sharp chisel and glue the inlay border in place. Locate knob screw holes, stack and clamp the drawer fronts and drill the holes.

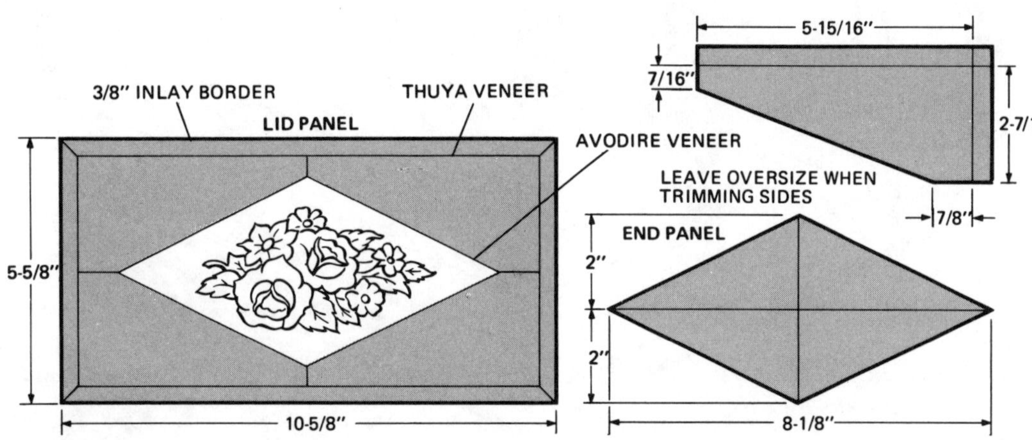

SEE ALSO

Comb boxes . . . Drawers . . . Gifts, Christmas . . . Gifts, Valentine . . . Jewelry . . . Marquetry . . . Veneering . . . Woods

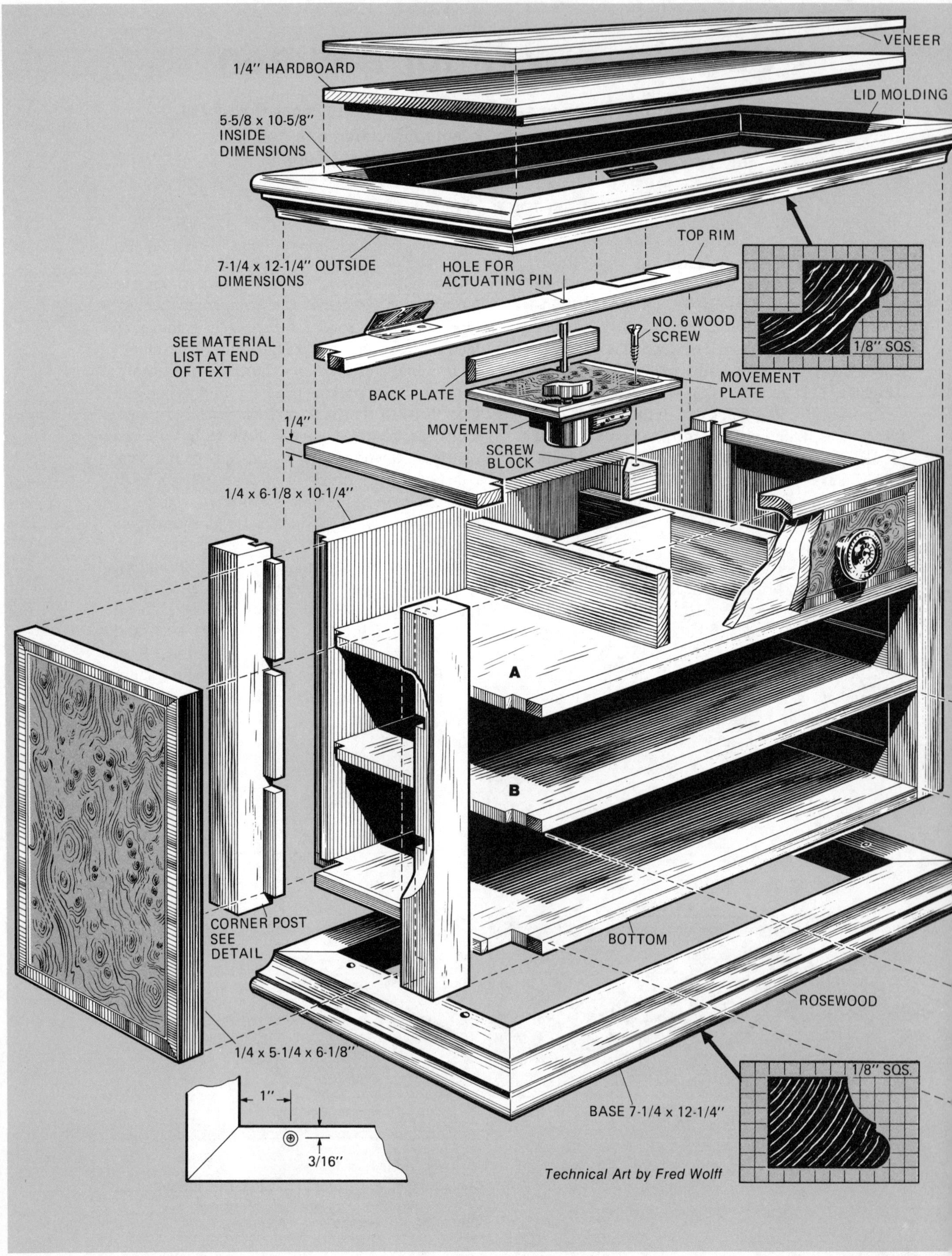
VENEER
1/4'' HARDBOARD
LID MOLDING
5-5/8 x 10-5/8''
INSIDE
DIMENSIONS
7-1/4 x 12-1/4'' OUTSIDE
DIMENSIONS
TOP RIM
HOLE FOR
ACTUATING PIN
NO. 6 WOOD
SCREW
1/8'' SQS.
SEE MATERIAL
LIST AT END
OF TEXT
BACK PLATE
MOVEMENT
PLATE
MOVEMENT
1/4''
SCREW
BLOCK
1/4 x 6-1/8 x 10-1/4''
A
B
CORNER POST
SEE
DETAIL
BOTTOM
ROSEWOOD
1/4 x 5-1/4 x 6-1/8''
1''
3/16''
BASE 7-1/4 x 12-1/4''
1/8'' SQS.
Technical Art by Fred Wolff

Drawer parts are of ¼-in. mahogany and ⅛-in. plywood. Glue drawer fronts to the drawers with the bottom edges flush. Redrill the knob screw holes and countersink them on the inside (later a layer of velveteen will cover the screwheads).

• *Lid and base.* Select the portion of floral inlay to be used and carefully trim away mahogany background and unwanted portions with a sharp chisel. Then, lay out the pattern for the avodire diamond shape on white paper. Center the floral inlay and trace the outline with a sharp pencil. Cut avodire veneer and two pieces of scrap veneer and glue the pattern to one piece of the scrap veneer. Sandwich the avodire veneer between the scrap pieces and tape the edges securely.

With a fine blade in your scroll saw, cut out the floral pattern and taped veneers together. After you cut to the outside of the diamond pattern, carefully separate the avodire veneer from scrap.

• *Movement.* A little trial-and-error fitting is in order here. Before cutting blanks or drilling any holes, refer to the movement that you have on

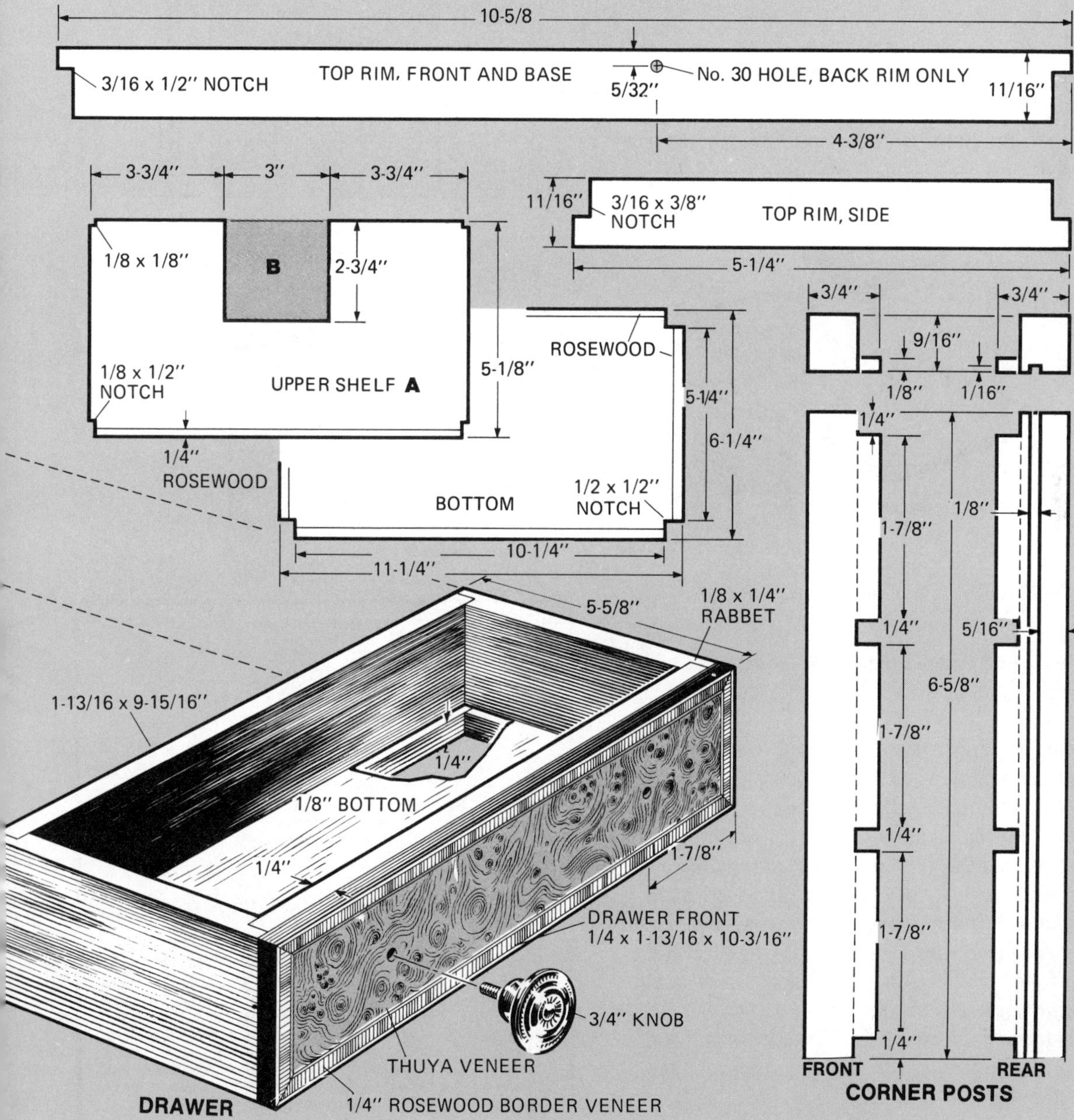

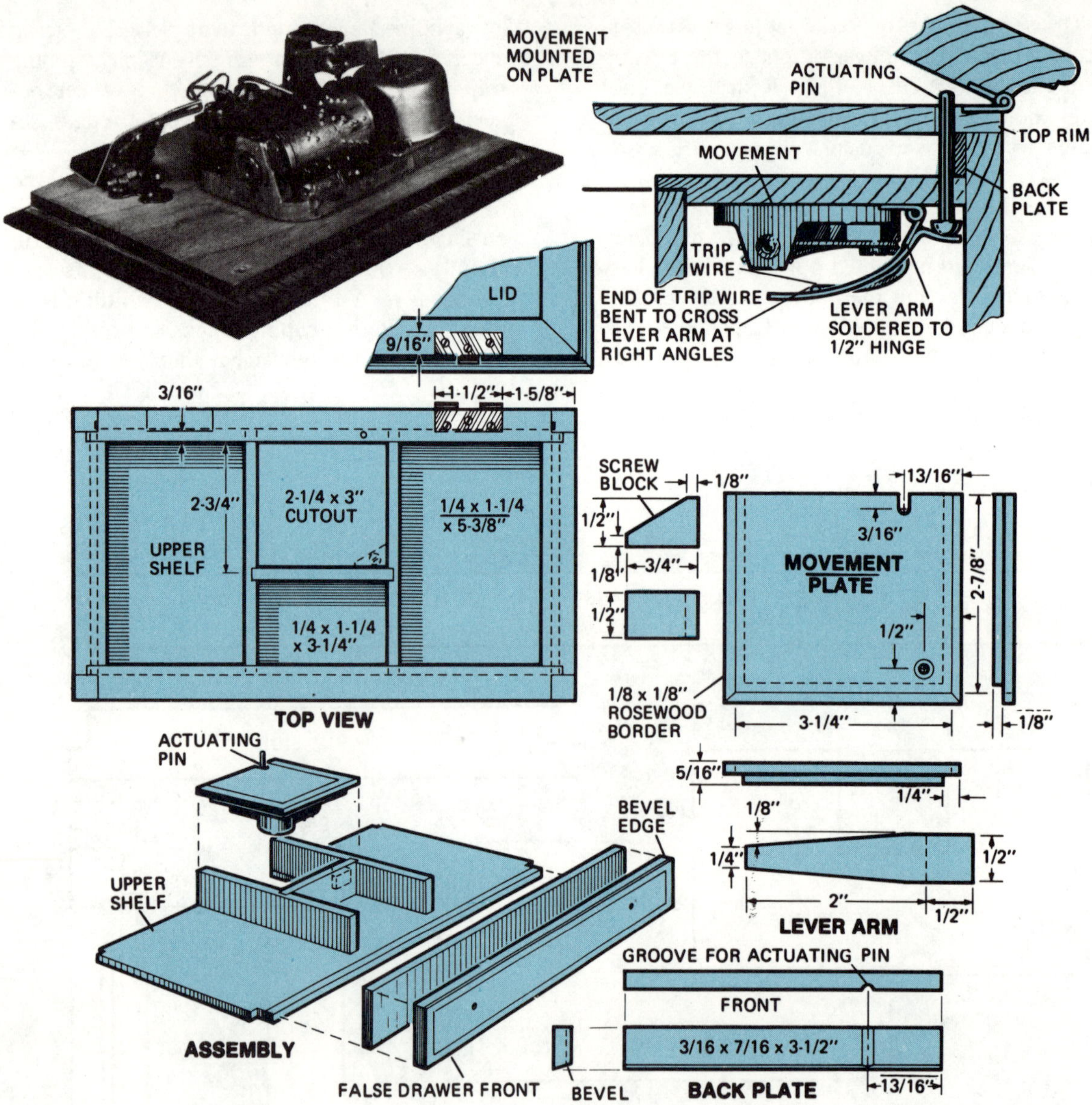

hand and determine dimensions from it. (They may vary from those of the model used in the prototype.)

• *Finish.* To finish your jewel box fill any imperfections with a wood paste such as Duratite, using colors to match adjacent wood. After sanding, dust thoroughly and apply five coats of clear lacquer diluted 20 percent with lacquer thinner. Allow each coat to dry completely, then sand lightly with 8/0 paper and dust with a tack-rag. Finally rub down the last coat with pumice and water, follow with rottenstone and water and wipe away all traces of powder.

Attach the hardware, line the drawers and top tray with velveteen glued over cardboard, then attach the base and hinge the lid to the box. Finally, install the movement and pin.

MATERIALS LIST

Amount	Description
5 sq. ft.	Thuya veneer
1 sq. ft.	Rosewood veneer
1 sq. ft.	Avodire veneer
1	Floral inlay (M111A)
15 ft.	¼" inlay border (56)
3 ft.	⅜" inlay border (6)
2 sq. ft.	¼" hardboard
2 sq. ft.	¼" birch plywood
3 sq. ft.	⅛" birch plywood
1 sq. ft.	¼" Honduras mahogany
1 pc.	¾ x 6 x 36" rosewood
1	Single-tune Swiss musical instrument
1 pr.	Narrow 1½" butt brass hinges
6	Brass knobs
1	Miniature brass hinge
1 pc.	.016 x ½ x 2½" brass sheet
Misc.	Red velveteen (for lining), white glue

Note: Numbers in parentheses are from catalog of Albert Constantine & Son, Inc., 2050 Eastchester Rd., Bronx, N.Y. 10461. Musical movements are available from Constantine, from Craftsman Wood Service, 2727 S. Mary St., Chicago, Ill. 60608, and other woodworking supply mail-order houses. Rearrangement of parts on the movement panel may be necessary to compensate for different locations of trip wires in various movements.

You can make these stunning jewel boxes as a gift or for yourself. Either way your craftsmanship and the beauty of the hardwood will make them projects to treasure

Two beautiful jewel boxes

By EVERETT JOHNSON

■ RUMMAGING AROUND in a large dresser drawer for a tiny cuff link is silly, but we all do it. How much smarter it would be to have one of these handsome man-size jewel boxes handy.

The miniature version of a full-size chest shown above appears to have nine individual drawers. Actually it's a fooler, it has only three. But they're long ones which make them all the more perfect for handkerchiefs, checkbooks and passport cases.

While having only two drawers, the jewel box on page 1568 also serves as an overnight caddy for holding the contents of one's pockets. Recesses in the top provide shallow trays for parking such things as a lighter and comb, a watch and wallet, loose change and a money clip.

Only choice cabinet woods should be used for such elegant boxes and nothing but your best craftsmanship. The box shown above was made of cherry; the other, of walnut. Both were hand-rubbed to a beautiful semiluster fininsh. The drawers are lined with plush velveteen.

The recessed top of the walnut box shown and detailed on page 1568 is a full inch thick. If you have trouble finding this thickness, you can build it up by gluing ¼-in. fir plywood to the bottom of ¾-in. walnut. The plywood will not be seen when the top is faced with the ⅜-in. strip across the front.

The sides fit rabbets cut in the ends of the top, and the ¼-in. drawer shelves fit dadoes and rabbets in the side members. The back also is housed in rabbets.

No knobs are used on the drawers, as finger grips are formed at the ends. The drawer fronts lap the side members as well as the shelves on which they slide.

The recessed trays in the top are made with a round-bottom, core-box bit chucked in a portable router. The router's fence attachment is used to keep the recesses parallel to the edges of the top. Work carefully, taking light cuts as you go until you reach a depth of ⅜-in. Then sand the recesses smooth. The drawers are made to slide freely in the openings, and a 1/16-in. clearance is left between the drawer fronts. For a somewhat different version of this same chest, including a different drawer—front treatment—see Vol. 9, page 1352.

The stunning cherry chest is actually the simpler of the two. The dadoes for the two notched shelves are stopped ¼-in. from the front, while

SEE ALSO

Drawers . . . Gifts, Christmas . . . Gifts, Valentine . . . Jewelry . . . Joinery . . . Marquetry . . . Routers

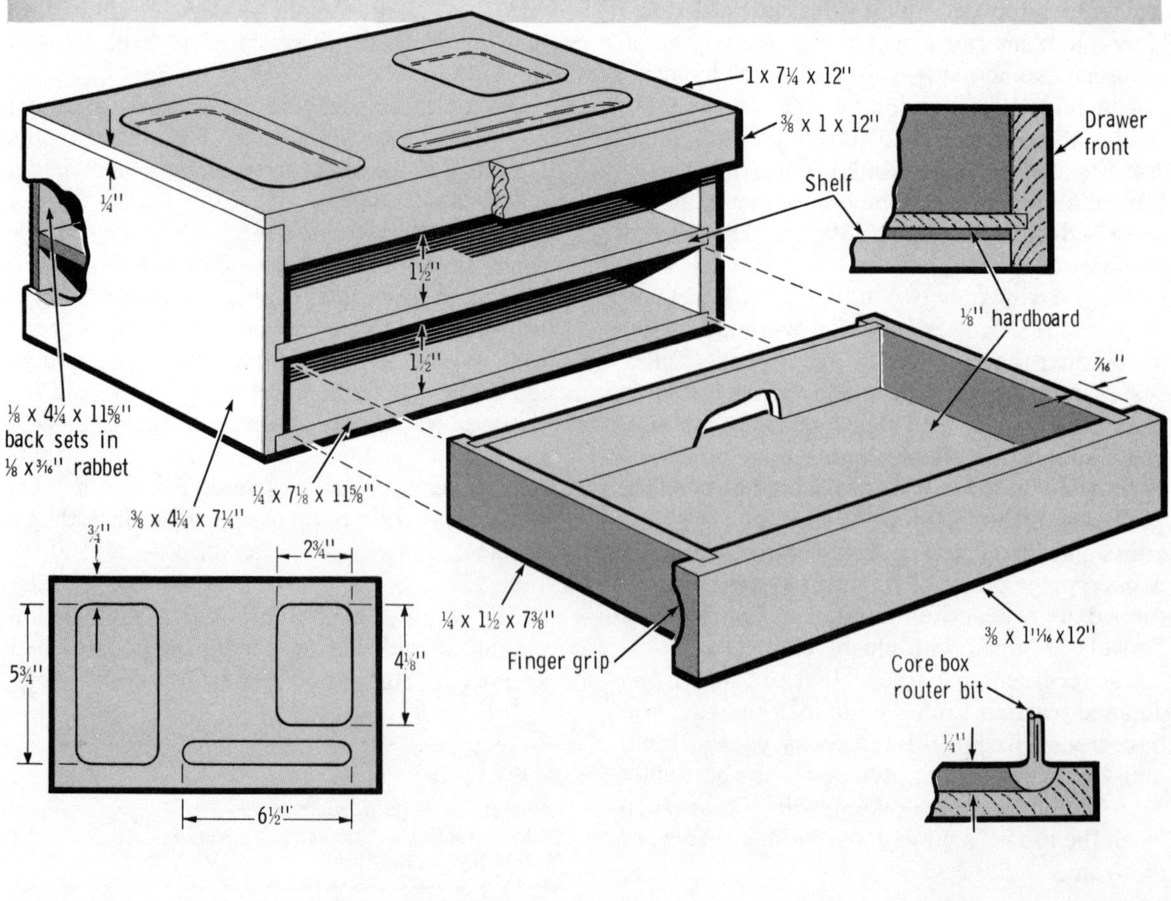
1 x 7¼ x 12''
⅜ x 1 x 12''
Drawer front
Shelf
¼''
1½''
1½''
⅛'' hardboard
7/16''
⅛ x 4¼ x 11⅝'' back sets in ⅛ x 3/16'' rabbet
¼ x 7⅛ x 11⅝''
⅜ x 4¼ x 7¼''
¾''
2¾''
5¾''
4⅛''
¼ x 1½ x 7⅜''
⅜ x 1 11/16 x 12''
Finger grip
Core box router bit
¼''
6½''

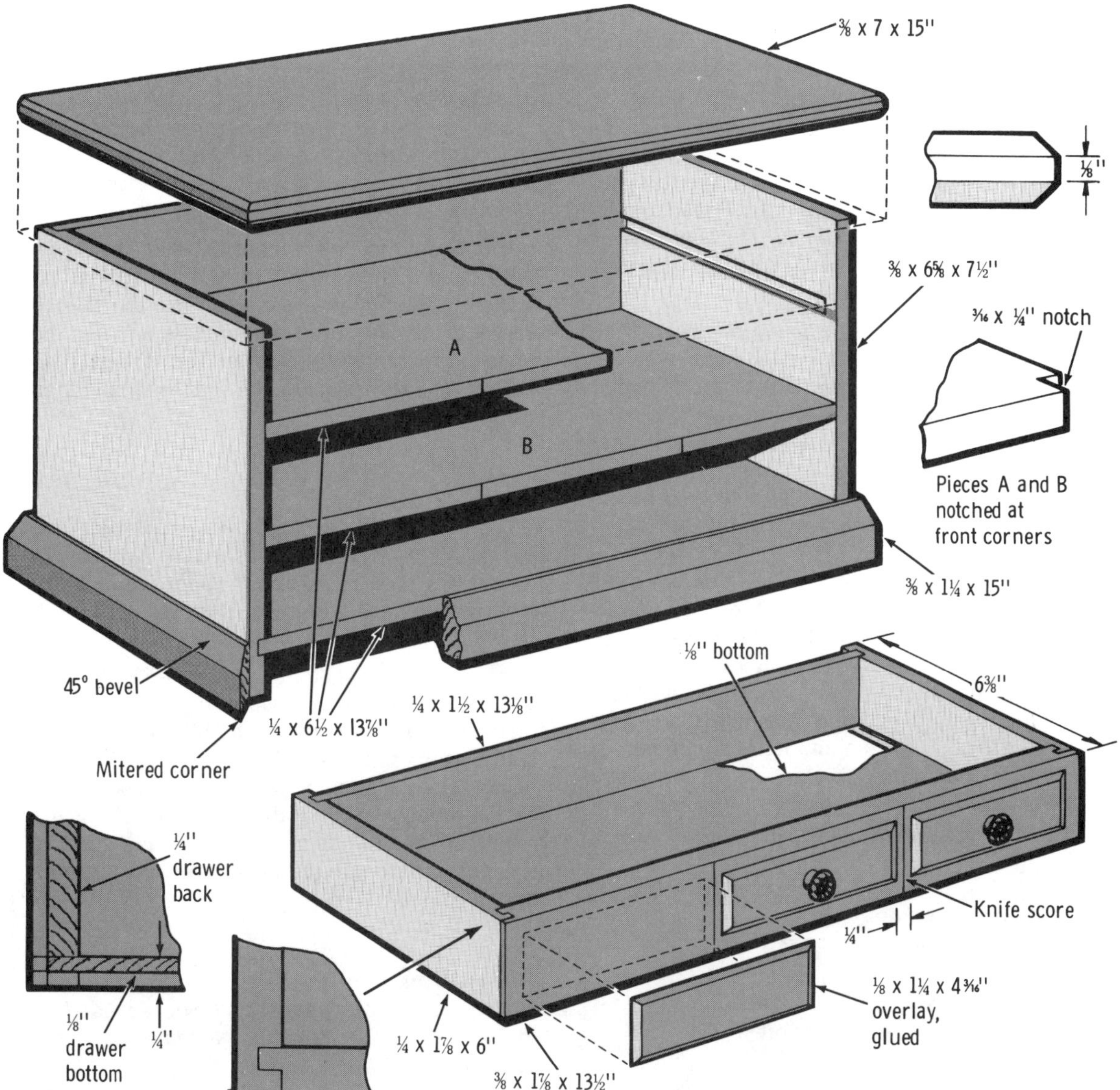

CORNER JOINT

the bottom dado runs through. The ⅛-in. back joins the sides in rabbets. The flush-fitting drawers differ from the others in the way the side join the fronts.

Beveled glued-on overlays create the look of individual drawers. Knife cuts scored across the faces of the drawers, as well as the dividing rails, make the illusion even greater. Actually, the drawers are set in ⅛ in.

The top can be pinned to the sides with short dowels or glued in ¼-in. dadoes cut on the underside. In the latter case, the height of the end members is made ¼ in. greater than that dimensioned. The back is likewise made ¼ in. higher to fit a stopped rabbet cut along the rear edge.

When you have the chest completed, sand the surfaces glass-smooth, using progressively finer grades of garnet paper. Sand the drawers before adding the overlays. Finally, stain and finish as desired, then drill the holes for tiny knobs.

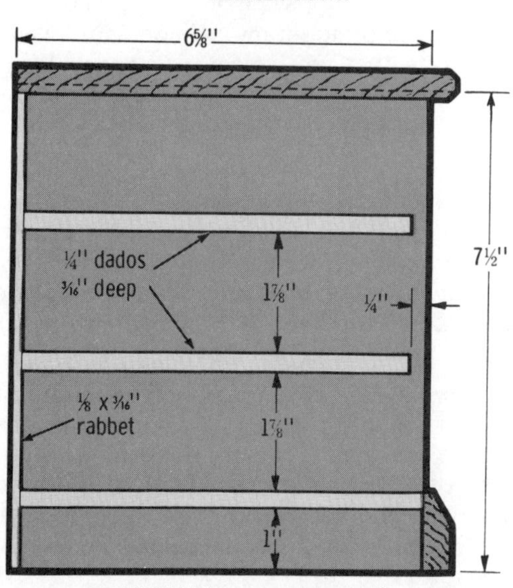

SECTION VIEW (end removed)

Cedar shakes over old roof

My asphalt-shingle roof is nearing the end of its normal life and I want to install a cedar-shake roofing. The deck, of boards laid edge-to-edge, seems to be in good condition. Do I need to take off the old shingles or can I lay the shakes over them? Should I replace the felt undercovering? If so, with what?—N.O., Ohio.

I would remove the old shingles—everything right down to the decking—then go over the decking to make sure no boards are loose or cupped. The latter should be replaced and the former nailed securely. Any deck boards that seem deteriorated, rotted, full of knots or otherwise defective due to aging should also be replaced. It's important to provide a solid nailing surface for shakes.

While you can use an ordinary felt undercovering, or liner, this may tend to prevent the underside of shakes from drying. I would, rather, install the "breather-type" liner usually recommended for use under shakes. This should be available through your local building materials dealer, and laid according to the manufacturer's recommendations. If you do the job yourself, be especially careful to avoid splits or hammer dents and make sure you use the right nails.

Unwinding lipped door

I have a grandfather's clock with a lipped access door so warped it can't be closed easily. The door is in one piece, without glass, and has two hinges and a lock. I want to preserve the original, but how can I get rid of the warp?—G.M., Va.

By "warp" you mean the "wind" or twist; that is, if you remove the door and lay it on a flat surface, it will rock when touched on alternate high corners. To eliminate it, run saw kerfs diagonally across the back of the door from low corner to low corner. Space kerfs ½ to ¾ in. apart for a width of 3 to 4 in., depending on the door's size and width. If you have no table saw, try to enlist the help of a friend who has one. You'll have to improvise a guide and then space the cuts by moving the ripping fence after each pass. Ordinarily, the cuts should be run to a depth of ¾ in. or slightly less than the door thickness. As a rule, such cuts will relieve the stresses that produced the wind.

Lay the door on a flat surface, weight it down and rip thin strips that will just drop into the kerfs without wedging. Glue these into the strips and let the glue dry thoroughly. Then trim and sand the strips flush. You can color them to match the old wood by rubbing them with a combination of artists' oil colors.

Shades stay up

Several large window shades in my home won't stay down—they won't catch and hold in any position. The shades are not old, torn or discolored. What's wrong?—Mrs. R. M. Lamb, Chicago.

It is likely that the ratchet ends of the rollers have been filled with lint, or that the springs installed in them have loosened. Take the shades down, brush lint out of the ratchets and use the tines of an old fork to retighten the springs. If no parts are bent or missing, the shades should then work properly.

Veneer lifting

I've stripped a chest of drawers which is veneered. With the remover washed off, some of the veneer has come loose and the edges have lifted. What happened, and what do I do next?—R. Dewey, Tulsa, Okla.

It is quite possible that you dampened the glue under the veneer and, thus, softened it enough to make it let go in places. I'd try lifting the veneer with a sharp chisel, and forcing new glue underneath. Then clamp plywood on top, with wax paper in between, until the glue dries. If blisters result, slit each at its center, force glue through the slits underneath the veneer, and weight until dry.

The best shade tree

What would you suggest as the best shade tree to plant to provide maximum shade?—Ralf Cozzens, Indianapolis.

I'd plant sugar maple. It's a slow-growing hardwood to be sure, but if well cared for, it develops a spreading, symmetrical top and its autumn leaf coloring, in my opinion, is unrivaled. Make sure that you select a well developed, balled specimen and remember to ask your nurseryman for tips on planting it.

Paint peels from plaster patch

A roof leak has led to a plaster patch on a bedroom ceiling. I painted this patch with the same paint that was used originally on the ceiling. Now the paint is peeling. How can I solve this problem?—J.E. Snelling, Denver.

I'm afraid you didn't wait long enough for the plaster to dry thoroughly. This takes time, as much as two months or more, depending on local conditions. Scrape and sand off all the loose paint, wait another month or so, then apply an undercoater or shellac, and repaint it. You'll likely have no further trouble.

Minicourse: the rabbet and dado

DADO AND RABBET joints increase contact area and thus are stronger than butt joints. For dado joint, one board should be a slip fit in the groove—too tight a joint can produce undue stress.

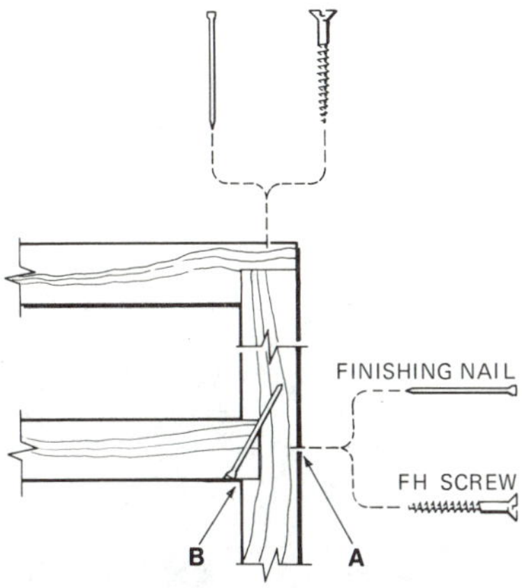

JOINTS ARE SECURED with glue and either nails or screws (dowels can be substituted if preferred). Dado can be fastened using method A or B. The latter technique makes the joint fastening invisible.

SIMPLE WAY to attach a drawer front: Sides are let into L-shaped rabbet in front and nails are driven through sides into and parallel to front to assure maximum resistance against pullout.

THREE WAYS to make a butt joint strong. The metal corner brace is store-bought. The triangular and square glue blocks can be made right in the shop. Use these where they won't show.

AFTER THE BUTT JOINT, it's a pretty safe bet that the two most common joints in woodworking are the rabbet and dado.

The L-shaped rabbet is used in most simple projects, cases, boxes and the like. If you work with sharp cutters and saw blades, you can produce very neat-looking rabbet joints using either two passes on the table saw, or a rabbet cutter in your router. Plough the groove slightly wider than needed and sand smooth the 1/32 in. or so overhang after the glue has dried.

The U-shaped dado provides gripping action of the groove and more gluing surface than the butt joint.

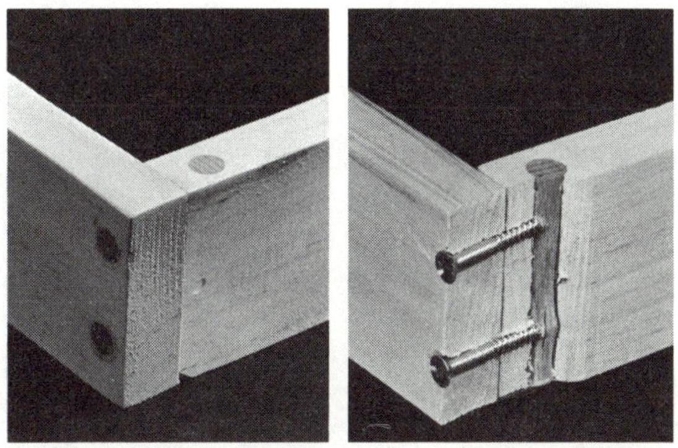

A BUTT JOINT is weak because fasteners have a tendency to pull out. Dowel in the second piece, at 90° to fastener, eliminates this problem (left). Joint to the right was cut away on the bandsaw to show how screws get a bulldog bite.

NEATER-LOOKING drawer joint is obtained by ploughing an L-shaped rabbet across ends of drawer front and sides. Joint is stronger because end-grain contact for both pieces is cut by 50 percent.

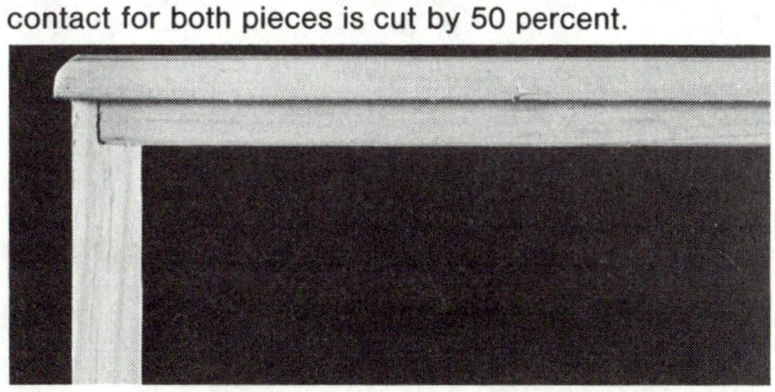

SEE ALSO

Dovetail joints . . . Drawers . . . Miter boards . . . Miter joints . . . Moldings . . . Shop techniques

How to make professional dowel joints

By DAVID WARREN and HARRY WICKS

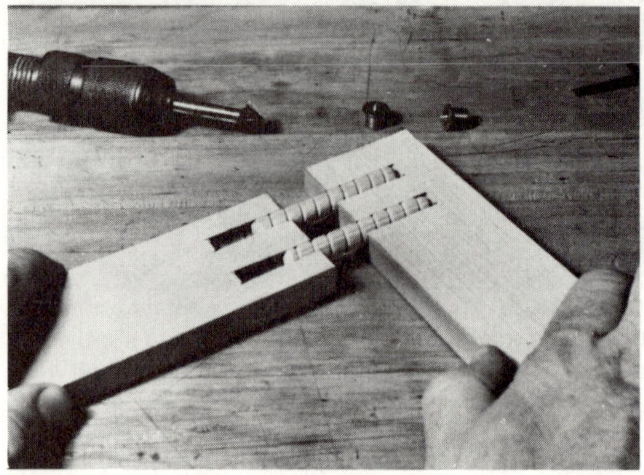

FOR MAXIMUM shear strength, dowel diameter should be half the thickness of the wood being joined and dowel length six to eight times its diameter.

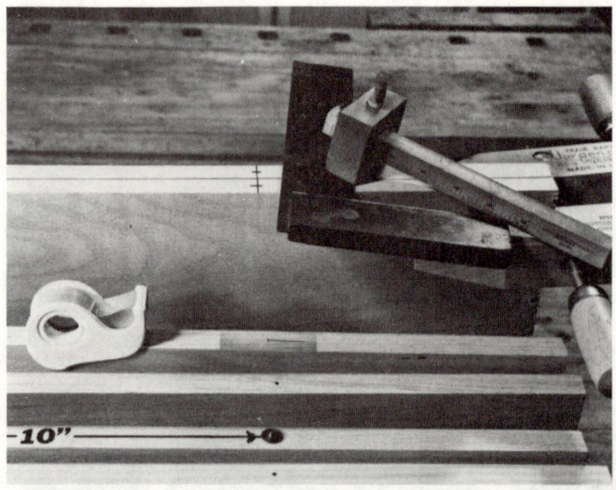

THREE WAYS to lay out dowel centers: (at top) gauge and try square, (in middle) tape and pinheads, and (at the bottom) drilled holes and dowel centers.

COUNTERSINK DRILLED holes to remove any burr that might hold joint apart, also to facilitate the board assembly and to permit excess glue to escape.

■ THE FAMILIAR dowel joint, now centuries old, is a good substitute for a mortise-and-tenon or a tongue-and-groove joint and, of course, is superior to screws and nail joinery. And the investment in power tools for doweling is less than that for mortising tools.

A dowel butt joint isn't quite as strong as a mortise-and-tenon, but that difference can be minimized by using good doweling techniques and modern plastic-resin glue. That's why you find that most of today's commercially manufactured furniture is doweled. With equipment that is presently available and a little know-how your projects can be just as strong.

alternate annular rings

Before starting any doweling operation there are a few points to have in mind. When you're edge-gluing stock, the annular growth rings in each board (they're visible on the ends) should curve alternately. Viewed from an end, for example, if rings on the first board arch, they should dip on second board—and so on. Such care to alternate the rings will offset the tendency of each board to cup and give you a flat

SEE ALSO

Clamps . . . Dovetail joints . . . Drawers . . . Drill press techniques . . . Drills, portable

FOR MAXIMUM torque strength, use at least two dowels. For a tight joint when edge-joining boards, dowels should be more than 20 in. apart (maximum).

DOWEL CENTERS are slipped in holes bored in first board; to transfer centers to second board, both boards are lined up and tapped with a mallet.

FAST WAY to bore precise holes is with a spur bit chucked in a portable drill or drill press. Wrap piece of tape around shank as a depth stop.

STUBBY SPUR BIT won't drift from center point as metal bits often do, and it will also drill deeper than a spade bit without piercing the other side.

FOR SHOP-MADE dowel pins, measure the bored holes with a depth gauge and then mark the length. To make a neat cut use a fine-tooth hacksaw.

DOWEL SHARPENER is used to taper both ends of the dowels, simplifying the job of inserting them into the holes. The model chucked in brace above is from Stanley.

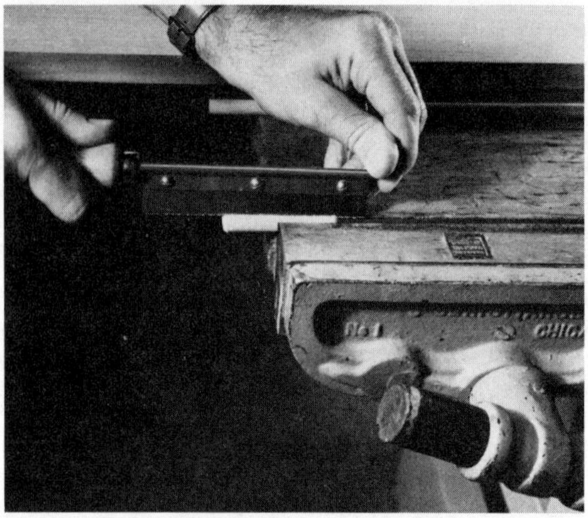

WHEN USING SOLID dowels, cut a groove the length of each pin to let the air and glue escape. Without such relief the wood may split.

TO SCORE a spiral along dowel, you just apply a sliding-rolling pressure on the dowel with the edge of a small mill file. Spiral helps spread glue evenly.

BOARDS ARE edge-joined by dripping glue in each hole, twisting the dowels in place and applying glue to the mating edge. Then clamp boards until glue sets.

overall project. Also, when the edges of two boards touch, the middle two-thirds of the joint should show a sliver of light. Then, when the bar clamps draw the joint tight, the glue-line at the ends will be especially fine.

And, before picking up the drill to bore those dowel holes, sight along the edges of the boards to be joined. If a board shows even a slight bow or warp, it should be trued-up on the table saw. Doing this now will save a lot of aggravation later.

As a final step before drilling, lay out the boards to be joined to get the most pleasing grain design. The ultimate, of course, (for perfectionists) is to achieve a finished surface that appears to be one wide plank. Here you will be restricted by how careful you were when you selected the planks at the lumberyard. In other words, don't let the yard man foist material upon you exactly as he takes it from the pile. Take a good look at the grain of each piece before you make your purchase.

choosing correct size dowel

The six basic doweling steps are shown in the photos. As a rule of thumb for the size dowel to use, the dowel's diameter should equal one-half the thickness of the wood being joined. As for dowel length, you are safe if you cut it about six times the dowel diameter. Thus, to join ¾-in. stock, you would use ⅜-in. dowels cut to 2½-in. lengths.

Lay out the holes to be bored so that they are registered perfectly. You can do this with one of the simple hand methods shown on page 1696 or, if your shop projects call for a lot of doweling, with a dowel jig. Five models are shown and countless other versions are probably available.

assembling board

With dowel pins cut to length, chamfered and kerfed for glue ooze-out, assembly can be started. Dribble glue in the holes in the first board and tap the dowels in place. After applying glue to the board-edge and mating drill holes, press the boards together and finish with bar clamps. Don't overtighten clamps or you might cause bowing. Finally, wipe off all excess glue before it sets and set the workpiece aside overnight to dry. Next day, use a plane if necessary to smooth the surface and then finish the job with a thorough sanding.

If you take a reasonable amount of care along the way, you will have professional-looking—and fitting—dowel joints at a minimum cost.

FIVE JIGS THAT MAKE DOWELING EASIER

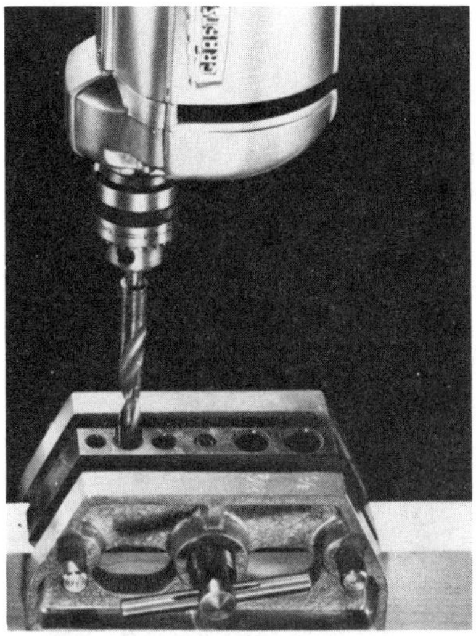

SELF-CENTERING drill guide that boasts a heat-treatment feature will accommodate six drill sizes ranging from ¼ through ½ in. The Model A Dowl-It jig is manufactured by the Dowl-It-Co., 515 North Hanover St., Hastings, MI 49058.

DRILLING IS SIMPLIFIED with this jig because its revolving turret adjusts quickly and eliminates loss of loose sleeves or parts. Model 840 with auger bit stop is made by General Hardware Manufacturing Co., New York, NY 10013.

THIS DRILLING JIG provides the means to drill properly aligned holes to depths of 1 1/16 in., adapts to various board thicknesses. It comes with full instructions and is manufactured by Elder's Manufacturing Co., Box 322, West Des Moines, IA 50265

INEXPENSIVE VERSION available at building-supply houses and hardware stores, this unit accommodates most common dowel sizes, requires registration lines made with a try square. The Model 59 is manufactured by The Stanley Works, New Britain, CT 06050.

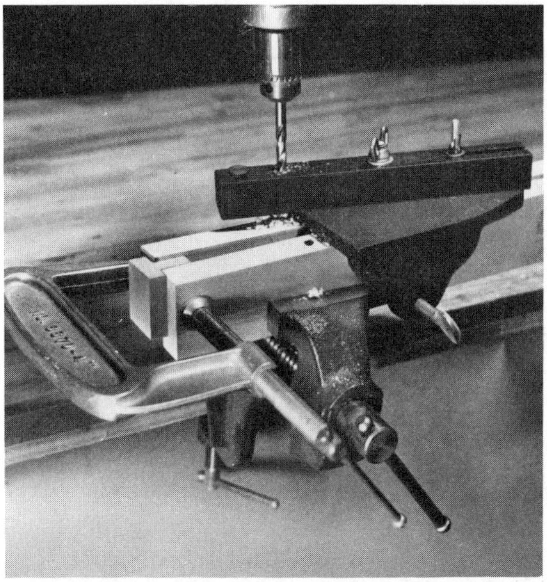

LATEST DOWEL JIG on the scene is this model by Home & Industry Tool Distributors, 2867 Long Beach Rd., Oceanside, NY 11572. With a guide clamped in position, the top bar swings two ways for perfectly matched holes. The C-clamp is not included in the set.

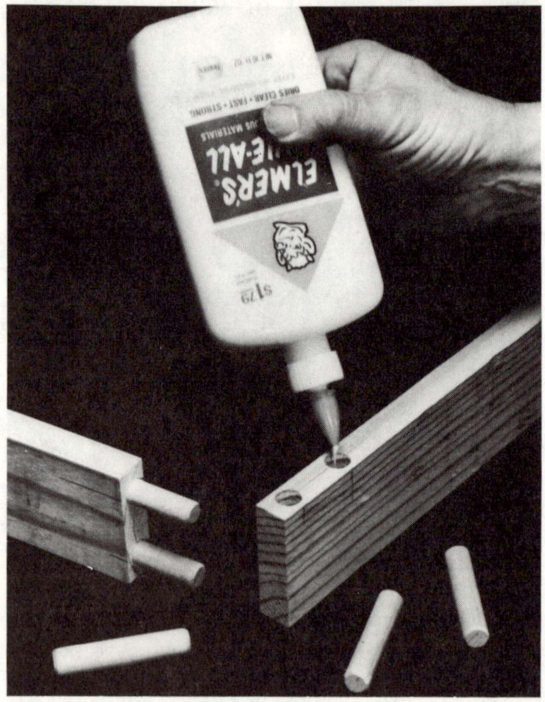

Here are a few hints that will help you save time and trouble in making strong, permanent joints on your next project, whether it be a table, a box or a drawer

A short course in wood joinery

By WAYNE C. LECKEY

COMMON MORTISE-AND-TENON JOINTS

WILL THAT TABLE you just completed last a hundred years or more, like the fine pieces produced by cabinetmakers of old? Much will depend on how well you put it together—but even more importantly, on what joinery was used. The joints and the way you put them together do make a big difference in the lasting strength of your work.

Furniture that relies on mere butt joints will never make it, for wood shrinks and is affected by moisture and humidity. Gradually poor joints will loosen up as age sets in. Only when the parts are integrated into a unit through carefully fitted joints can you expect your cabinetry to "live" to a ripe old age.

As you see here, many different kinds of joints can be used in assembling furniture. The one you pick depends a great deal on the piece itself.

SEE ALSO

Butler's tables . . . Cabinet furniture . . . Children's furniture . . . Coffee tables . . . Desks . . . Dining tables . . . Drawers . . . Finishes, wood . . . Hutch tables . . . Occasional tables

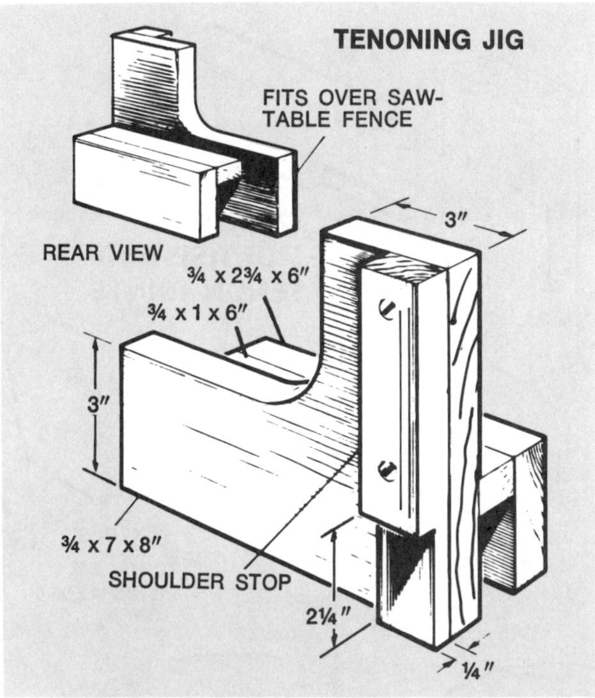

DESIGNED TO STRADDLE a saw fence, this homemade tenoning jig lets you cut accurate-fitting tenons safely on narrow stock. Jig is made from scrap and work is clamped to it.

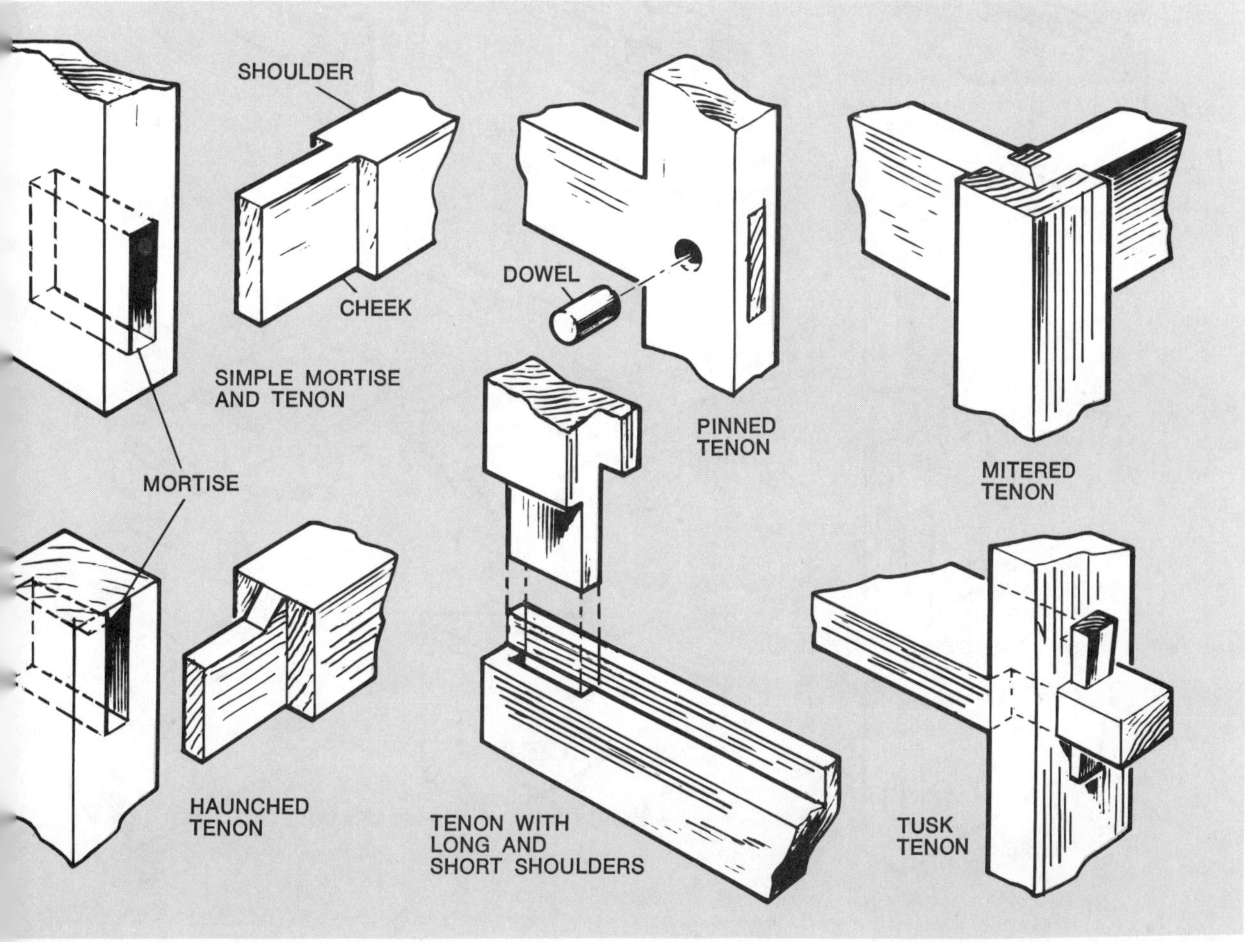

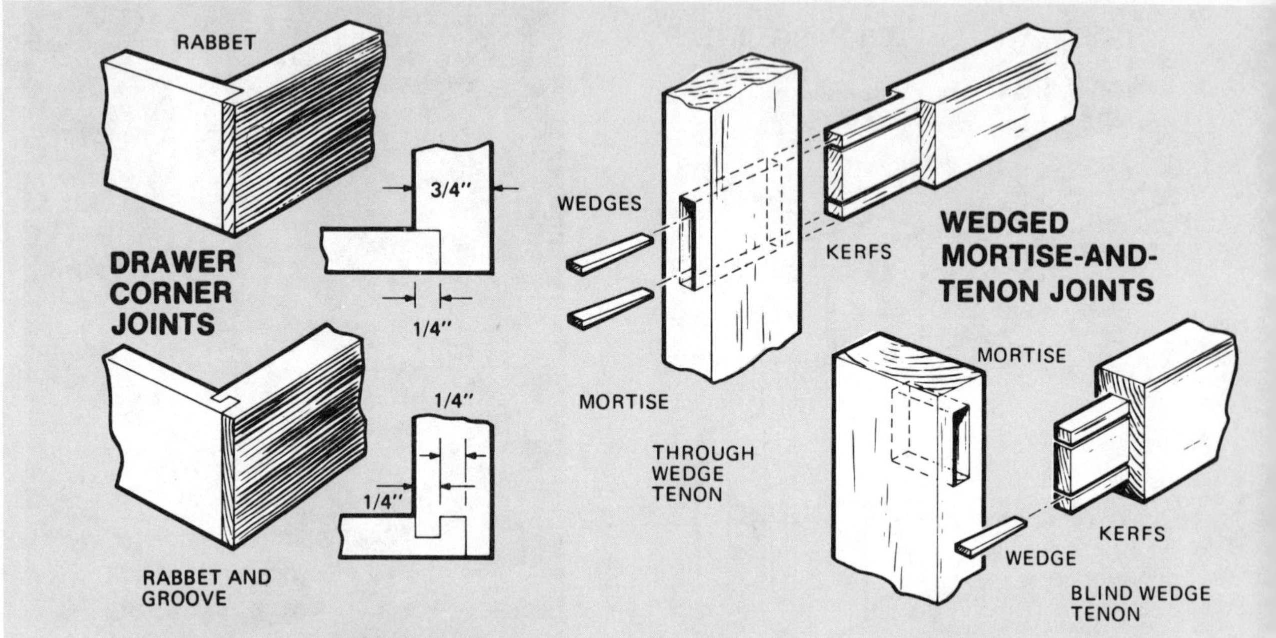
RABBET
3/4"
1/4"
DRAWER CORNER JOINTS
1/4"
1/4"
RABBET AND GROOVE
WEDGES
KERFS
MORTISE
THROUGH WEDGE TENON
WEDGED MORTISE-AND-TENON JOINTS
MORTISE
KERFS
WEDGE
BLIND WEDGE TENON

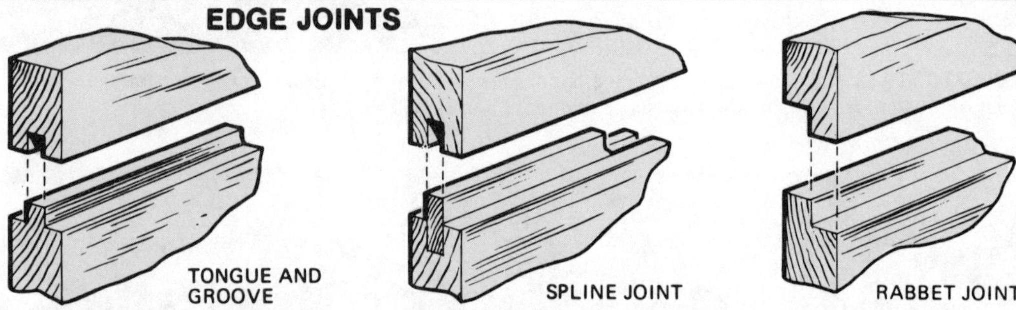
EDGE JOINTS
TONGUE AND GROOVE
SPLINE JOINT
RABBET JOINT

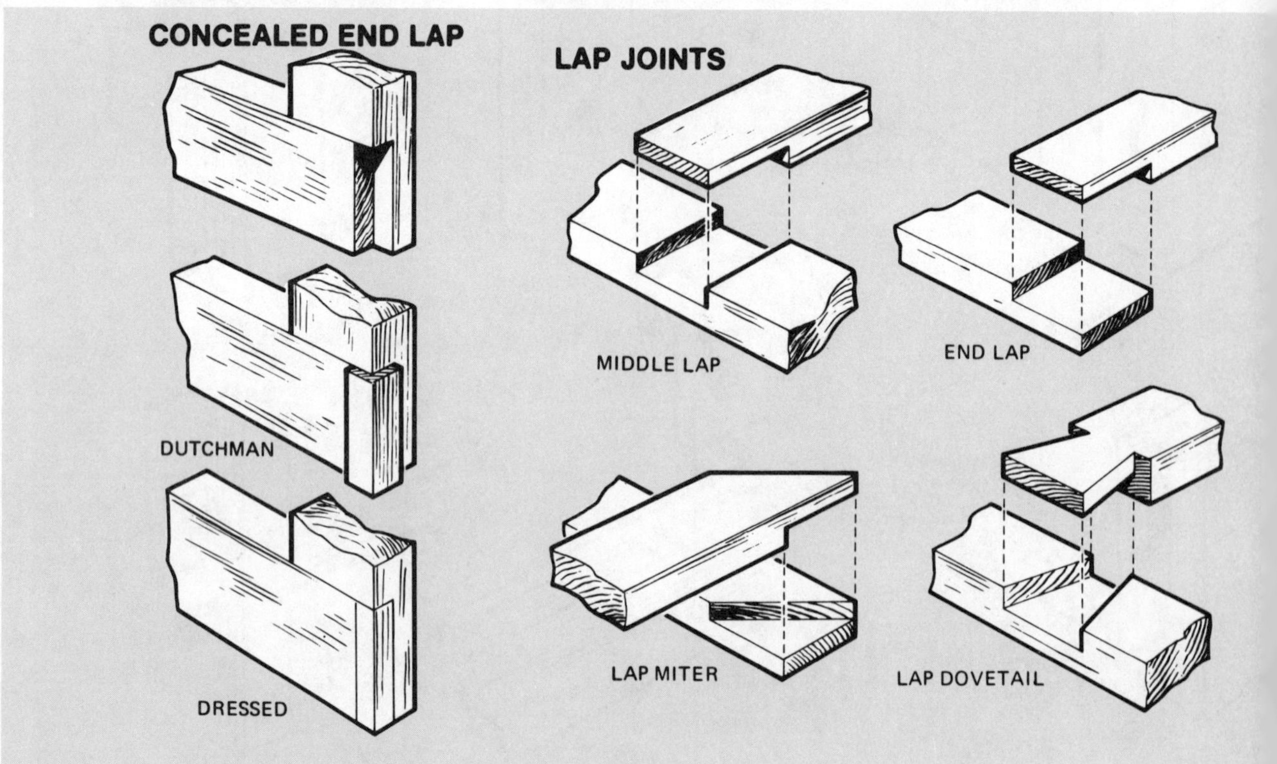
CONCEALED END LAP
DUTCHMAN
DRESSED
LAP JOINTS
MIDDLE LAP
END LAP
LAP MITER
LAP DOVETAIL

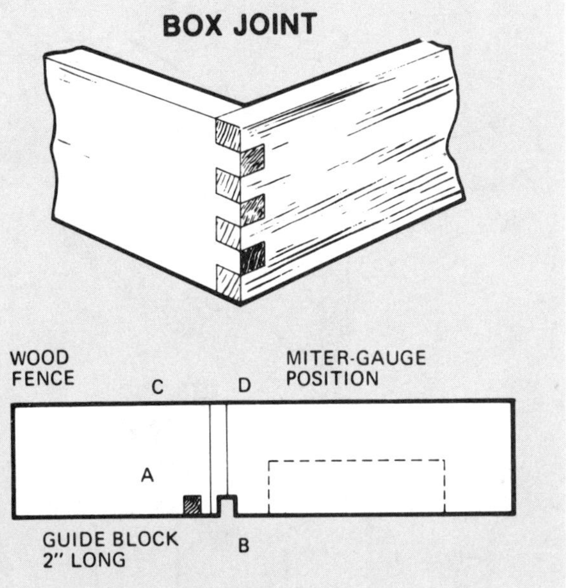

BOX JOINT JIG attached to miter gauge spaces dado cuts made on table saw.

Often you have a choice, one joint being as strong as the other but requiring a special tool to make it. There are dowel joints, mortise-and-tenon joints, lap joints, spline joints, pinned joints, miter joints, rabbet joints, dado joints and lock joints, to name only a few of the many different kinds. There are special joints to put drawers together, conceal corners and glue table-tops. Each shares a place in making you a master craftsman.

One of the handiest fixtures you can make for cutting tenons on a table saw is a tenoning jig.

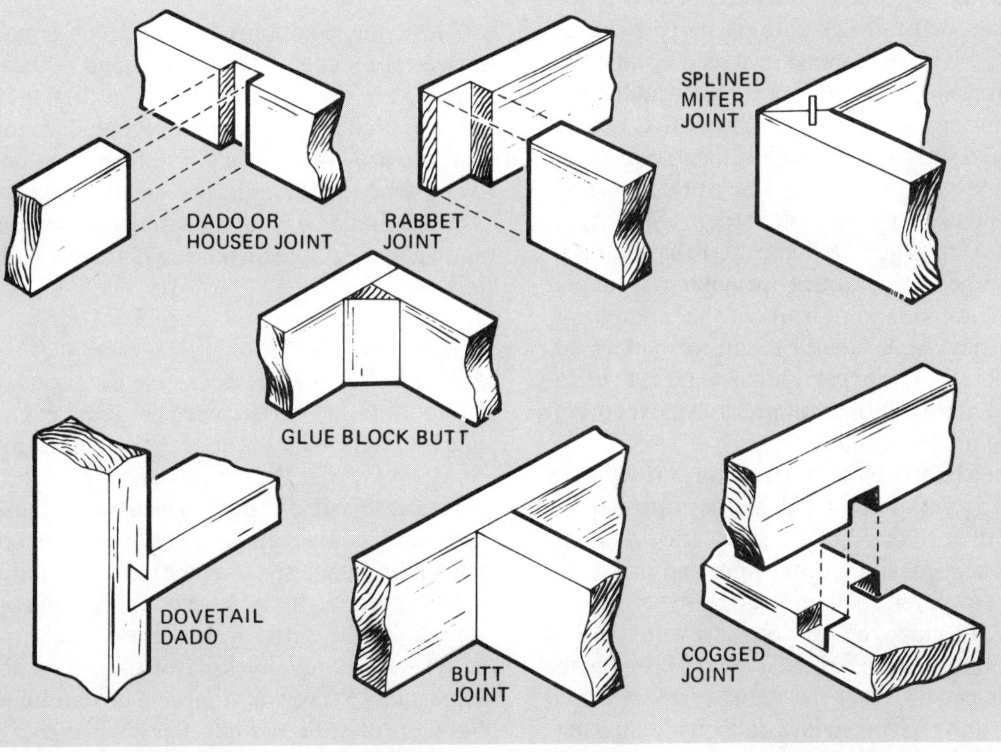

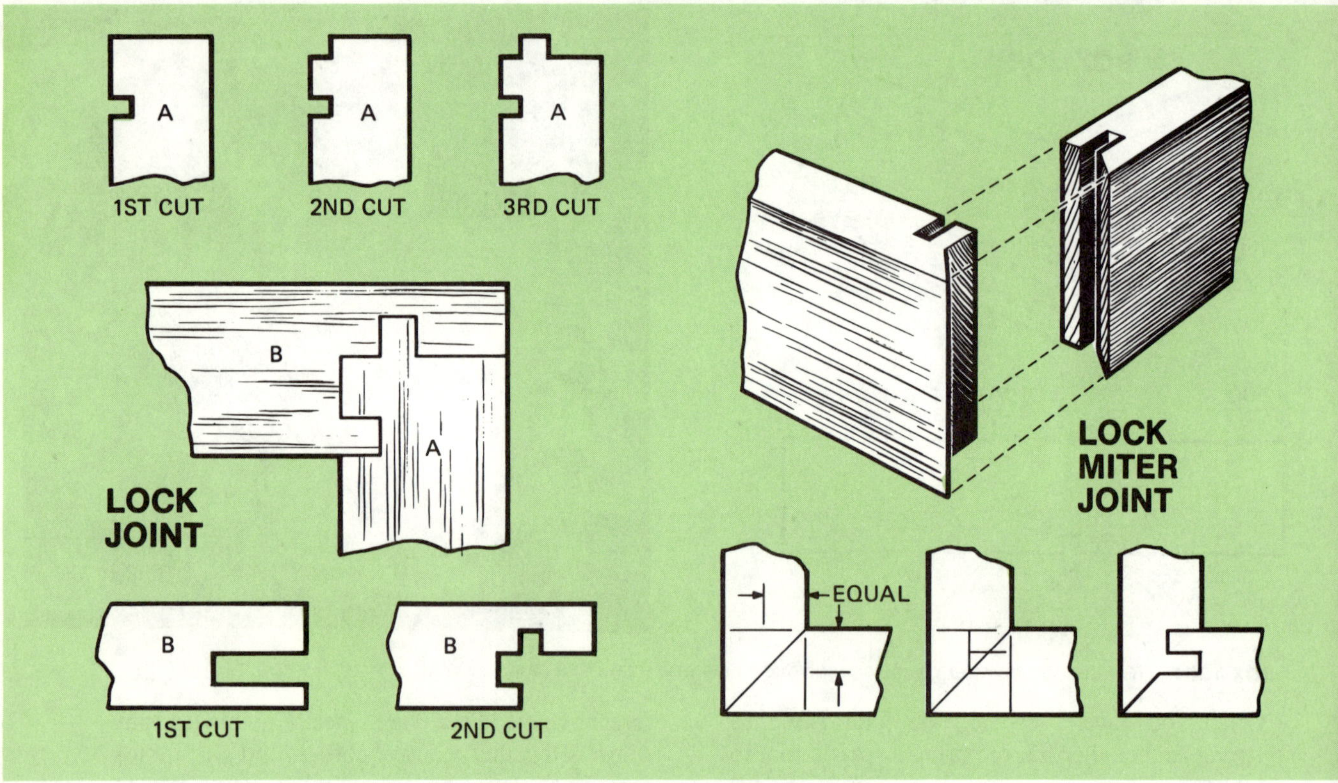

wood joints, continued

Detailed at the top of page 1577, the jig is designed to straddle and slide along the saw fence so you can make cheek cuts on narrow pieces safely. Work to be tenoned is placed against the shouldered stop on the jig, clamped and then passed through the saw. Then the work is turned around and the cut is repeated to make the second cheek cut, and finally, the work is turned end for end to cut the opposite tenon. Cheek cuts on a tenon are generally made after the shoulder cuts, and general practice in making a simple mortise-and-tenon joint is to cut the tenon first, then the mortise. While the tenon can be formed on the table saw, the mortise has to be cut with a mortising chisel on the drill press. An exception would be an open-end mortise.

Another table-saw jig for cutting perfect box, or finger, joints is detailed at the top of page 1579. Similar to the dovetail joint, the box joint makes a neat-looking corner joint and is exceptionally strong since it presents lots of gluing surfaces. To make the jig, you start with a ¾-in. wood auxiliary fence, which is screw-fastened to the miter gauge. Then the regular saw blade is removed and replaced with a dado blade. In most cases the width of the cut is equal to or slightly less than the thickness of the stock, and likewise when determining the depth. Make initial cut A in the wood fence, then remove it from the miter gauge.

Mark the position of second cut B so it is spaced the same width as cut A and at the same time mark lines C and D, centering them as shown. Nail a little square of wood 2 in. long in cut A to provide a guide pin and finally attach the wood fence to the miter gauge and make cut B. The jig should be ready now and you can use it as shown in the photo on page 1579 to make the box joint.

making the box joint

Mating pieces of stock are set against the fence, the edge of one piece being set even with line D and the edge of the second piece even with line C. Now pass the offset work across the saw. To make the second cut, as well as the third and succeeding cuts, carefully shift the work so that the cut just made sits over the guide pin and again pass the work across the saw. Repeat the operation along the entire width of the stock.

When making any kind of joint it is always important to take your time and do careful work. Solid, precise cuts and edges will make your project last many years.

A PARTS HOLDER for your ladder can be made by screwing one or two soft plastic cups to the stepladder shelf in addition to boring holes into the shelf for tools. The cup lids will prevent spillage.—*Walter E. Burton, Akron, OH.*

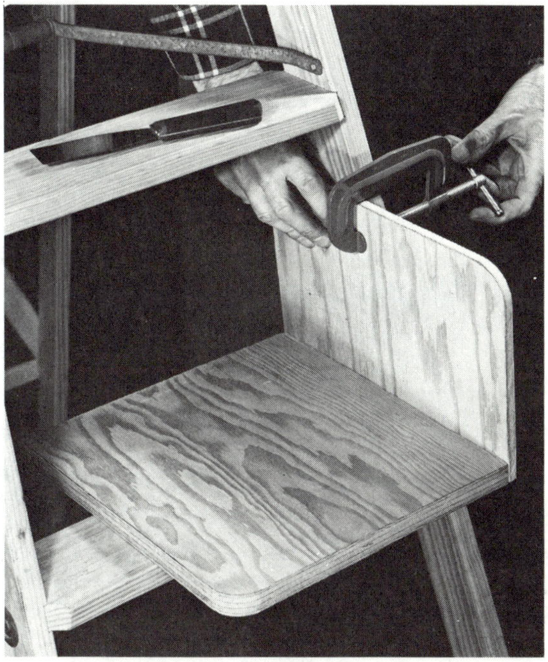

A PLATFORM FOR FOOTROOM on your stepladder wiil let you work more comfortably. Use ¾-in. plywood for the platform's bottom and ⅜-in. on the side. Clamp your platform firmly to the side of the ladder.—*Andrew Vena, Philadelphia.*

THIS HANDY CADDY will help organize your nails and make them more transportable. Bolt the cans together through a plywood handle. You can fashion your own handle or use a store-bought model.—*M. David Rubbo, Johnstown, PA.*

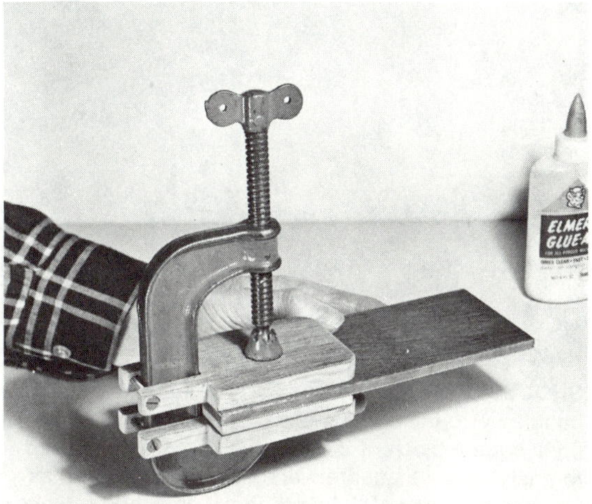

THIS C-CLAMP ENLARGER provides you with big jaws for gluing wide surfaces. First cut slots in the enlarger so that it fits over the clamp's back. Then, fasten it with a nut and bolt.—*Peter Legon, Malden, MA.*

13 bonus tricks for your jointer

By WAYNE C. LECKEY

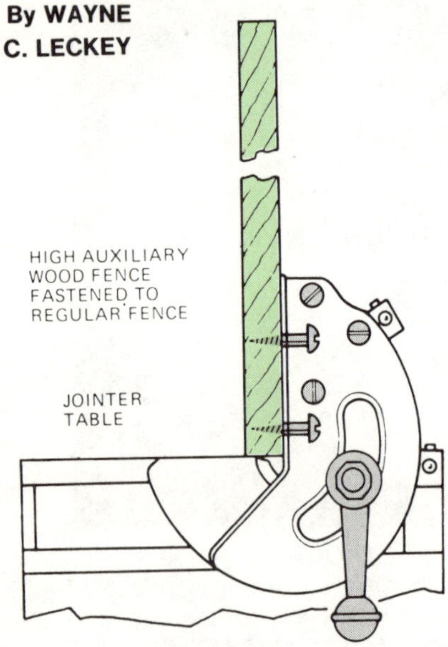

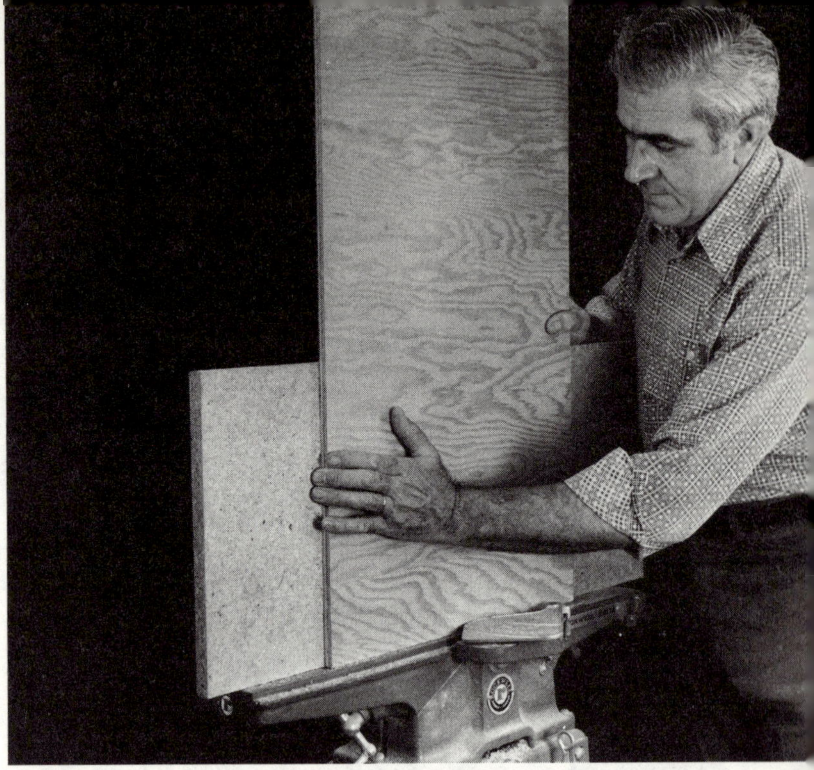

1 High fence for tall work

THE STANDARD 4-in. jointer fence should be fitted with an oversize auxiliary one to provide adequate, positive support when planing large work, as shown above. Select a perfectly flat piece of plywood, sand the face and apply a coat or two of sealer followed with a coat of paste wax to make it extra smooth. Use roundhead screws through the existing holes in the jointer fence to attach the plywood. Side pressure is essential to keep the work in full contact with the fence.

2 Shouldered tenons

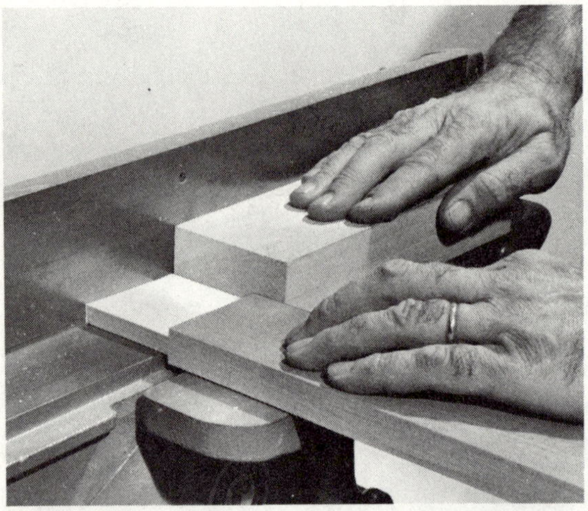

SHOULDERED TENONS on narrow stock are easily handled with the aid of a backing block. This is simply a square block of 2 x 4 or the like, which is used to push the work squarely across the cutter head as you keep the end of the work firmly against the fence. If the shoulder cut is fairly deep, make the cut in two or more passes. Flop the work with each cut before lowering the front table to make the next.

SEE ALSO

Dovetail joints . . . Joinery . . . Legs, furniture . . . Lumber . . . Miter joints . . . Moldings . . . Workbenches . . . Workshops

3 Push block for safety

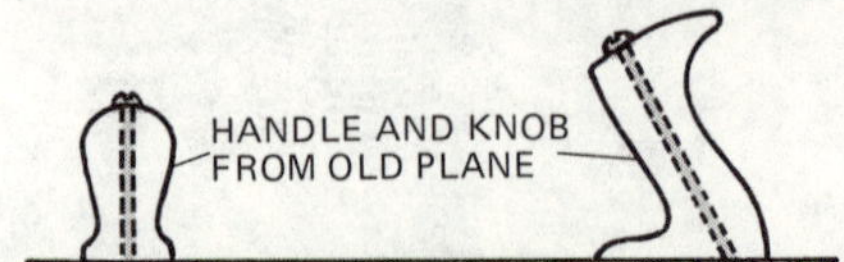

SURFACE PLANING should never be done without using a combination push block/hold-down to keep your hands clear of the cutter head. The push block shown makes use of parts from an old hand plane, but you could also use 1-in. dowels for handles. In use, the pusher is grasped by one hand on the knob, the other on the handle. A small cleat across the end on the underside hooks over the edge of the workpiece.

4 Stopped bevel chamfer

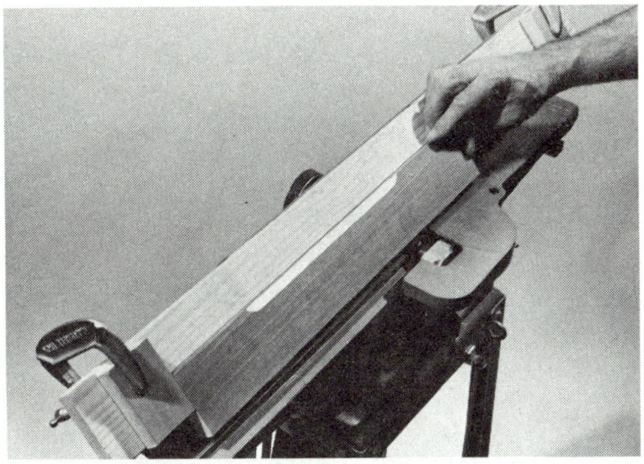

THIS HANDSOME cut is widely used for table and chair legs, posts and general cabinetry. It is made in the same way as a common stopped chamfer with the exception that the jointer fence is tilted 45° to form a beveled cut. Use an auxiliary wood fence with stop blocks attached, and lower both tables an equal amount. Elevate the lead end of the work while resting the opposite end against the right-hand starting block. Start the machine, lower the work into the cutter, then advance it slowly until it reaches the forward stop block. Important: Use *two* hands for this operation. (One hand is shown in the photo for the sake of clarity.) The operation requires the removal of the blade guard so watch your fingers when making cut.

5 How to plane end grain

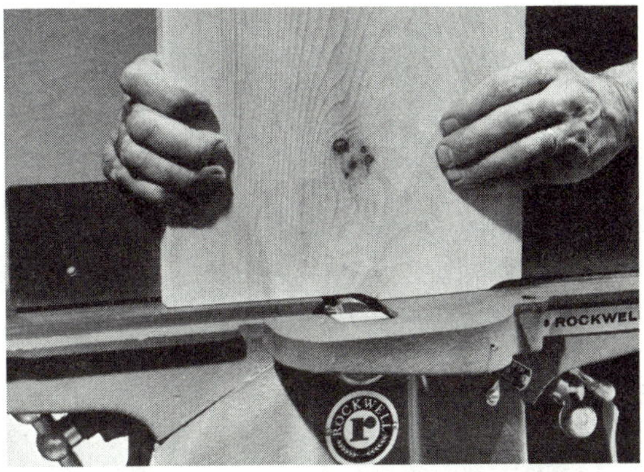

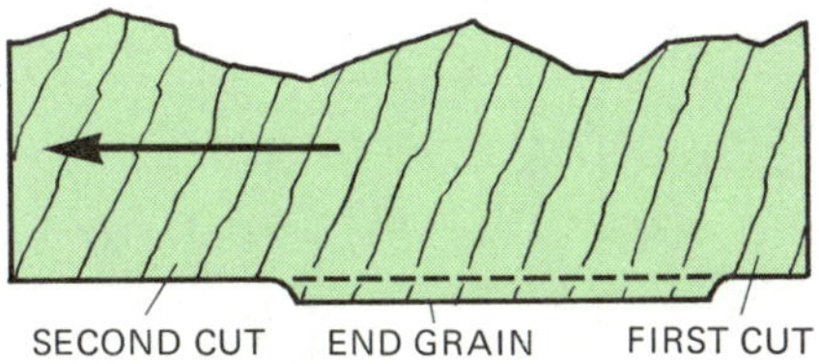

PLANING END GRAIN with a jointer will usually chip and splinter the wood at the end of the cut. But not if you first make a short cut with the jointer and then reverse the work to complete the cut. The knives of the cutter head merely pass over the initial cut without cutting, resulting in a chip-free corner. End grain of a board should always be planed first, then the side grain for best results.

6 How to make novelty molding

DECORATIVE MOLDING can be produced with the jointer by making a series of cove cuts in the surface of the work. To do this, clamp a wooden stop block to an auxiliary wood fence and mark the fence with equally spaced index lines. Butt the end of the work squarely against the stop, then slowly and carefully lower it face down into the rotating cutter head. Shift and reclamp the stop for each cut. Both the front and rear tables must be lowered an equal amount for this operation. You can use your imagination to create different designs by varying the spacing of the index marks.

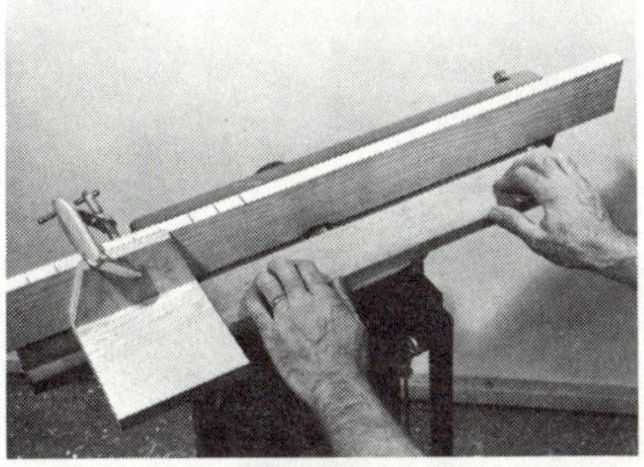

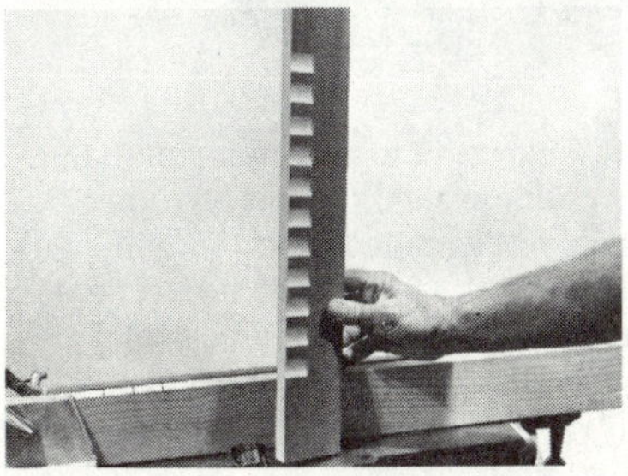

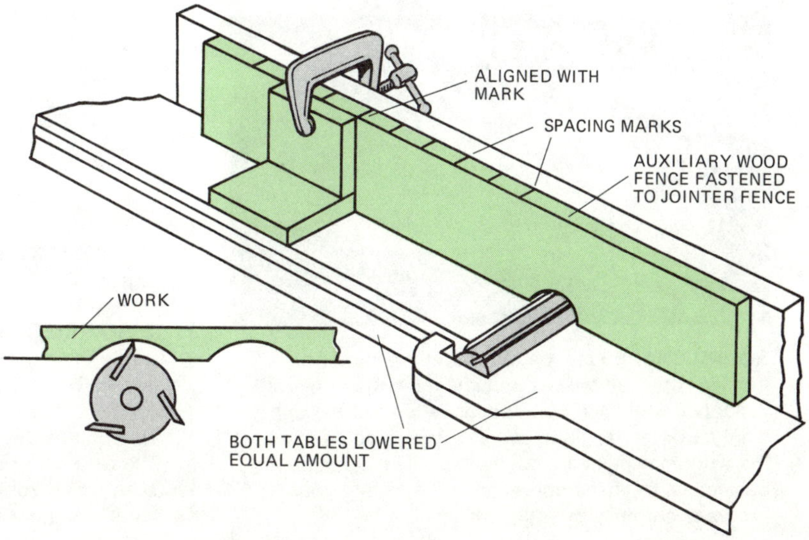

7 Cutting raised panels

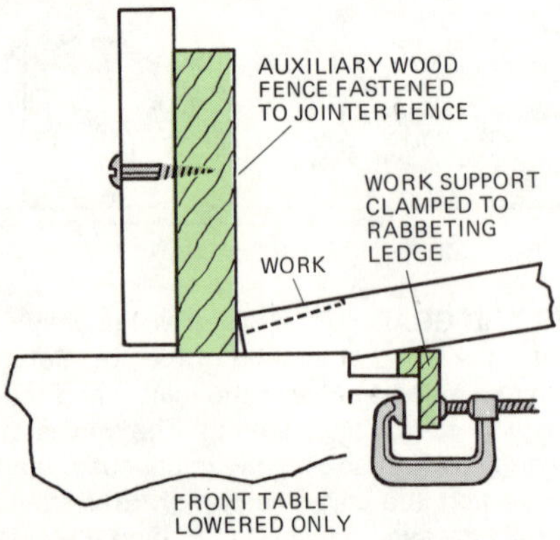

RAISED DOOR panels can be formed neatly with the jointer. First clamp an auxiliary wood fence to the jointer fence, letting it just clear the tables. Set the fence for the desired width of cut, then clamp a strip of wood to the rabbeting ledge of the rear table. This supports the wood at an angle to produce the desired amount of bevel as the work is passed over the cutter. Take small bites, about 1/16 in. at a time, and make cross-grain passes first, then the straight grain, to avoid chipping as you pass over the corners.

9 Freehand rounding

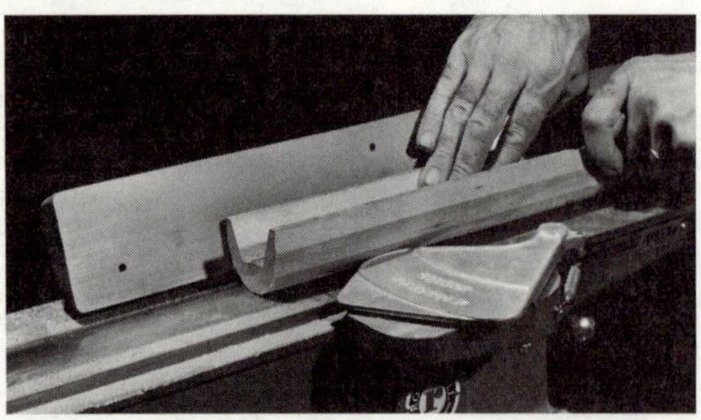

ROUND SHAPES can be formed with a jointer by making repeated passes and changing the angle of incidence with each cut. The fence is adjusted to a single arbitrary angle to serve only as a guide to keep the work moving in a straight line. The procedure is basically a freehand operation so ''eyeball'' your progress carefully as you work.

8 Big and little rabbets

WHEN THE JOB calls for a rabbet that must be made by planing, it's a simple operation for a jointer whether it be an edge rabbet or a surface one. You simply position the fence to set the rabbet's length or width and adjust the front table to set its depth. Rabbet depth is limited, of course, to the rabbet ledge on your particular machine, and when the depth required is greater, you will be forced to cut such rabbets on your table saw. An extra smooth rabbet can be cut with a hollow-ground planer blade. Certain dado cutters will produce a smooth rabbet too. In the case of a dado cutter, it's often necessary to add a wood facing to the saw's fence.

10 Shouldered tenons

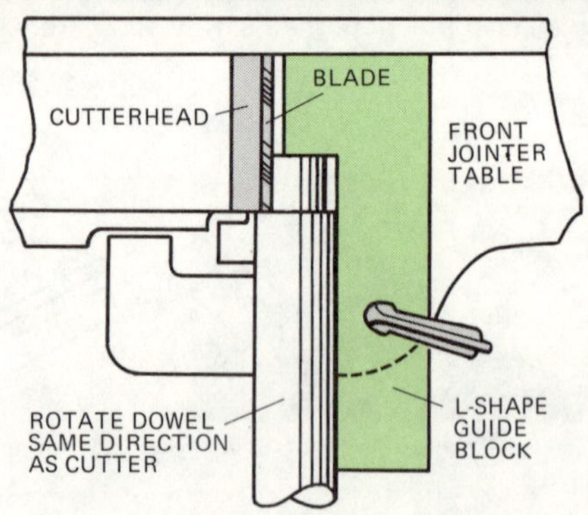

A NOTCHED BLOCK clamped to the rabbeting ledge of a jointer permits cutting round tenons on round stock. The position of the clamped block sets the length of the tenon, while the front table adjustment determines the depth of cut. To turn a tenon, push the work into the spinning cutter from the side and then slowly rotate the work in the same direction of rotation as the cutterhead.

11 How to cut stopped chamfers

A STOPPED CHAMFER can add an interesting shape to a square chair leg. Here's how it's made on a jointer. Lower front and rear tables equally. Then clamp start and stop blocks to an auxiliary wood fence to limit length of cut. Place the end of the leg against the front-table stop block and start the machine. Lower the raised end of the work into the rotating cutter and advance the work until it touches the rear-table stop block. Be sure the front-table stop block is clamped securely in place because there is a forceful kickback thrust to the work at the start of the cut.

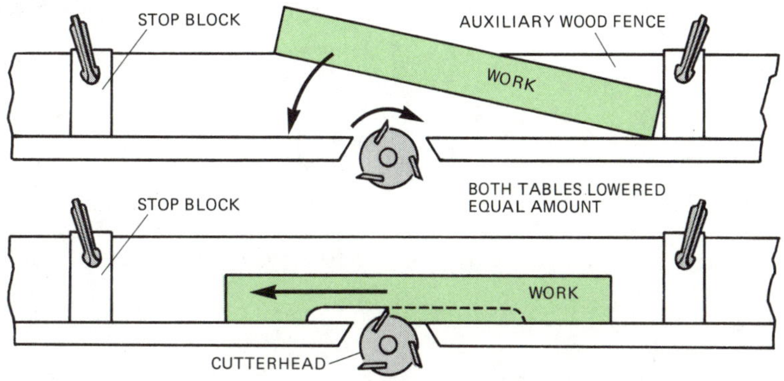

12 How to make bevels

BEVELS ARE CUT running work against a tilted fence in an "in" or "out" position. The outward tilt shown is safer because fingers are in full view. When working with wild grain, an inward tilt is needed for a smooth cut. Several passes with adequate downward and sideward pressure are usually required.

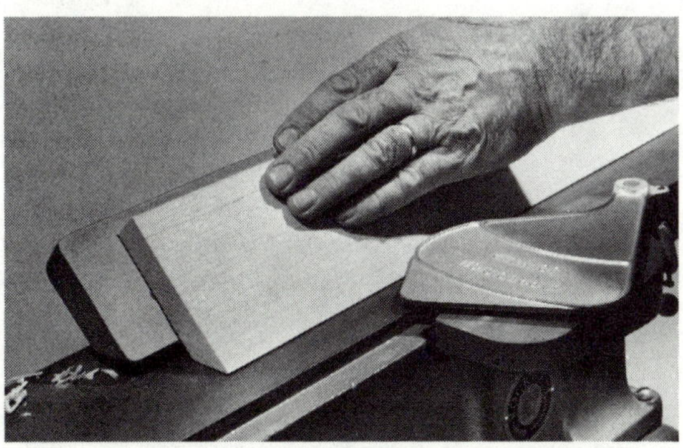

13 Tapering square stock

TO SHORT-TAPER the four faces of square stock, you pull the work over the cutterhead. Lower the front table to suit the amount of taper. Then mark stock where the taper is to start and center mark directly over the cutter. Press down so the corner of the work contacts the front table and slip a block under the raised end of rear table to hold work at an angle. Mark block location on each face with a try square, then lightly brad block to one face. To start cut, rest front end against a clamped block that prevents kickback and assures the same starting point for each pass. Rebrad block to the work for each of the four cuts.

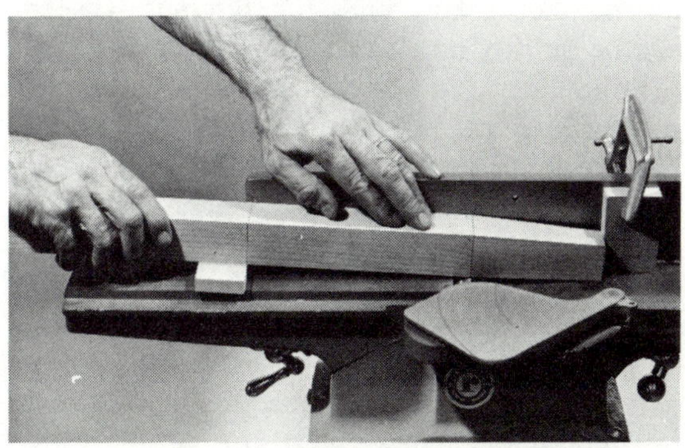

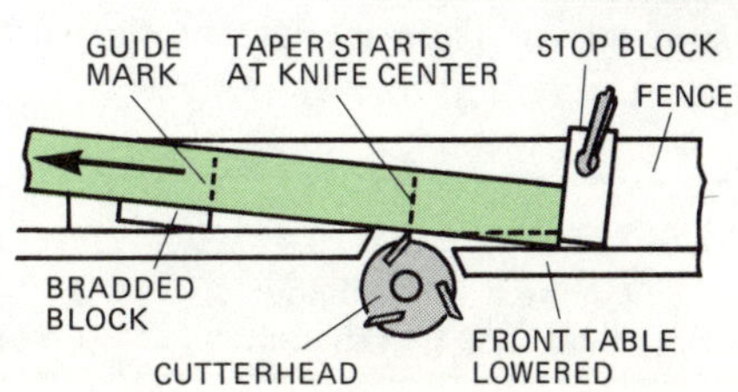

STAND'S LEGS are splayed in two directions for vibration-free operation. Beneath the jointer is a sawdust drawer and push block shelf.

Mobile stand for a 6-in. jointer

■ THIS STURDY, vibration-free jointer stand is suitable for all 4- and 6-in. jointers. It's easy to keep clean and can be rolled into position on casters. The sawdust drawer collects chips and has handles at both ends for dumping. Casters can be quickly raised or lowered by foot levers.

Build the stand's frame first. The prototype was made of oak, but fir can be substituted if rail lumber dimensions are increased to 1½ x 2½ in. and legs to 1½ x 3½ in. Note the legs are splayed. Thus, dadoes (U-shaped notches for lower rails) and end rabbets (L-shaped cutouts for top rails) in legs must be made with 7° angle crosscuts. To lay out joints accurately, first cut the legs to length. (Compound 7° cuts are required at both top and bottom of legs.) Next, cut rails to overall dimensions given. Then lay legs on flat surface, in proper relationship to each other.

SEE ALSO

**Joinery . . . Lumber . . . Moldings . . .
Power-tool stands . . . Workbenches . . . Workshops**

Position the upper and lower rails and trace for the cutouts. Do the same for each face on the stand. The top edge of the upper rails (B and C) must be beveled 7° to achieve a level mount for the tool.

mounting the jointer

All joints should be glued as well as bolted. Use 5/16-in.-dia. lagscrews where bolts are not feasible. The plywood drawer is assembled with glue and nails. For most jointers, the motor may be swung from a rod located between the top stretchers. The weight of the motor maintains the proper belt tension.

Bolting the jointer to the stand will also vary from model to model. Steel-plate and bar supports for heavy models distribute weight on rails; ¾-in. plywood will distribute weight of lighter units. Cut a hole in the plywood to allow cutter chips to shoot into sawdust drawer. In mounting a Shopsmith jointer, mounting tubes should be cut off so that they won't extend into the drawer area.

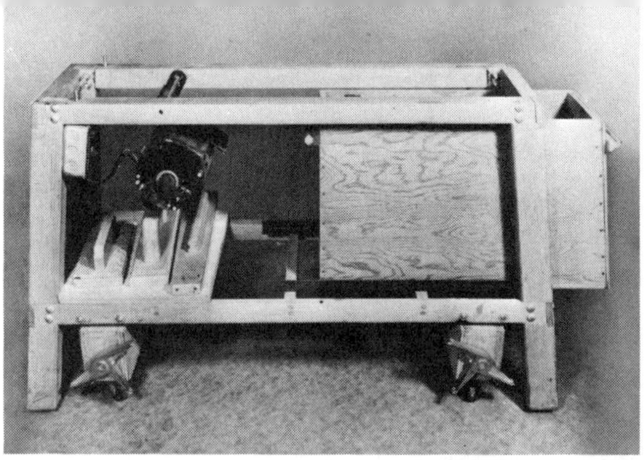

LARGE SAWDUST drawer slides easily on the angle-iron tracks for removal and emptying.

SHOPSMITH 4-in. jointer can also be accommodated by this stand that includes retractable casters.

MATERIALS LIST—JOINTER STAND

Key	No.	Size and description (use)
A	4	1¾ x 2½ x 26″ oak (leg)*
B	2	1½ x 1¾ x 38¼″ oak (upper side rail)*
C	2	1¼ x 1¾ x 12″ oak (upper end rail)*
D	2	¾ x 1¾ x 44″ oak (lower side rail)*
E	2	1¼ x 2 x 18″ oak (lower end rail)*
F	3	1 x 1¾ x 15″ oak (brace)*
G1	1	¾ x 11¾ x 15″ plywood (drawer front)*
G2	1	¾ x 11¾ x 13¾″ plywood (drawer back)*
H	2	⅜ x 15 x 24¼″ plywood (drawer sides)*
I	1	⅜ x 11⅜ x 23⅛″ plywood (drawer bottom)
J	1	¾ x 1 x 10¼″ oak (pull and stop)*
K	1	¾ x 1 x 7″ oak (handle)*
L	4	3/16 x 1½ x 1½ x 6″ angle
M	2	¾ x 3¼ x 15½″ oak
N	4	¾ x 4¾ x 15½″ oak
O	4	¾ x 2½ x 4″ oak
P	4	retractable casters (Shopsmith)
Q	1	½″-dia. x 11¾″ steel rod
R	1	motor mount (Sears)
S	2	⅜″-dia. x 2½″ carriage bolts
T	8	No. 8 x 1½″ fh machine screws, washers, lock washers, nuts
U1	4	5/16″-dia. x 3″ carriage bolts, washers, nuts
U2	16	5/16″-dia. x 2¼″ carriage bolts, washers, nuts
V	4	5/16″ x 2½″ carriage bolts with Teenuts
W	12	No. 8 x 2″ fh wood screws
X	2	⅛ x ¾ x ¾ x 24½″ angle irons

Misc.: White glue, 4d nails, sandpaper.
* These are overall dimensions, pieces must be cut to fit.

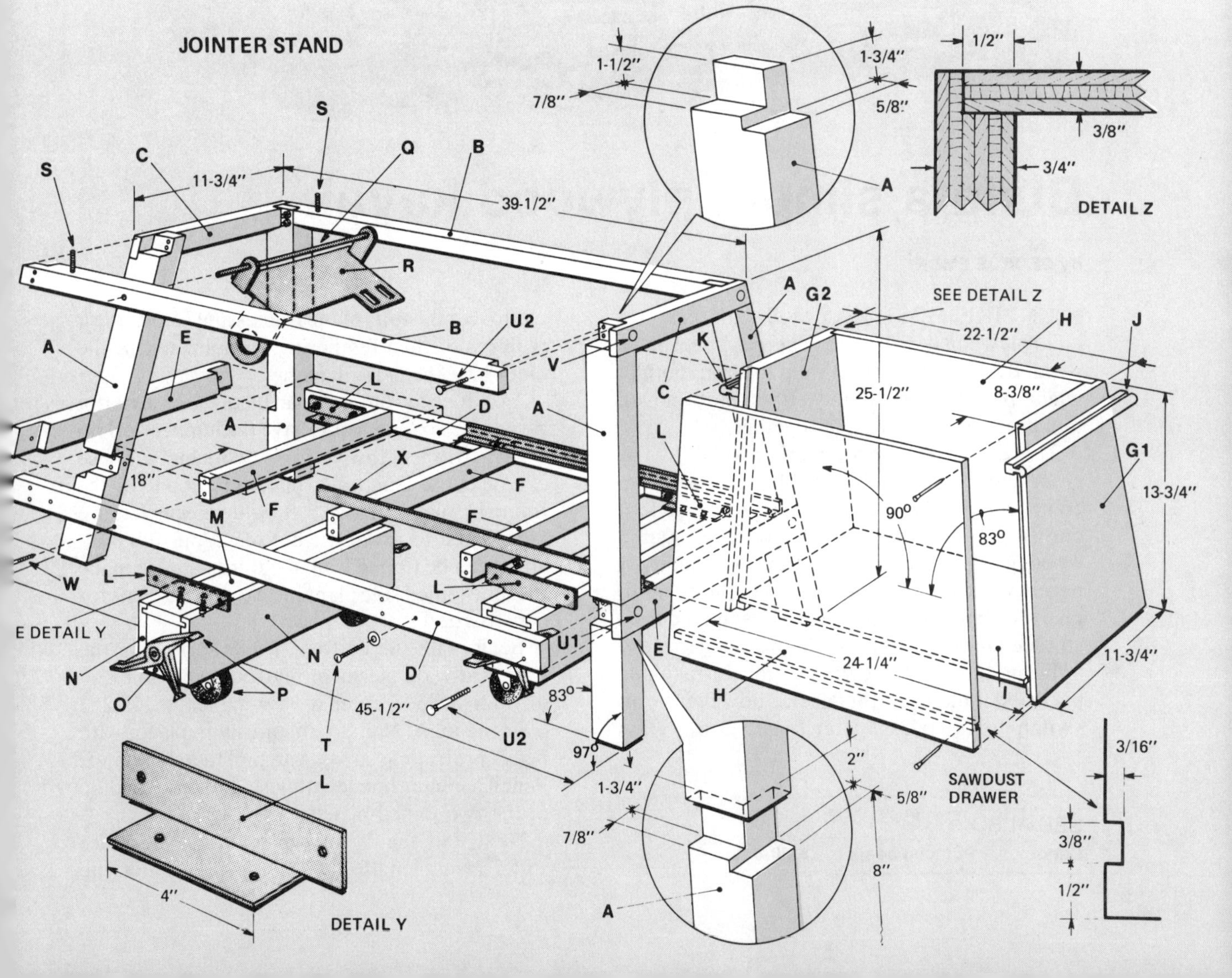

Build a simple plywood kayak

By GEORGE EMORY

■ UNLIKE MOST KAYAKS, this easy-to-build plywood design has a generous beam and a perfectly flat bottom from stem to stern, both of which increase the stability. Even more novel, though, is the way it's put together.

There's no tricky toolwork involved. The sides and bottom are ¼-in. plywood with uncomplicated 90° chines and simple fore-and-aft curves. To keep the weight down, ¼-in. plywood is also used for the frames, making it necessary to add stiffening cleats to the edges to give them more rigidity and provide the required surface area for mounting the planking.

From the sheer down, it's an ultrasimple plywood hull. For the deck, however, you switch to fiberglass, stretching 7½-oz. glass cloth over the tops of the frames and saturating it with resin, then feathering the joint where the cloth laps the side planking.

You'll need four 4x8 panels of ¼-in. exterior plywood. To save work, have the lumberyard rip a 1-ft. strip lengthwise from two panels. These can be cut to lengths to make all but one of the frame blanks. The two 3-ft.-wide pieces left are butt-joined to make the bottom. Four full 8-in. strips can be ripped from the third panel to make the butt-joined side planking. Complete plans for construction start on page 1590.

Begin with the bottom. Temporarily join the two yard-wide pieces of plywood with an 8x36-in. butt strip. Center a 34½-in. length of 2x2 over the joint. Nail it temporarily in place, with heads protruding so you can pull them out later. Pencil a center line lengthwise down the middle of the two joined panels.

Next, cut the ¾ x ¾-in. chines. These are 15-ft. 10-in. lengths of clear pine. Center the

SEE ALSO

Canoes . . . Pontoon boats . . . Sailboats

midpoints on the ends of the 2x2 crosspiece and bend the ends in toward the center line. Two scraps of lumber can be nailed temporarily over the center line to serve as the stems. Mark the ends of the chines for angle cutting so they will fit flush to the stems. After cutting the ends, nail them temporarily.

Pencil in the frame positions at right angles to the center line and check width measurements at each location against those in the plans. If necessary, spring the chines in or out to get the proper curvature. Temporarily nail the chines to the plywood at each frame location, then pencil the outline of each one on the plywood bottom. Be sure to carry the inner lines across the butt strip since this must be cut to fit between the chines.

Now pull the temporary chine nails far enough out to remove the chines from the plywood. (Leave the nails in the chines for alignment later.) Use a sabre saw to cut the plywood bottom. This done, you can remove the butt strip and trim it along the inner chine lines.

Use a resorcinol resin glue, such as Weldwood, when assembling the boat. Begin by replacing the butt strip joining the two pieces of bottom planking. Coat all mating surfaces with glue and retighten all screws in their original holes.

Next, mount the chines on the bottom. Gluecoat all mating surfaces and push the temporary nails back into their original holes to re-align the chines. Then drive 1-in. copper nails through the plywood into the chines, spacing them roughly 6 in. apart.

Now you can cut and assemble the frames. On the cockpit frames (3, 4 and 5), leave a cross brace between the cockpit stringer notches. These will provide the necessary rigidity to hold the frames in proper alignment until the stringers have been installed.

While not shown this way in the frame drawing, frames 4 through 7 should have the stiffening cleats mounted on the rear surface, while frames 1 through 3 should have them on the forward surface. Thus, the stemward edge of each vertical cleat will protrude slightly beyond the chine and gunnel stringers. When this edge is planed flush the cleats will provide ample gluing surface for side planking.

Position each frame on the bottom and drive a 1¼-in. fine wire nail down through the stiffener strip and bottom near each end, leaving the heads protruding so you can pull them out later. Now, turn the hull over and draw a straight line between the two nail points. Drive a ⅝-in. No. 4

LEEBOARDS PIVOT to permit beaching boat. Wing nuts and carriage bolts lock them in "up" position.

LITTLE BEAVER

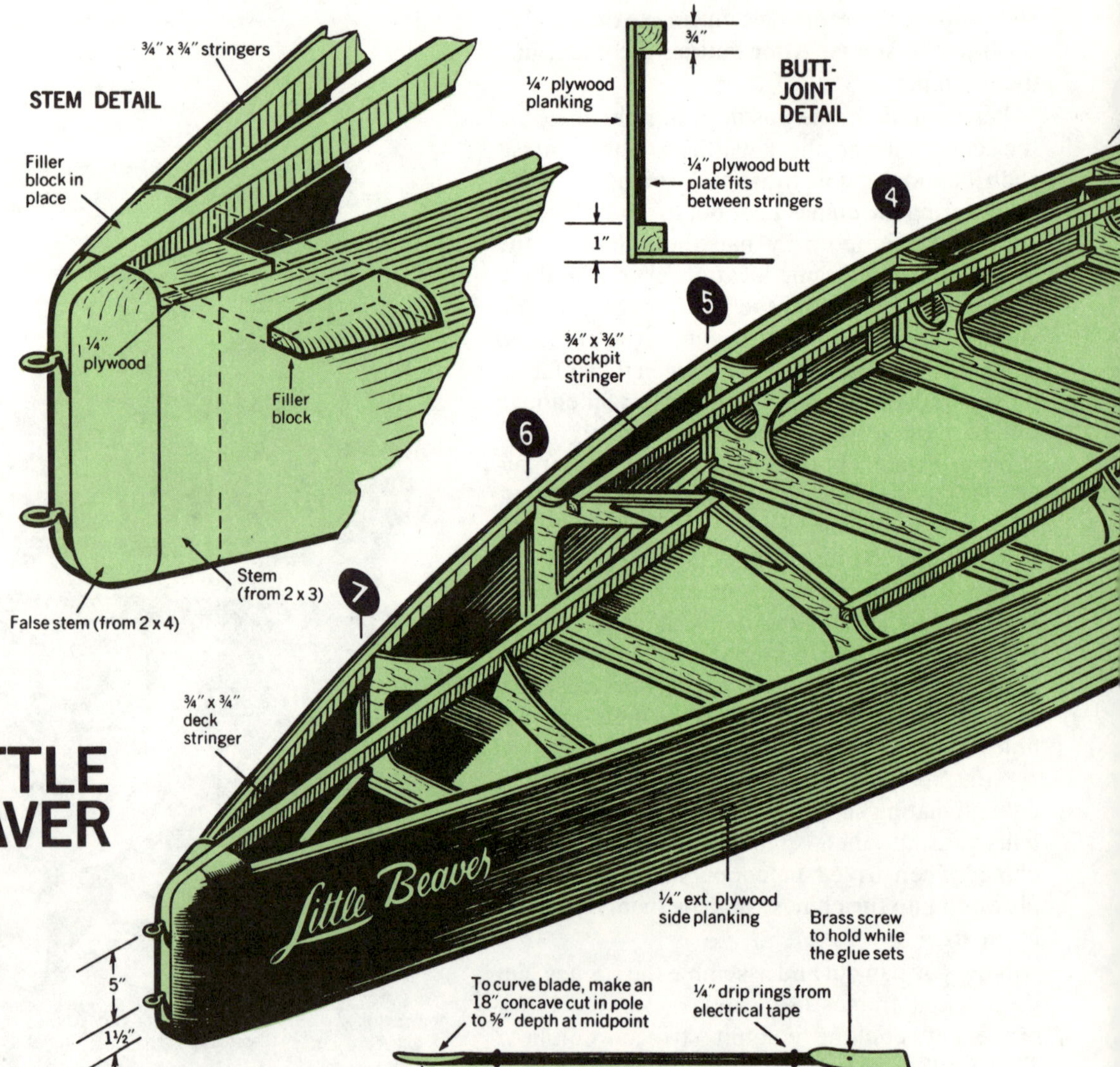

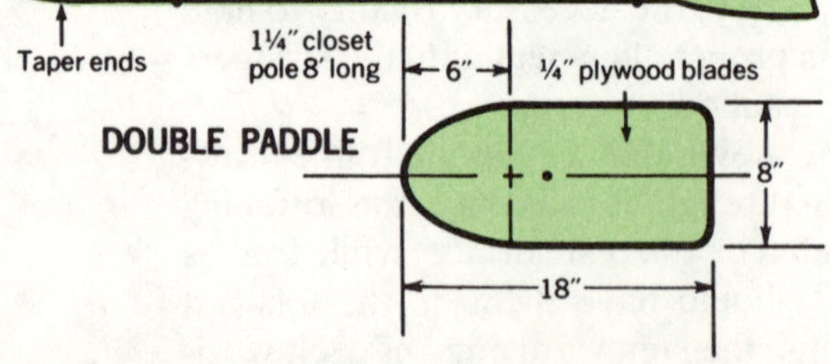

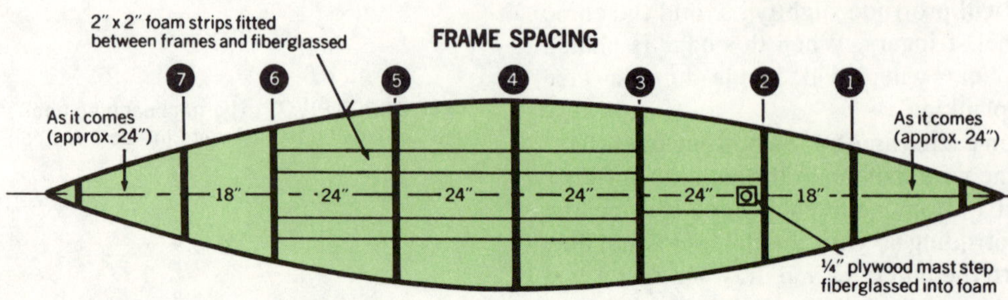

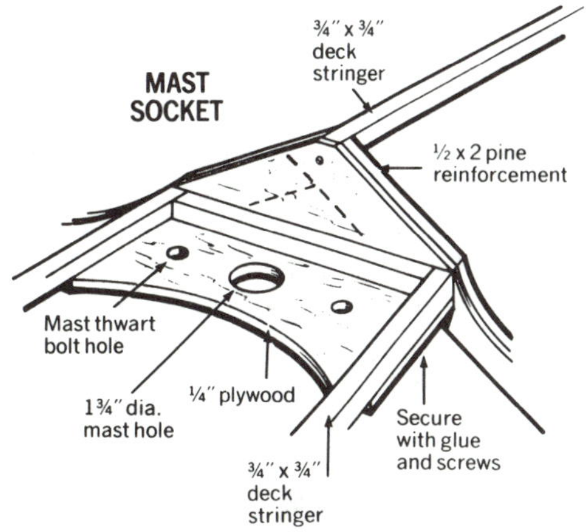

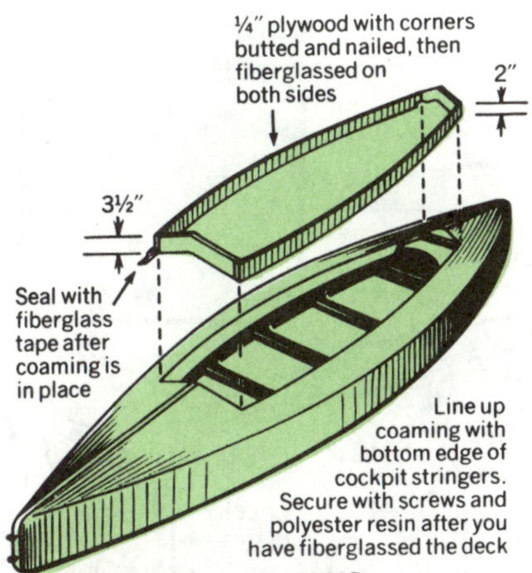

COCKPIT COAMING

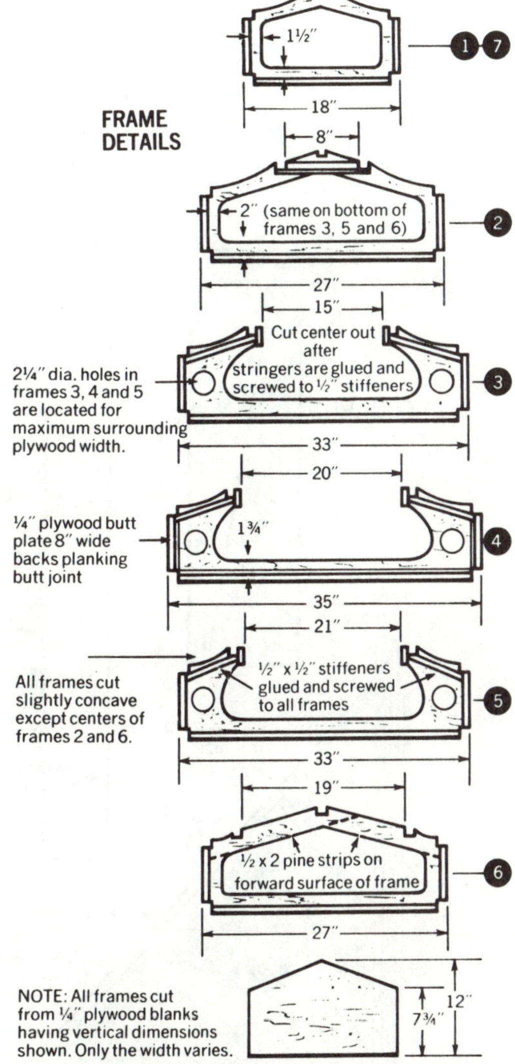

flathead brass screw through the bottom into the cleat at the midpoint of this line. Then pull out one nail at a time and replace it with a similar screw. As in all other joints, coat mating surfaces with glue. If additional screws are needed to draw the bottom snug against the frame, drive them along the penciled line.

The stems are also mounted at this time. Drive a 1½-in. No. 8 flathead brass screw up through the plywood into the end of the 2x3. The false stem is actually a nose-piece shaped from a 2x4 to continue the hull line and provide a sharper bow. You can mount this along with the various filler pieces which complete the stem assembly after the side planking and deck stringers have been installed. Now you are ready to attack the deck. Use a continuous length of fiberglass. Draw it moderately taut lengthwise and staple at the stems.

Do the same thing crosswise, stapling at 1-in. intervals just below the gunnels. Cut V-notches where necessary to eliminate wrinkles where cloth overlaps sides. Flow on three coats of resin with a soft brush, sanding lightly between coats and featherning the fabric edge to the plywood. Now you can install the plywood cockpit coaming.

Drawings of the paddle, controls and sailing accessories are generally self-explanatory. Control pedals are hinged to the floor and equipped with short lengths of screen-door spring or heavy rubber bands cut from an inner tube. The aluminum rudder is mounted on the hull with large eyebolts at the stern "stem." Use steel or aluminum rod as a rudder pin.

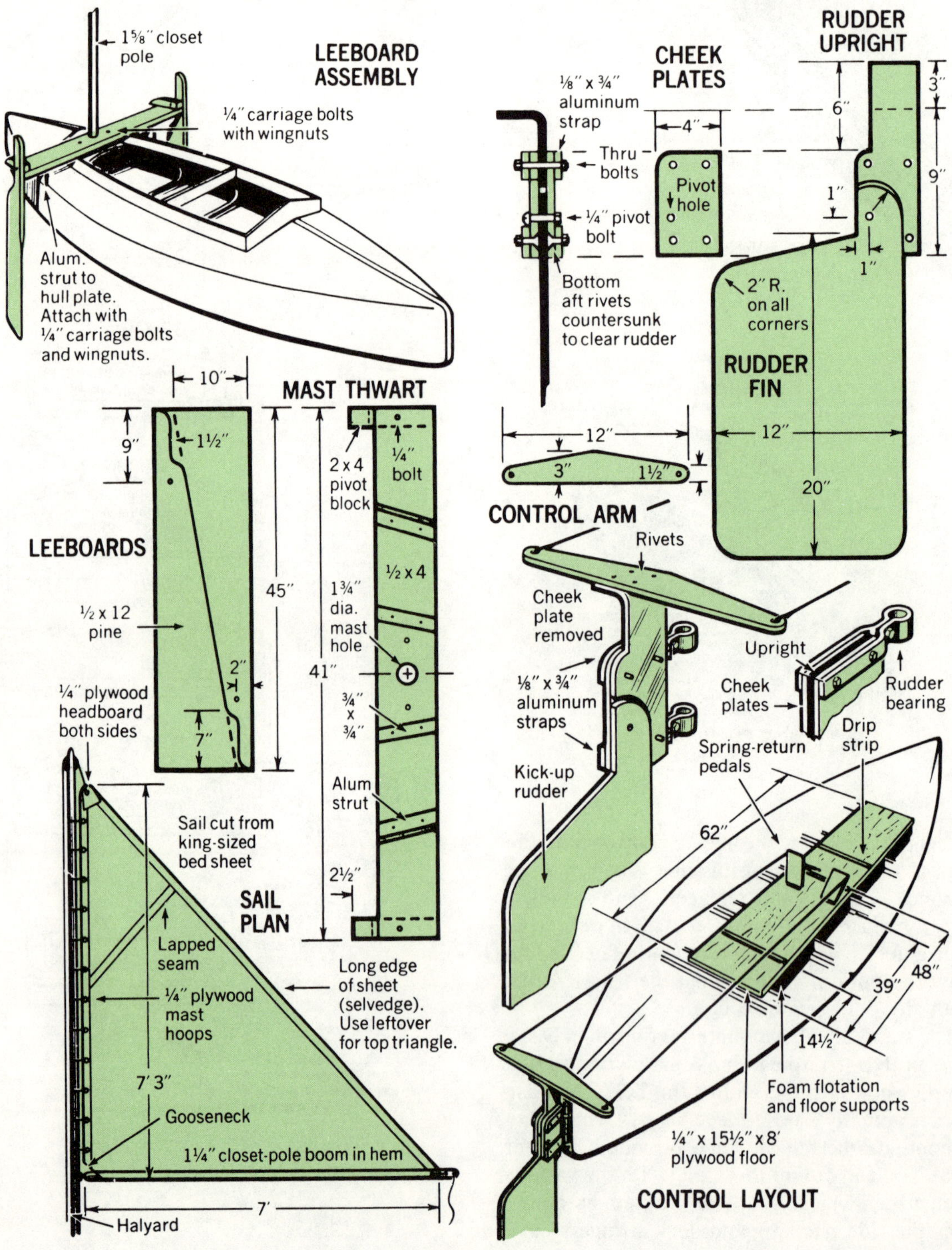

Kiln-dry your lumber with solar heat

■ TO BEAT THE COST of small quantities of kiln-dried hardwoods, Curtis Johnson found a way to dry his own green wood using solar energy. The retired Forest Service employee has been using solar kilns for several years. His latest model, with an 800-board-foot capacity, is shown here.

Collectors on this version have been rotated on their 40°-from-vertical axes to collect more early-morning and later-afternoon sun.

Operating in southern Wisconsin (43° north latitude), the kiln can dry a load of 1-in.-thick (4/4) walnut from 85-percent moisture to 8 percent (same as kiln-dried and right for interior use) in 50 summer days, with the interior temperature often reaching 130° F. Wintertime drying does take considerably longer, but output can be upped by starting with air-dried wood.

Operation of this solar kiln is simple. Solar collectors fitted 1½ in. behind glazed sash are broad, flat ducts—black-painted sheet metal on the side facing the glass and ⅛-in. hardboard on the other. Air enters the collectors through floor vents cut off from the interior by plastic film. Warmed air rises in the collectors, escapes out the tops, and is circulated through the stacked and spaced wood by two thermostatically governed fans (set to go on at 80° F.) Electricity for the fans is the only operating expense.

A free booklet on building and using the solar kiln is available from State and Private Forestry, United States Forest Service, Dept. PM, Box 5130, Madison, WI 53705.

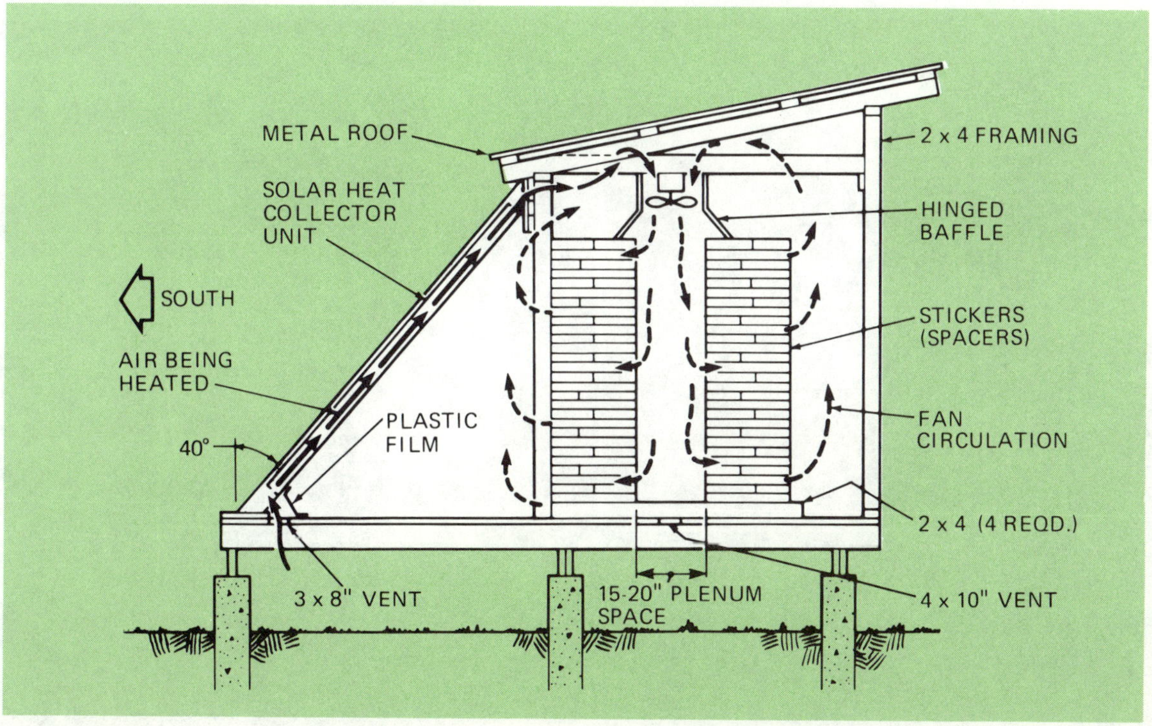

Easy projects add spice to your kitchen

By ROSARIO CAPOTOSTO
By MARTIN HIGGINS

OLD-TIME GROCERY-BIN CANISTER

SILVERWARE-AND-NAPKIN CADDY

YOU'LL FIND lots of use for this silverware and napkin caddy—it's extra-handy when serving a buffet meal. Except for the turned handle, the caddy is made of ½-in. walnut throughout. Both ends are identical and cut out at one time, the holes bored for the handle and the edges rounded. With the turned handle in place, the ends are fastened squarely to the center member with small screws in counterbored holes, later filled. Then the bottom is added.

The two dividers are made to fit the round edge of the center piece by forming a ¼-in.-radius lip at the top with a round file. They're screwed in place from the back. The two slanting sides are added last. I finished the caddy with Danish-walnut stain, followed by two coats of clear satin polyurethane.

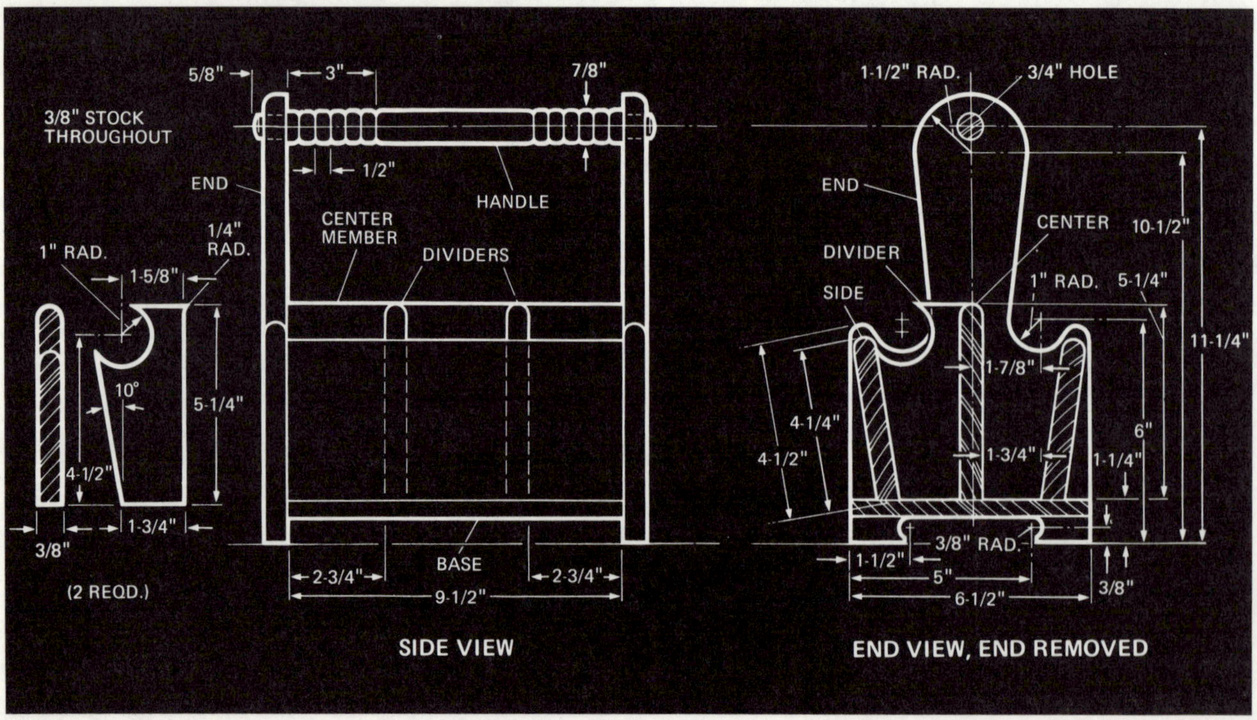

THIS MINIATURE version of an oldtime grocery-store bin will add a charming accent to your kitchen in the form of a five-in-one canister. It's made to hold half-gallon plastic food containers you can buy in housewares departments. You have the option of making five separate lids or a one-piecer that looks like five. The window openings are made in one strip.

Windows are cut out by drilling ⅜-in. holes at corners of the openings, then jigsawing from hole to hole. Rabbets for 1/10-in. Plexiglas are formed with ⅛-in. thick strips. I used dabs of quick-setting epoxy to hold the plastic in place and ⅝ x ¾-in. brass butts from Brainerd Mfg. Co., East Rochester, N.Y., to hinge the lids. You'll need 10 for 5 lids, 3 for one lid.

BUTT-JOIN, glue and nail ¼-in. bottom to the six compartment dividers.

DOUBLE-UP top's thickness with second ¼-in. layer beveled at the front.

USE homemade sander in jigsaw to smooth the window openings' edges.

SEE ALSO
Gifts, Christmas . . . Kitchens . . . Lazy Susans . . . Plexiglass projects . . . Rolling-pin catchalls . . . Salt-and-pepper shakers . . . Telephone centers

FORM rabbets for window panes by adding ⅛-in. strips around openings.

HALF-GALLON plastic food containers are placed in the compartments.

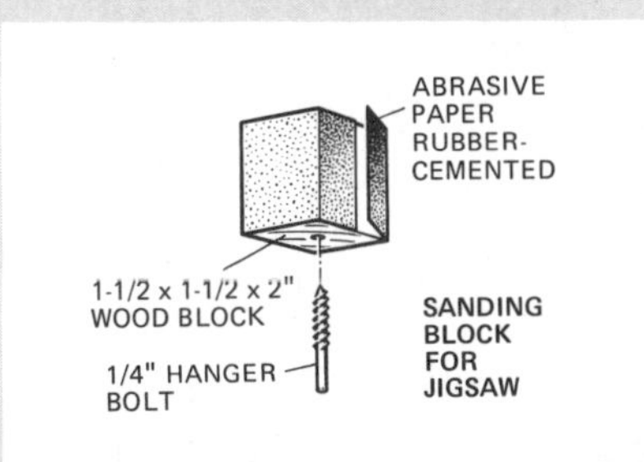

HANGER bolt in abrasive-covered block is chucked in jigsaw for sanding.

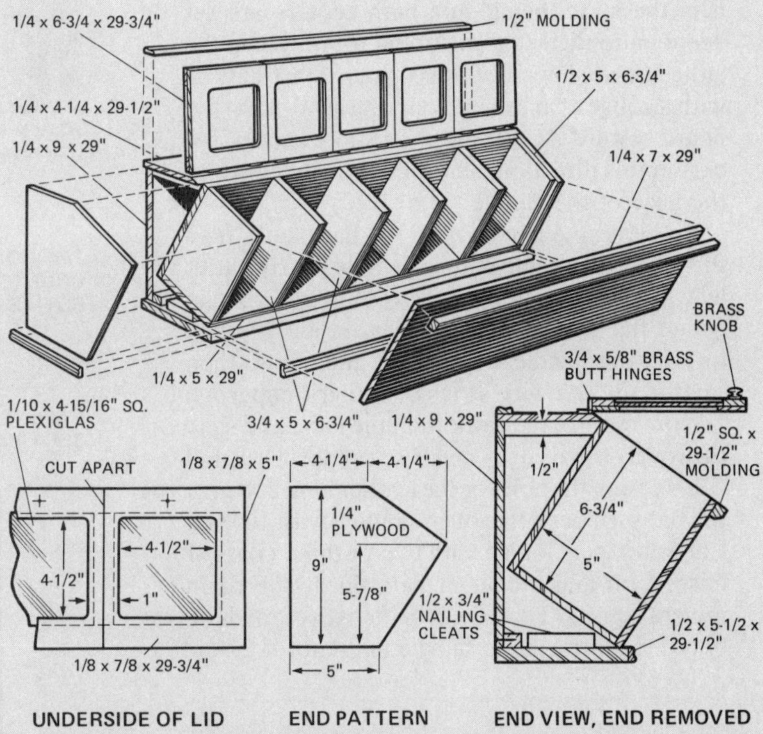

Turned-handle cutting board

By DAVE WARREN

HERE'S A GIFT you can turn out in a few hours—though it will last a lifetime. Start by preparing a 1½-in.-thick piece of cherry, rock maple or walnut and a full-sized cardboard template. Center the template accurately on the hardwood slab and mark the outline. Drill 1-in. holes at the base of the handle, then cut the blank to shape with a sabre saw or a bandsaw.

Find the precise center of the blank and mount it in the lathe, being sure both centers are set deeply into the end grain of the wood. Keep the lathe speed slow—about 900 rpm. Start cutting with a gouge at midpoint, working away from the board toward the handle end. Make successive cuts in this direction, starting each bite closer to the base of the handle.

To blend the handle with the flat blank, hold the gouge on its side with its handle nearly parallel with the sloped slides. As you slice in, roll the gouge flat and toward the handle end. Finish turning the handle with gouge and skew, then sand it smooth with strips of 120-grit paper.

Now remove the work from the lathe and sand the rough-sawn edges on a disc sander. Drill and countersink the hole for the leather loop and give the flat surfaces a thorough sanding with 100 and 120-grit paper. Finish with two or three coats of linseed oil and a coat of paraffin dissolved in mineral spirits. Thread a 24-in. length of rawhide boot lace through the handle and knot it.

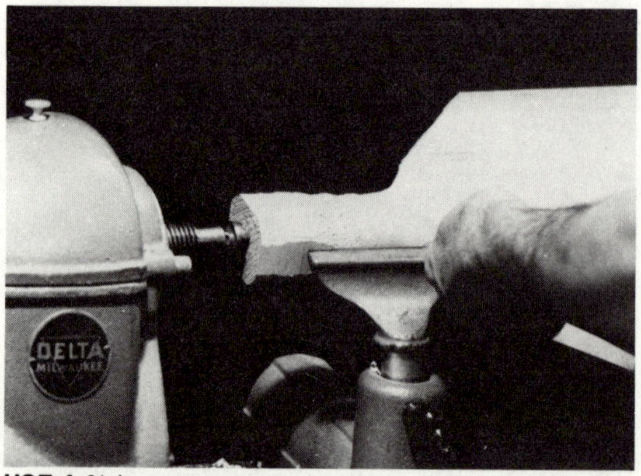

USE A ¾-in. gouge to begin turning handle section round. Keep hands clear of whirring blank.

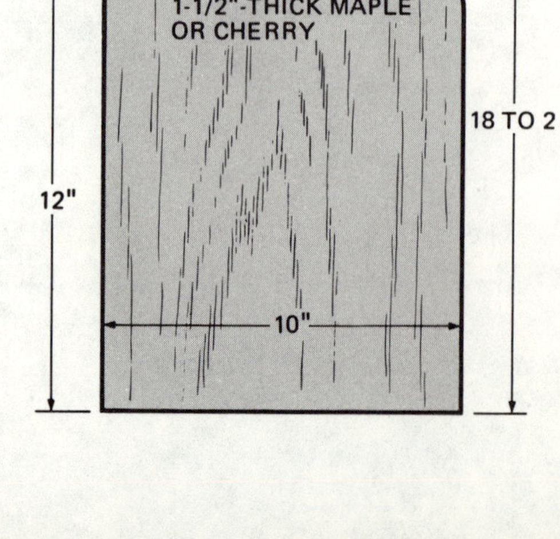

SEE ALSO

Butcher blocks . . . Cutting boards . . .
Gifts, Christmas . . . Kitchens . . . Lazy Susans . . .
Letter racks . . . Servers . . . Serving carts . . .
Snack tables . . . Wine racks

Cookbook caddy

By ROSARIO CAPOTOSTO

■ THIS HANDSOME SHELF will add a touch of interest to your kitchen and keep your wife's cookbooks handy at the same time. Its drawer can store recipes galore.

There are no fancy joints to bother with; nothing but butt joints, glued and nailed, are used. The back and the drawer interior are cut from plywood, but ½-in. solid pine is used for the rest. Set your rip fence to make 12-in. cuts and run all at one time to insure a perfect fit for all inside pieces and to save yourself time. Saw the curves, then use your router with a ¼-round bit to round the edges where indicated. Sand all surfaces as smooth as you will want them before you begin the assembly.

Assemble the parts with glue and 1½-in. finishing nails in this order: First attach the base apron to the drawer shelf. Then attach the back to both shelves and add the sides. Set the nailheads and fill the holes. Make the plywood drawer as a box with four sides and a bottom, then add the pine false front and the knob. For an interesting finish, that is not too difficult, try a wood graining or antiquing kit.

SEE ALSO
Bookcases . . . Bookends . . . Bookracks . . . Bookstands . . . Cupboards, china . . . Drawers . . . Dry sinks . . . Gifts, Christmas . . . Joinery . . . Lazy Susans . . . Magazine holders . . . Servers . . . Serving carts . . . Snack tables . . . Towel racks

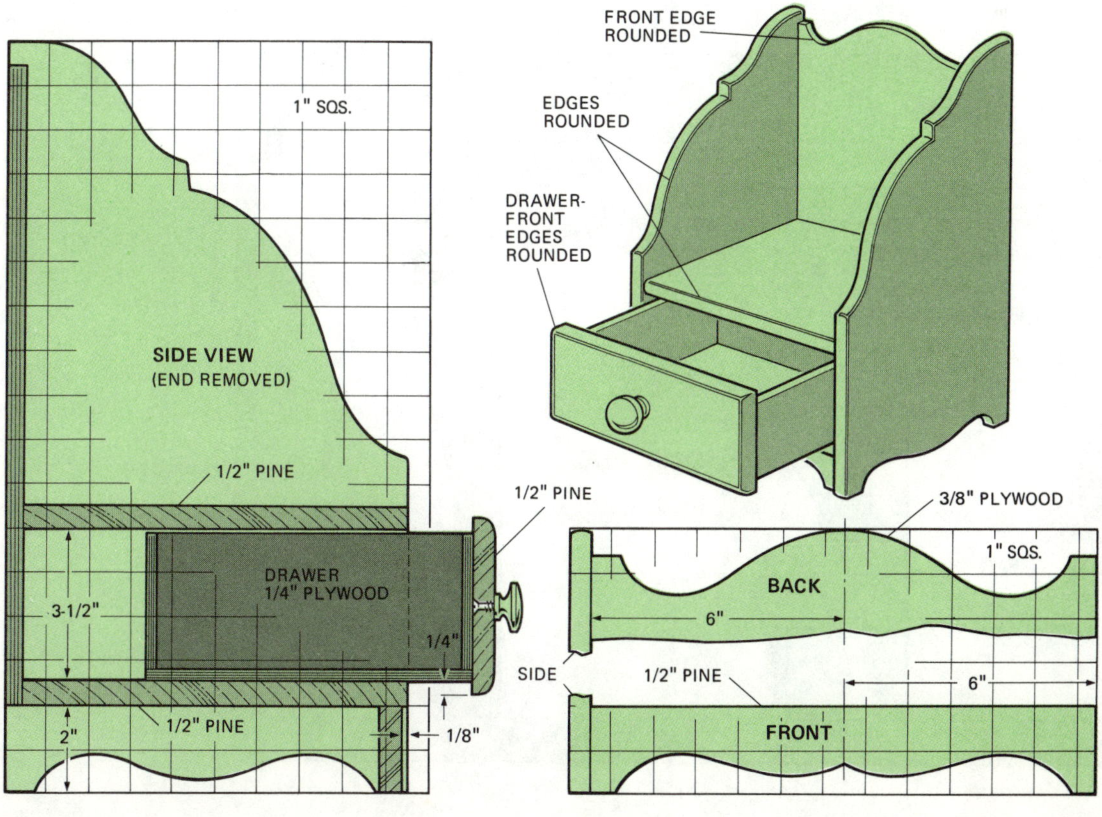

A tray for your best silver

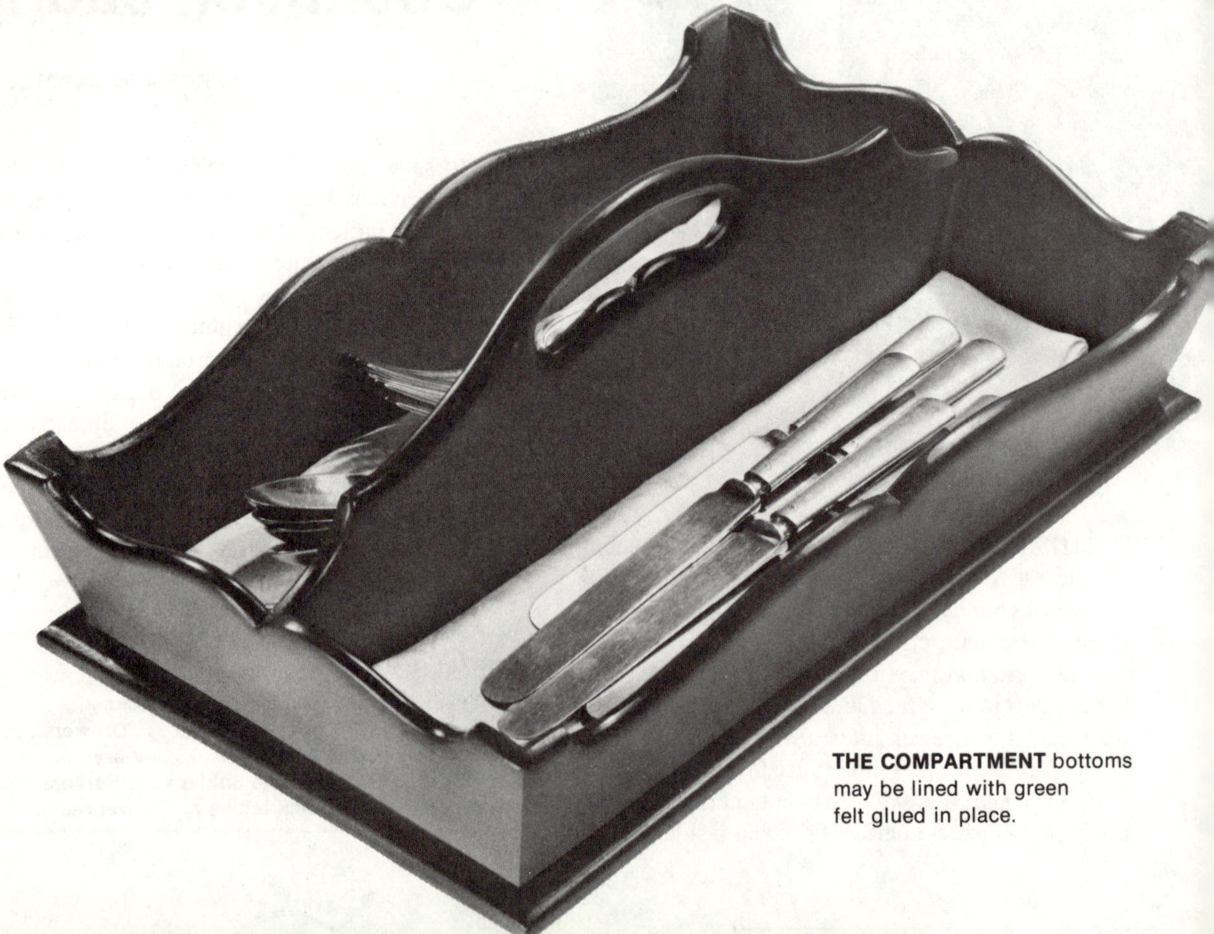

THE COMPARTMENT bottoms may be lined with green felt glued in place.

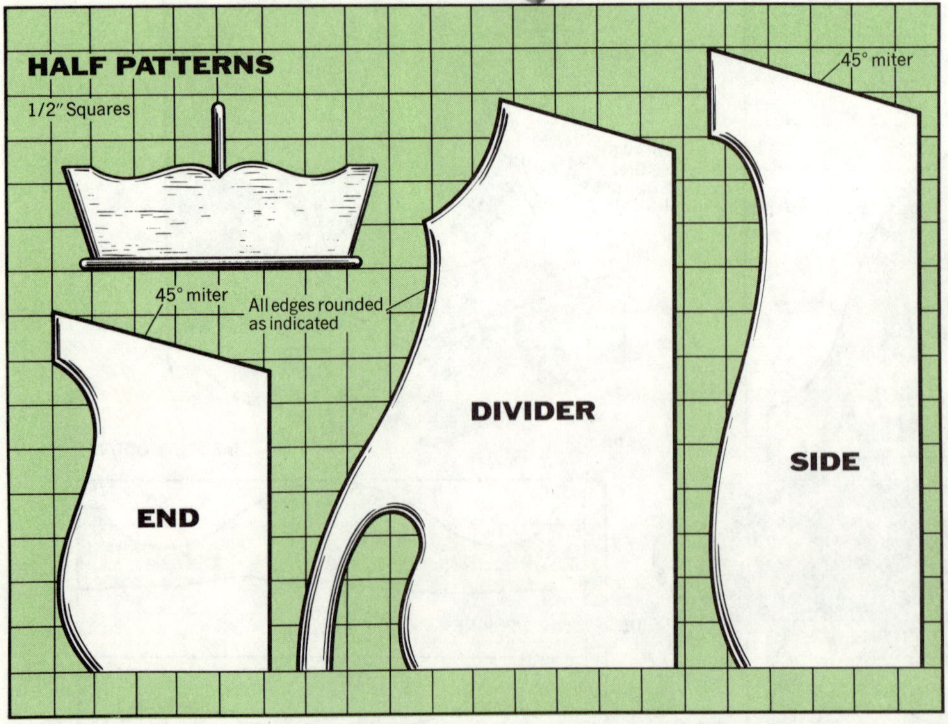

THE HANDSOME TRAY pictured to the left looks complicated to make but it's actually very easy. Constructed of 3/8-in. poplar, this attractive silverware holder is basically simple in design and construction. Though assembly ordinarily would be difficult (because of the tray's angular sides), it's a snap here because of a simple gluing jig that eliminates otherwise difficult clamping.

Start by laying out the patterns on a sheet of heavy paper, then cut them out with scissors or a razor blade. Using the templates as a blade-setting guide, set the table-saw blade to coincide with the angle of the patterns and rip one edge of lumber at this angle. Cut enough to make up the two sides and two end panels. After the bevel has been cut, return the blade to the 0° setting.

Align the bottom edge of the pattern with the beveled edge of the wood and trace the outline. Do this for ends and sides. The divider is traced onto a square piece of wood. All parts are cut on the jigsaw. The gluing jig, with its beveled cutout, simply slips over the assembled tray and holds the parts together until dry. After the glue has set, remove the piece from the jig and glue on the bottom. Finish the tray with stain and two coats of shellac.

SEE ALSO
Butcher blocks . . . Candle stands . . . Cupboards, china . . . Gifts, Christmas . . . Kitchens . . . Lazy Susans . . . Plexiglass projects

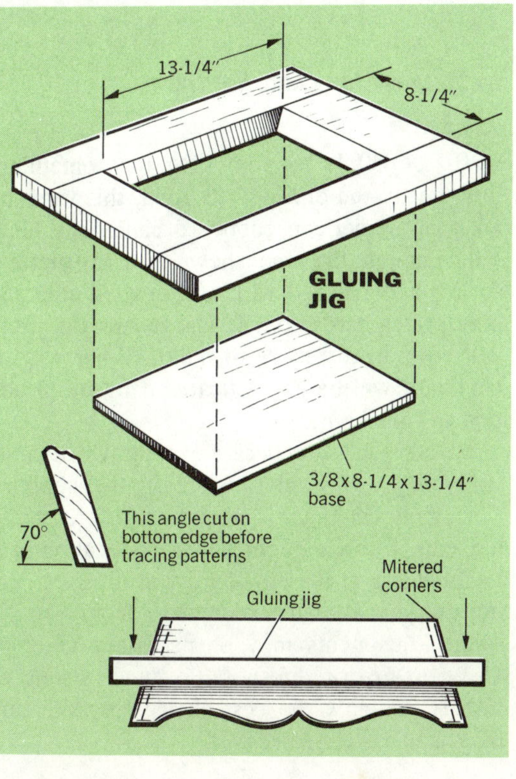

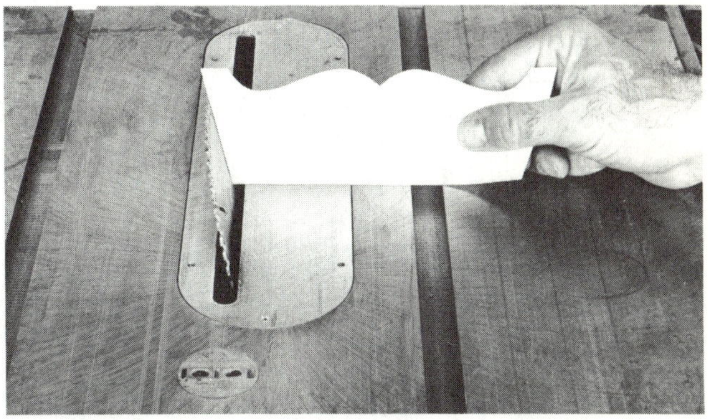

MAKE THE templates and set the blade to the right angle for ripping the edges of the sides and ends.

THE SCROLLS are cut on a jigsaw. For a smooth cut use a very fine blade, high speed and a slow feed.

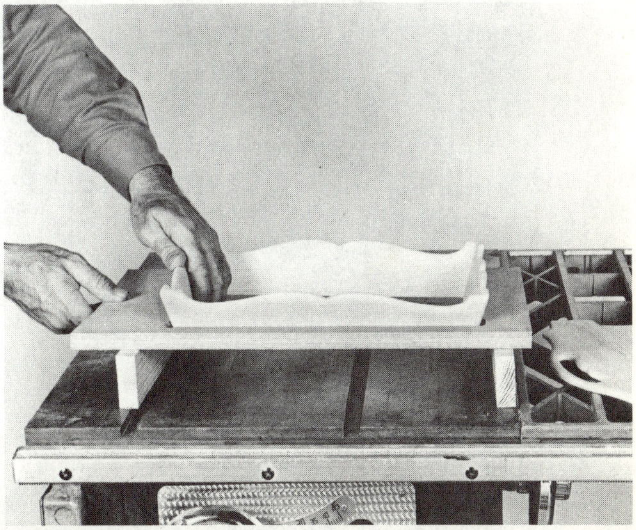

THE GLUING jig consists of a piece of plywood with a beveled cutout. No nails are used in the assembly.

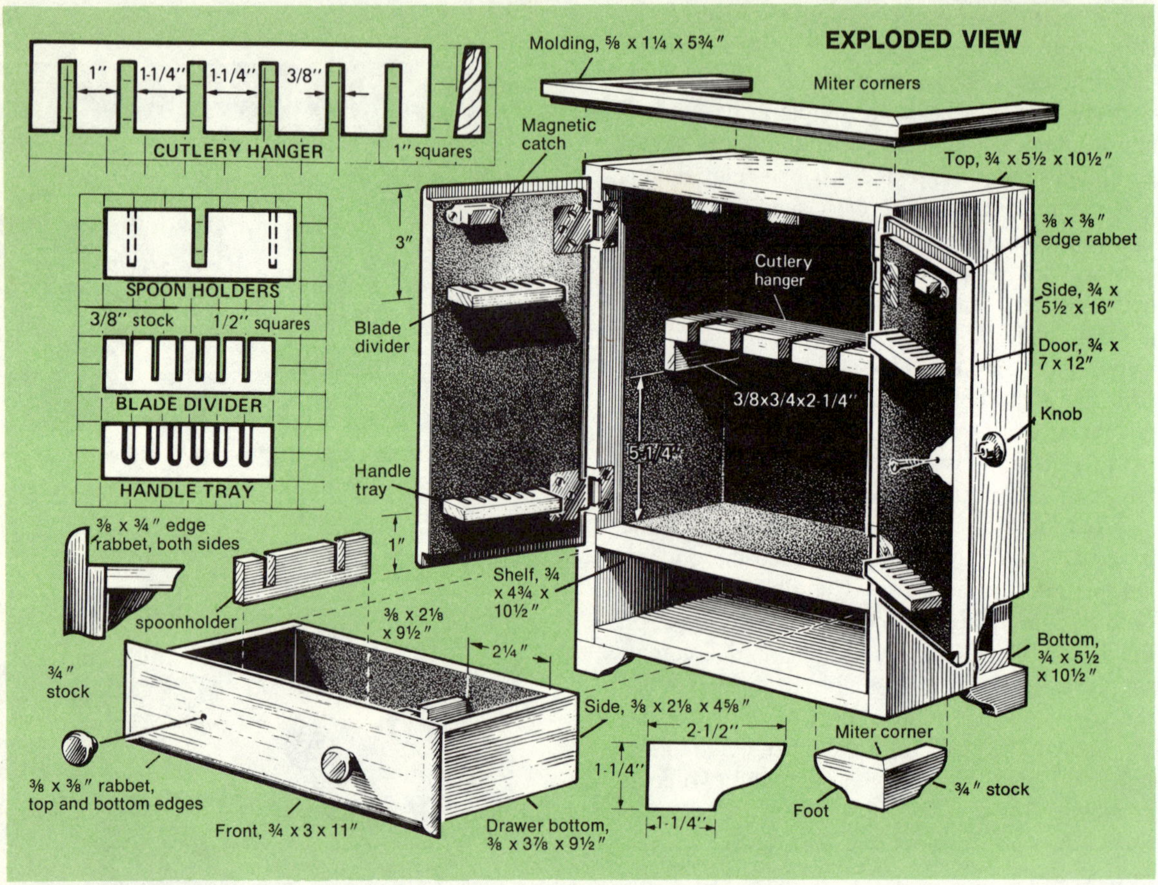

Colonial cutlery cupboard

By ELMA and WILLARD WALTNER

■ IF YOU'VE been looking for something a little out-of-the-ordinary to build, this version of an Early American cupboard can easily fill the bill. Though the one shown is constructed of spruce and finished with a fruitwood stain, you may prefer hardwood. It just means the project will cost slightly more to build. Either way, the cupboard will be a practical and beautiful addition to your home.

Before you start, decide exactly which cutlery your wife will want to store in the cupboard. Then you can alter dimensions before making any cuts. Equally important is the location of the knifeholders in the cupboard and drawers. Your inventory may vary somewhat from ours, so some adjustments may be necessary here, too. Use your favorite finish, but a tough, strong varnish is probably the best choice for both durability and appearance.

SEE ALSO

Chests . . . Cupboards, china . . . Drawers . . . Gifts, Christmas . . . Kitchens . . . Lazy Susans . . . Planters . . . Servers . . . Serving carts

METRIC CONVERSION

Conversion factors can be carried so far they become impractical. In cases below where an entry is exact it is followed by an asterisk (*). Where considerable rounding off has taken place, the entry is followed by a + or a - sign.

CUSTOMARY TO METRIC

Linear Measure

inches	millimeters
1/16	1.5875*
1/8	3.2
3/16	4.8
1/4	6.35*
5/16	7.9
3/8	9.5
7/16	11.1
1/2	12.7*
9/16	14.3
5/8	15.9
11/16	17.5
3/4	19.05*
13/16	20.6
7/8	22.2
15/16	23.8
1	25.4*

inches	centimeters
1	2.54*
2	5.1
3	7.6
4	10.2
5	12.7*
6	15.2
7	17.8
8	20.3
9	22.9
10	25.4*
11	27.9
12	30.5

feet	centimeters	meters
1	30.48*	.3048*
2	61	.61
3	91	.91
4	122	1.22
5	152	1.52
6	183	1.83
7	213	2.13
8	244	2.44
9	274	2.74
10	305	3.05
50	1524*	15.24*
100	3048*	30.48*

1 yard = .9144* meters
1 rod = 5.0292* meters
1 mile = 1.6 kilometers
1 nautical mile = 1.852* kilometers

Fluid Measure

(Milliliters [ml] and cubic centimeters [cc or cu cm] are equivalent, but it is customary to use milliliters for liquids.)

1 cu in = 16.39 ml
1 fl oz = 29.6 ml
1 cup = 237 ml
1 pint = 473 ml
1 quart = 946 ml
= .946 liters
1 gallon = 3785 ml
= 3.785 liters
Formula (exact):
fluid ounces × 29.573 529 562 5* = milliliters

Weights

ounces	grams
1	28.3
2	56.7
3	85
4	113
5	142
6	170
7	198
8	227
9	255
10	283
11	312
12	340
13	369
14	397
15	425
16	454

Formula (exact):
ounces × 28.349 523 125* = grams

pounds	kilograms
1	.45
2	.9
3	1.4
4	1.8
5	2.3
6	2.7
7	3.2
8	3.6
9	4.1
10	4.5

1 short ton (2000 lbs) = 907 kilograms (kg)
Formula (exact):
pounds × .453 592 37* = kilograms

Volume

1 cu in = 16.39 cubic centimeters (cc)
1 cu ft = 28 316.7 cc
1 bushel = 35 239.1 cc
1 peck = 8 809.8 cc

Area

1 sq in = 6.45 sq cm
1 sq ft = 929 sq cm
= .093 sq meters
1 sq yd = .84 sq meters
1 acre = 4 046.9 sq meters
= .404 7 hectares
1 sq mile = 2 589 988 sq meters
= 259 hectares
= 2.589 9 sq kilometers

Kitchen Measure

1 teaspoon = 4.93 milliliters (ml)
1 Tablespoon = 14.79 milliliters (ml)

Miscellaneous

1 British thermal unit (Btu) (mean) = 1 055.9 joules
1 calorie (mean) = 4.19 joules
1 horsepower = 745.7 watts
= .75 kilowatts
caliber (diameter of a firearm's bore in hundredths of an inch) = .254 millimeters (mm)
1 atmosphere pressure = 101 325* pascals (newtons per sq meter)
1 pound per square inch (psi) = 6 895 pascals
1 pound per square foot = 47.9 pascals
1 knot = 1.85 kilometers per hour
25 miles per hour = 40.2 kilometers per hour
50 miles per hour = 80.5 kilometers per hour
75 miles per hour = 120.7 kilometers per hour